“Destined to become a modern-day clas
Assessment and Interpersonal Neurobiolog
the Longing to Be Known should be on every
rigorous empirical evidence with clinical wisdom and richly elaborated case material, the author provides a compelling introduction to one of the most important innovations in contemporary clinical psychology. Readers experience first-hand the nuances of Therapeutic Assessment, and how it helps strengthen the empathic connection between client and therapist. Graduate students, early-career psychologists, and experienced clinicians will all benefit from this remarkable book.”

Robert F. Bornstein, *PhD, University Professor, Adelphi University, USA*

“Nearly two decades after his classic *In Our Clients' Shoes*, Stephen Finn gifts assessment psychologists another gem. I cannot recall another volume from which I have learned so much that was not only immediately and pragmatically applicable to my assessment practice but also prompted such constructive reflection on how I think about my work and what I might do differently—and more effectively—with future patients. Finn is a master at making complex intrapsychic and interpersonal concepts accessible without diluting their sophistication. His capacities for creative, integrative thinking— here, involving theory and research in assessment, psychotherapy, attachment, and neuroscience—and communicating these ideas lucidly are remarkable. Finn's new book teems with evocative, empathic case illustrations that bring his ideas to life, modeling an assessment stance that is humane, collaborative, shame-sensitive, and clinically transformative. I highly recommend this book to all assessment psychologists and students who value a depth-oriented, relational approach, regardless of whether they practice formal Therapeutic Assessment.”

Anthony D. Bram, PhD, FABP, ABPA, Harvard Medical School, USA; Boston Psychoanalytic Society and Institute, USA; (co-) author of *Psychological Testing That Matters: Creating a Road Map for Effective Treatment* and *Psychological Assessment of Emotional Dysregulation in Children and Adolescents: The Bipolar Spectrum and Beyond*

“Nobody combines empirical rigor, thoughtful reflection, and a deep concern for human experience the way Stephen Finn does. That rare integration is what makes him one of the most inspiring voices in clinical psychology—and why I eagerly anticipate each of his books, often returning to them again and again. In this sequel to *In Our Clients' Shoes*, Finn connects his groundbreaking approach to psychological assessment with recent advances in science and clinical practice. He reflects on the neurobiological foundations of therapeutic change, empathy, trauma, multimethod assessment, shame, epistemic trust, and the work of many of the most influential thinkers in psychological assessment. As always, the book is written in clear, accessible, and clinically rich prose, brought vividly to life through abundant clinical examples. It invites readers not only to deepen their clinical skill but also to reconnect with their own humanity, sensitivity, and curiosity."

Christopher J. Hopwood, *PhD, Professor of Psychology, University of Zurich, Switzerland*

"In this book, Finn expertly integrates scholarship and his unparalleled clinical acumen to produce a tour de force treatise on the neurobiological underpinnings of Therapeutic Assessment. Scholars will find in it an erudite review of a broad and extensive literature, and clinicians will benefit from the rich clinical vignettes that draw on the author's decades of research, practice, and teaching in this field."

Yossef S. Ben-Porath, *PhD, Professor Emeritus, Kent State University, UK; co-developer of the MMPI-3*

"Dr. Finn weaves a tapestry using his decades of clinical experience, intertwined with contemporary theoretical and research foundations of interpersonal neurobiology, attachment, shame, and human memory, into the therapeutic domain where assessment serves as the framework for new effective approaches to therapeutic change. Case examples demonstrate how multimethod assessment used in Therapeutic Assessment helps clients feel respected, seen, understood, and accepted, setting the stage for the therapist as a 'secure base' promoting intersubjectivity, empathy, and therapeutic change."

Carol George, PhD, Professor Emerita, Mills College, USA; co-author of *The Adult Attachment Projective Picture System: Attachment Theory and Assessment in Adults*

"At a time when psychological assessment is declining in practice and graduate schools, this powerful sequel to *In Our Clients' Shoes* clarifies how and why the therapeutic use of psychological assessment creates lasting change. Finn's easy-to-read chapters clarify often difficult-to-understand concepts in neurobiology, polyvagal theory, memory reconsolidation, shame, and attachment. His many case examples beautifully illustrate these constructs and demonstrate the therapeutic growth and shame reduction created by using tests therapeutically. This volume will no doubt invigorate the clinical work of assessors and therapists from all orientations."

Julie Cradock O'Leary, PhD, co-author of *Thurston Cradock Test of Shame*

"Finn's exquisite evolution of his Therapeutic Assessment model, with the melding of neurobiological research findings and weighty psychological concepts, shines through in this rich compilation of his recent works. This compendium will propel readers to transfigure their psychological assessment practice into a fundamentally restorative offering."

Radhika Krishnamurthy, *PsyD, ABAP, Clinical Psychology Professor, Florida Tech, USA; Former President, Society for Personality Assessment*

"Psychological assessment as a process, as well as resulting conclusions, carries a great deal of power. What Finn understands better than most is how this also means that assessment carries a great deal of potential—potential for healing, potential for growth, and potential for relief from both struggles and suffering. What he did for theory in *In Our Clients' Shoes*, he solidifies in research in this volume. He weaves in research ranging from affective neuroscience to interpersonal neurobiology to illustrate possible mechanisms for the transformative power of Therapeutic Assessment. Perhaps even more powerful, he illustrates these processes through deep and authentic case examples that bring them to life in a way that allows the reader to internalize them deeply. For the practitioner of psychological assessment, this book offers clear ways to deepen and improve the practice toward deep transformation."

A. Jordan Wright, PhD, ABPP, ABAP, Clinical Associate Professor, New York University, USA; author of *Conducting Psychological Assessment: A Guide for Practitioners*

Adult Attachment Projective Picture System (AAAP); Alessandro Crisi, whose Wartegg system is remarkable for identifying split-off aspects of the personality and who has become a close friend; and Constance Fischer—to whom this book is dedicated—for providing a philosophical grounding for Therapeutic Assessment and for her personal encouragement. Only recently have I fully appreciated how brave she was in putting forward ideas that challenged the prevailing view of psychological assessment.

Two international organizations provided venues in which I could test my ideas and offered wonderful opportunities to meet others passionate about assessment: the Society for Personality Assessment and the International Society of the Rorschach and Projective Methods. Some chapters in this book grew out of presentations first given at meetings of these organizations.

Carol Middelberg has supported me as a friend and was the first person to tell me about memory reconsolidation. I am also indebted to her brilliant written summary of the revolution in modern psychotherapy. Recently, Tori Olds and Bruce Ecker have confirmed that Therapeutic Assessment is a way of achieving memory reconsolidation and have been teaching me about Coherence Therapy. Julie Cradock O'Leary is my shame "buddy," and I am grateful for our many discussions and for her wonderful test, the Thurston Cradock Test of Shame.

Anthony Bram read earlier versions of many chapters of this book and provided valuable suggestions, as well as an endorsement. Yossi Ben-Porath, Robert Bornstein, Carol George, Chris Hopwood, Radhika Krishnamurthy, Julie Cradock O'Leary, and Jordan Wright also read the initial draft and offered endorsements that helped me believe in this book.

Over many years, my therapy buddies, Rich Armington and John Driggs, have listened attentively to my stories about clients and helped me put words to my feelings. Truly, I would not be the psychotherapist I am without their camaraderie. My amazing husband, Hal Richardson, has supported me emotionally and practically as I traveled around the world, maintained a busy practice in Austin, and took time away from our home life to write this book. I am thankful every day that he is in my life.

Finally, I wish to thank the many clients who shared their lives with me over the years and helped me grow wiser and healthier. I am especially grateful to those individuals who gave me permission to tell their stories in this book. All of them hoped that reading about their struggles and victories would inspire and help others.

Therapeutic Assessment and Interpersonal Neurobiology

Therapeutic Assessment and Interpersonal Neurobiology shows how collaborative assessment can function as a potent therapeutic intervention—reducing shame, strengthening epistemic trust, and catalyzing meaningful change.

Integrating research on affect regulation, memory reconsolidation, and intersubjectivity with richly detailed case examples, the book demonstrates how psychological tests can be used not only to understand clients but to help them experience themselves differently. The author highlights common traps that therapists fall into and provides strategies for them to improve their practical skills and enhance the course of treatment to transform clients' lives. The book emphasizes the importance of client collaboration, secure attachment, mentalization, addressing shame, and epistemic trust during psychological interventions. Bridging psychological assessment and modern psychotherapy, this volume provides assessment professionals and trainees with a rigorous, humane, and clinically actionable framework for using tests as instruments of psychological healing.

As a sequel to his influential book, *In Our Clients' Shoes: Theory and Techniques of Therapeutic Assessment*, the author offers a renewed and transformative vision of psychological assessment grounded in contemporary neuroscience, attachment theory, and decades of clinical practice. This is an invaluable resource for psychologists, particularly those who use the MMPI-2, MMPI-3, Rorschach, AAP, and EMP.

Stephen E. Finn, PhD, is an internationally recognized clinical psychologist, developer of Therapeutic Assessment, and author of influential books and articles shaping contemporary psychological assessment research, training, and practice.

Therapeutic Assessment and Interpersonal Neurobiology

Empathy, Intersubjectivity, and the Longing to Be Known

Stephen E. Finn

Routledge
Taylor & Francis Group
NEW YORK AND LONDON

Designed cover image: Getty Images © Kateryna Kovarzh

First published 2027
by Routledge
605 Third Avenue, New York, NY 10158

and by Routledge
4 Park Square, Milton Park, Abingdon, Oxon, OX14 4RN

Routledge is an imprint of the Taylor & Francis Group, an informa business

ISBN: 978-1-032-99093-4 (hbk)
ISBN: 978-1-032-99091-0 (pbk)
ISBN: 978-1-003-60223-1 (ebk)

DOI: 10.4324/9781003602231

Typeset in Times New Roman
by Deanta Global Publishing Services, Chennai, India

I dedicate this book to Constance Fischer in gratitude for her lighting the way.

Contents

Figures

Tables

Author Biography

Stephen E. Finn, PhD, founder of the Center for Therapeutic Assessment, is a licensed clinical psychologist in practice in Austin, Texas; a Clinical Associate Professor of Psychology at the University of Texas at Austin; Senior Researcher and Director of Training at the European Center for Therapeutic Assessment at Catholic University of the Sacred Heart, Milan, Italy; Director of Training at the Asian-Pacific Center for Therapeutic Assessment in Tokyo, Japan; and Honorary Professor at the Universidad Abierta Interamericana, Buenos Aires, Argentina. He has published 100+ articles and chapters on psychological assessment, psychotherapy, and other topics in clinical psychology, and is the author of *In Our Clients' Shoes: Theory and Techniques of Therapeutic Assessment* (2007; now translated into seven languages). He is co-author of *Therapeutic Assessment with Children: Enhancing Parental Empathy through Psychological Assessment* (2022, with Deborah J. Tharinger, Dale I. Rudin, and Marita S. Frackowiak) and *Therapeutic Assessment with Adults: Using Psychological Testing to Help Clients Change* (2022, with Francesca Fantini, Filippo Aschieri, Raja M. David, and Hale Martin). In 2011, Dr. Finn was given the Bruno Klopfer Award from the Society of Personality Assessment for distinguished lifetime contributions to the field of personality assessment. In August 2017, he received the award for Distinguished Contributions to Assessment Psychology from Section IX (Assessment) of the Society for Clinical Psychology (Division 12 of the American Psychological Association). In 2018, he received the Carl Rogers Award for an outstanding contribution to the theory and practice of humanistic psychology from the Society for Humanistic Psychology (Division 32 of the American Psychological Association). Also, in 2026 he recieved the John R. Graham Award for Distinguished Mentorship in Personality Assessment from the Society for Personality Assessment.

Acknowledgments

As this book was written over the past 19 years, there are many people to whom I am grateful for supporting me and contributing to my thinking. First, I thank my colleagues on the Board of the Therapeutic Assessment Institute (TAI) for collaborating with me in the ongoing development of Therapeutic Assessment: Filippo Aschieri, Raja David, Hilde De Saeger, Francesca Fantini, Marita Frackowiak, Jan Henk Kamphuis, Hale Martin, Noriko Nakamura, Ernesto Pais, Dale Rudin, Pamela Schaber, and J. D. Smith. Lionel Chudzik, Barton Evans, Diane Engelman, Melissa Lehmann, Lena Lillieroth, and Deborah Tharinger are former members of the TAI Board, and they too made important contributions to Therapeutic Assessment. In addition, Dale, Lionel, Marita, and Pamela are part of the Center for Therapeutic Assessment in Austin, along with Christopher Arrillaga, Lisa Lasater, Casey O'Neal, and Katherine Thomas. These colleagues are often the first to hear my new ideas about Therapeutic Assessment, and they have helped me make important decisions about what to include in this book.

Two other groups have worked tirelessly to develop Therapeutic Assessment and spread it around the world: the European Center for Therapeutic Assessment (Filippo Aschieri, Cristina Augello, Patrizia Bevilacqua, Camillo Caputo, Cristina Corvi, Erica Dell'Acqua, and Francesca Fantini) and the Asian-Pacific Center for Therapeutic Assessment leadership team (Mitsugu Murakami, Noriko Nakamura, Shin-ichi Nakamura, Yasuko Nishida, and Naoko Ogura), along with its members: Hisako Hoshide, Seiji Mabuchi, Sachiyo Mizuno, Masamichi Noda, Mikako Ohzeki, Mitsue Tomura, and Sho Yabugaki. In addition, Mette Kyung Reacroft, Qiwu Sun, and Anna Elisa Villemor-Amaral are introducing Therapeutic Assessment in Denmark, China, and Brazil, respectively, and I am excited to learn more about TA's fit within these cultures.

I have had the good fortune to be mentored after my Ph.D. by four brilliant assessment psychologists: Leonard Handler, who gave us the term "Extended Inquiry" and was always so supportive of my work; Carol George, who helped me understand attachment theory deeply and gave us her wonderful test, the

Chapter 1

Introduction

Bridging the Gap between Recent Developments in Psychotherapy and the Practice of Psychological Assessment

I have long aspired to publish a sequel to my previous book, *In Our Clients' Shoes: Theory and Practice of Therapeutic Assessment* (Finn, 2007) to describe my more recent thinking about Therapeutic Assessment (TA) and the therapeutic potential of psychological assessment more broadly. My inspiration for this volume comes largely from the revolution in psychotherapy theory and practice that has taken place over the last four decades. Fosha, Siegel, and Solomon (2009) described this new paradigm as "experiential clinical therapeutics," linking it to neuroscience and developmental research emphasizing the primacy of emotion and the importance of human attachment. As a result of this growing body of research, we now understand more than ever about how to help clients heal from trauma, insecure attachment, and genetically influenced emotional suffering. We know that when skilled clinicians create authentic relationships in which they act as attuned, invested auxiliary attachment figures, they help clients reduce shame, build epistemic trust, and open themselves to new experiences and information. Such relationships create the conditions for clinicians to offer "safe surprises" (Bromberg, 2012)—emotionally potent moments that yield bottom-up learnings, reconsolidate traumatic memories, and transform the unconscious emotional schemas that underlie clients' persistent struggles.

Unfortunately, because psychological assessment traditionally is seen as entirely separate from psychotherapy, few clinicians have understood how psychological tests can be used to create powerful therapeutic experiences. In most clinical settings around the world, tests are still used primarily to support diagnosis, guide treatment planning, and assess outcomes. The goal of this book is to bridge the gap between modern psychotherapy and psychological assessment and inform psychological assessors, psychotherapists, and psychiatrists about collaborative/therapeutic psychological assessment[1] and its relationship to interpersonal neurobiology and evolutionary/developmental psychology.

My thinking has been shaped by two main influences: (1) reading experts in interpersonal neurobiology and psychotherapy—Bonnie Badenoch, Louis Cozolino, Bruce Ecker, Peter Fonagy, Diana Fosha, Leslie Greenberg, Iain McGilchrist, Stephen Porges, Alan Schore, Daniel Siegel, Daniel Stern, Colwyn

DOI: 10.4324/9781003602231-1

Treverthen, Ed Tronick, and David Wallin, among others (all of whom will be cited in the pages to come)—and (2) reflecting on the powerful therapeutic experiences I have witnessed in my own and other colleagues' work with collaborative/therapeutic assessment (c/ta). Affective neuroscience has been an especially useful lens for understanding both the therapeutic successes and failures that occur during psychological assessment, and for refining techniques that facilitate positive change. Many practices developed by early pioneers of collaborative assessment (e.g., Fischer, 1985/1994; Handler, 2006; Purves, 2002), align naturally with principles of affective neuroscience. I believe this is because assessment psychologists working in the phenomenological and humanistic traditions had deep intuitive wisdom about human nature. Still, by intentionally integrating interpersonal neurobiology into Therapeutic Assessment, I have seen even more powerful transformations in my clients—experiences I will share throughout the book. My hope is that these insights will help clinicians find new, effective ways to help individuals who have not benefited from other forms of psychological intervention.

My thinking has also been enriched by experts working at the interface of psychological assessment and interpersonal neurobiology, including Anna Bucheim, Carol George, Luciano Giromini, Gregory Meyer, Julie Cradock O'Leary, and Donald Viglione. I am grateful for their contributions and will reference their work throughout this volume. I am also encouraged by the context in which this book is being written. In 2007, when *In Our Clients' Shoes* was published, collaborative psychological assessment was—quoting Constance Fischer—"common sense, but not common place" (Fischer, 2000). Today collaborative/therapeutic assessment has spread worldwide, with active clinical and research groups in Argentina, Brazil, Denmark, Italy, Japan, the Netherlands, the People's Republic of China, Sweden, and the United States. Continuing education courses sponsored over the past 20 years by the Asian-Pacific Center for Therapeutic Assessment, Asociación de Estudio y Investigación en Psicodiagnóstico, Centro Universitario de Evaluación Colaborativa y Terapéutica, Collaborative Assessment Association of the Bay Area, Colorado Assessment Society, European Center for Therapeutic Assessment, International Society of the Rorschach and Projective Methods, Society for Personality Assessment, Therapeutic Assessment Institute, and Viersprong Institute for Personality Disorders have exposed thousands of psychologists to Therapeutic Assessment. Three meta-analyses now show that c/ta has a significant positive effect on adult clients' symptomatology, motivation, and satisfaction with assessment and treatment, and self-views (Finn, 2023). The literature on collaborative/therapeutic assessment has also grown dramatically—to more than 1000 publications by my estimate. My hope is that this book will encourage even more psychologists to become interested in collaborative/therapeutic assessment and help those familiar with it to deepen their therapeutic effectiveness.

This volume brings together articles I published over the past 16 years along with previously unpublished works from conference presentations and TA training workshops. The pieces are presented roughly in chronological order so readers can follow the evolution of my thinking as I learned about interpersonal neurobiology—and as I had my own "bottom-up learnings" with clients. These clients were, as always, my greatest teachers, and their collaboration was essential to my understanding of how the theory I was reading was applicable to real assessment practice. All the clients described in this book have given permission for their stories to be included, and several contributed reflections about their experiences of Therapeutic Assessment. I am deeply grateful for their generosity.

Let me now provide an overview of the contents of this book. Chapter 2 stems from a paper presentation I gave in 2008 after reading Daniel Stern's (2004) account of mirror neurons and the human need for intersubjectivity. Stern's summary helped me understand important clinical interactions I had witnessed and think more deeply about the human longing to be seen and "feel felt" (Siegel, 1999). The implications of these ideas for psychological assessment were quickly evident to me. Chapter 3 is an exploration of three different meanings of "empathy" and how these different aspects are relevant to psychological assessment. This piece was written in 2009 as a tribute to the revered clinical psychologist, Paul Lerner, whose work in assessment and psychotherapy was well ahead of his time (Finn, 2009). Chapter 4 is a previously published case study (Finn, 2011a) of a young man I assessed multiple times during a long-term psychotherapy. The client had a history of severe medical trauma, and the Rorschach helped us work with this trauma. Neuroimaging studies of the Rorschach provided a basis for me to understand the client's fascinating test responses and for us to elaborate on an aspect of his story that he had never explored. Chapter 5 was first published in 2012 and is a precursor to this book in that I summarize the implications of neurobiological research for psychological assessment (Finn, 2012). The reader will be able to see my thinking on these topics at that time.

Chapter 6 is another account of the power of the Rorschach to elicit unresolved trauma so that it can be mentalized and healed. I tell the story of a young woman who had a longstanding pattern of dysfunctional romantic relationships and how the Rorschach shed light on the origins of this dynamic. Chapter 7 focuses on shame, a topic of great interest to me and one that has become central to Therapeutic Assessment over time. I summarize research over the past 40 years on the development and function of shame and how excessive shame is related to the psychological difficulties that bring many people for psychological assessment. I explain how shame is related to the dissociation of healthy affect states and how to recognize shame and dissociation when conducting psychological assessments, providing case examples. I then discuss how to use collaborative psychological assessment to help clients heal from problematic shame and reintegrate previously blocked emotions. The chapter ends with a letter from a client describing how her Therapeutic Assessment helped her overcome her shame. Chapter 8 is based on a webinar I gave in 2020 for the Therapeutic Assessment Institute. In it, I explore similarities between the work of Alexander Romanovitch Luria, Lev Vygotsky, and Constance Fischer. I explain how two concepts related to Vygotsky's work, the "zone of proximal development" and "scaffolding," are operationalized in Therapeutic Assessment, using two case examples as illustrations.

Chapter 9 is based on an article written with Jan Kamphuis and published in the *Journal of Personality Assessment* (Kamphuis & Finn, 2019). We explain how the evolutionary-based theory of epistemic trust (ET) and epistemic hypervigilance (EH) may help explain the somewhat surprising research showing that Therapeutic Assessment positively impacts clients who are typically very resistant to change, including those clients with personality disorders. The collaborative, intersubjective framework of TA and many of its specific techniques are highly relevant to restoring ET in clients. Chapter 10 is based on a presentation I gave to the Society for Personality Assessment in 2014. I begin by describing my psychotherapy with a traumatized 28-year-old woman, Jane, that failed because we became caught in reciprocal roles of "victim" (Jane) and "rescuer" (me). Using Karpman's (1968) well-known "drama triangle" of victims, rescuers, and perpetrators as a model, I explain how structural dissociation and projective identification are at the root of such enactments. Jane's psychological test results illustrate these personality adaptations and provide guidance for how to work with traumatized clients in a way that can be healing for both clients and assessors.

Chapter 11 is from an article published in the *Journal of Personality Assessment* (Finn, 2011b) and is the first of several chapters illustrating the clinical utility of the Adult Attachment Projective Picture System (AAP; George & West, 2012) and the importance of attachment theory for TA. I explain how I used the AAP as a mid-therapy intervention with a middle-aged man being treated for relationship difficulties. Reading an AAP-based description of his attachment status helped the man become aware of his characteristic defenses against painful affect and gave him the motivation to stay in therapy while experiencing and getting support for his unresolved mourning. Chapter 12 was written as a paper presentation in 2014 and is another case in which the AAP was central to helping a client face underlying grief that was being avoided and that caused severe relational difficulties. The 52-year-old client and I worked with her AAP stories during an Extended Inquiry, gradually undoing her preoccupied attachment defenses until she understood how they were protecting her from mourning unresolved pain from her childhood. This work was part of a couple's Therapeutic Assessment and eventually led to a major positive shift in the couple's dynamic.

Chapter 13 is new for this volume and demonstrates how Porges's (2011) *polyvagal theory* is useful for understanding our clients' experiences of overwhelming emotions. I recount the TA of Mary, a 51-year-old woman, who had a pattern of forming intimate relationships with men who were physically violent. During the administration of the AAP, Mary began to dissociate and was able to connect this experience to an unresolved sexual trauma that occurred when she was 15 years old. As I explained polyvagal theory to Mary in simple terms, she was able to change her narrative about the traumatic event from one of shame and personal responsibility to one of self-compassion and acceptance of normal human neurobiology. Chapter 14 concerns a new area of interest of mine, memory reconsolidation, a natural neurobiological process through which animals and humans "update" their mental models, and which many experts have proposed as a possible mechanism for transformational change in different psychotherapies. I explain the necessary steps for memory reconsolidation to occur, how these take place in Therapeutic Assessment, and then recount a case in which memory reconsolidation most likely was the active therapeutic agent. I offer suggestions for how to actively facilitate memory reconsolidation during psychological assessment.

In the concluding chapter, I consider why many psychologists still resist viewing psychological assessment as a powerful therapeutic intervention. I analyze the institutional and professional/personal forces that contribute to this resistance and propose strategies for addressing it—including rooting TA explicitly in a human science perspective that is compatible with affective neuroscience and interpersonal neurobiology. I end by imagining a training program for modern psychological assessment that would help the field reach its potential.

Note

1 I will use the term "collaborative/therapeutic assessment (c/ta)" to refer to a general approach to psychological assessment that aims to involve clients as collaborators and use psychological assessment to help with their problems-in-living. I will use "Therapeutic Assessment" for the semi-structured model of collaborative psychological assessment developed by myself and my colleagues and for which a certification program exists through the Therapeutic Assessment Institute (TAI, 2025).

References

Bromberg, P. M. (2012). *The shadow of the tsunami and the growth of the relational mind.* Routledge.

Finn, S. E. (2007). *In our clients' shoes: Theory and techniques of Therapeutic Assessment.* Routledge.

Finn, S. E. (2009). The many faces of empathy in experiential, person-centered, collaborative assessment. *Journal of Personality Assessment, 91*, 20–23.

Finn, S. E. (2011a). Journeys through the Valley of Death: Multimethod psychological assessment and personality transformation in long-term psychotherapy. *Journal of Personality Assessment, 93,* 123–141.

Finn, S. E. (2011b). Use of the Adult Attachment Projective Picture System (AAP) in the middle of a long-term psychotherapy. *Journal of Personality Assessment, 93,* 427–433.

Finn, S. E. (2012). Implications of recent research in neurobiology for psychological assessment. *Journal of Personality Assessment, 94,* 440–449.

Finn, S. E. (2023). What we have learned from 30 years being in our clients' shoes. *The TA Connection, 11*(1), 4–12.

Fischer, C. T. (1985/1994). *Individualizing psychological assessment.* Routledge.

Fischer, C. T. (2000). Personal communication.

Fosha, D., Siegel, D. J., & Solomon, M. F. (2009). *The healing power of emotion: Affective neuroscience, development, and clinical practice*. Norton.

George, C., & West, M. (2012). *The Adult Attachment Projective Picture System: Attachment theory and assessment in adults.* Guilford.

Handler, L. (2006). The use of therapeutic assessment with children and adolescents. In S. Smith & L. Handler (Eds.), *Clinical assessment of children and adolescents: A practitioner's guide* (pp. 53–72). Erlbaum.

Kamphuis, J. H., & Finn, S. E. (2019). Therapeutic Assessment in personality disorders: Toward the restoration of epistemic trust. *Journal of Personality Assessment, 101*(6), 662–674.

Karpman, S. B. (1968). Fairy tales and script drama analysis. *Transactional Analysis Bulletin, 7*, 39–43.

Porges, S. W. (2011). *The polyvagal theory: Neurophysiological foundations of emotions, attachment, communication, self-regulation.* Norton.

Purves, C. (2002). Collaborative assessment with involuntary populations: Foster children and their mothers. *The Humanistic Psychologist, 30,* 164–174.

Siegel, D. J. (1999). *The developing mind: Toward a neurobiology of interpersonal experience*. Guilford.

Stern, D. N. (2004). *The present moment in psychotherapy and everyday life*. Norton.

Therapeutic Assessment Institute. (2025). *Full certification process*. Downloaded from www.therapeuticassessment.com.

Chapter 2

Empathy, Intersubjectivity, and the Longing to Be Known

Why Personality Assessment Works*

Please consider the following real clinical scenarios and think about what they have in common:

1) It is my first year in clinical psychology graduate school, and Lloyd Sines, the professor teaching the lab for my psychopathology course, takes us six students each week to interview different people admitted to the inpatient psychiatric ward at the University of Minnesota hospitals. One week my classmates and I are brought to see an elderly man, Mr. Olson, sitting in a chair in his hospital room, almost completely catatonic. The head nurse tells us Mr. Olson has not moved or uttered a word since his children brought him in the day before, and that he has been severely depressed since the death of his wife one month ago. As we observe, Dr. Sines pulls up a chair and moves in close to Mr. Olson. He introduces himself in a quiet voice and then takes Mr. Olson's hand very gently in his. He says, "Mr. Olson, I would like to say some things about what I think you are experiencing right now. If I'm correct in what I say, please squeeze my hand to let me know that I'm right. If you understand and agree to this, please squeeze my hand right now." Mr. Olson responds as requested. Dr. Sines then continues, "You are feeling that life is not worth living right now" *(squeeze)*, "that you wish you could just lay down and die" (squeeze), "that you wish people would just leave you be" *(squeeze)*, "and that you can't go on living without your wife." Mr. Olson squeezes again, and a tear silently runs down his cheek. Dr. Sines continues in this fashion and within 15 minutes, Mr. Olson is crying and talking to Dr. Sines in a strained voice about his wife's death. In less than 30 minutes, Mr. Olson is able to stand and walk to his bed and lie down. We students are in awe at Dr. Sines' clinical mastery.

* This chapter is adapted from a paper presented at the annual meeting of the Society for Personality Assessment, March 28, 2008, New Orleans, LA, as part of a symposium "Conceptual Innovations in Personality Assessment," C. G. Overton (Chair)

DOI: 10.4324/9781003602231-2

2) Lucy is a 21-year-old college student who has suffered numerous traumatic experiences in her childhood that her family has never acknowledged, including her parents' highly conflictual marriage and subsequent vicious divorce, her mother's alcoholic binges, her younger brother's frequent rages, and her father's attempts to turn her against her mother after their separation. Lucy's mother and stepfather have referred her for a psychological assessment because they are concerned about her alcohol use and the fact that her grades in college are much lower than they ever were in high school. Lucy agrees to participate, and in our initial session, my post-doc and I learn that Lucy is the consummate "party girl," who lives for the string of parties each weekend where she gets drunk and after which she frequently can't remember what happened. Still, Lucy confesses to us that she is bothered by not knowing what she wants to do in life. She feels lost, she says, and embarrassed that she hasn't already decided on a college major. We agree to do some career and personality testing, and Lucy subsequently comes to every one of the scheduled sessions, eagerly participating in each test we give.
3) Mr. B is on probation, referred against his will for an MMPI-2 assessment, and when I first meet him, he is resistant, skeptical, and hostile. After 10–15 minutes of trying to establish his own goals for the assessment—with little success—I ask him instead about his experiences on parole. I listen carefully as he launches into a heated diatribe about how "disrespected" he feels by Ms. Jones, his probation officer. He complains vehemently that Ms. Jones has told him he is an angry person, but that he is not; he insists he is simply more forthright and "honest" than most people. I sympathize with how awful it can be to feel mischaracterized, especially by people who have power over us. After a while, Mr. B agrees to take the MMPI-2, saying he wants to see who is right—he or Ms. Jones. After this point in the interview, he becomes calmer and more vulnerable and asks me if the MMPI-2 can tell what kind of job he should look for. He then goes on to tell me about his problems meeting women. His subsequent MMPI-2 profile is quite unguarded.
4) Marion is 50 and tells me in the first few minutes of our initial session that she is having a classic "mid-life crisis" brought about by "empty nest syndrome." I learn that she got married at age 19, gave up plans to go to college, and instead stayed home to raise 5 children. Now her youngest child has left for college, and Marion says she is depressed, doesn't know what to do with herself, and no longer "knows who she is." I find out that she has spent much of the past year reading self-help books and filling out sample "personality profiles" in women's magazines. Her husband finally suggested she go for a "real" psychological assessment and got my name from a friend. Marion arrives eager and full of questions about herself. Her main question is: "Who am I? I became so 'de-selved' in my relationships

with my husband and my children that I no longer know who I am. Is there still hope I can 'find myself' at age 50?"

To me, these four case excerpts illustrate a phenomenon I have witnessed and been fascinated with for years: there is a basic human longing to be known, understood, and accepted for who we are (see Finn, 2009). In the first scenario, it was Dr. Sines' accurate empathy for Mr. Olson's inner world that reached through his despair and eventually gave him the energy to reenter the world of human relationships and resume his grieving. With Lucy, the "party girl," you can imagine the difficult underlying emotional states she was managing with her wild and superficial social behavior—emotional states that eventually became clear to us through her Rorschach responses. Yet, Lucy so wanted to know more about herself that she eagerly took part in a process that she knew—on some level—would elucidate those difficult emotions.

Some of you have seen the video of my interview with Mr. B—the man on probation. When I watch it I am always struck by how upset he is that Ms. Jones has misunderstood him, and how cooperative he becomes with me as I sympathize with his plight and offer a way for us to assess whether he is an "angry person." And finally, with Marion, the 50-year-old woman, I marveled at how hard she had worked to try to "find herself" by reading self-help books and filling out various rating scales. She was so eager for feedback from me that I decided to be especially thoughtful about what I said to her about her, lest my comments become part of some new, hastily constructed self-definition.

As I hope you could read, each person was struggling with a desire to be understood and known by themselves and by me and was willing—precisely because of this motivation—to enter into the unknown and to them mysterious process called psychological assessment. In fact, I would suggest to you that without this motivation, none of these assessments would have been successful or even possible. And I think a similar force is at work in all successful psychological assessments.

My goal in this chapter is to explain how the motivation to be known, understood, and accepted is crucial to our work as psychological assessors and basic to our make-up as human beings. I will talk about recent research in developmental neurobiology that helps explain this motivation and then draw implications for the practice of psychological assessment.

One-Way and Two-Way Intersubjectivity

I have written before about intersubjectivity theory as it applies to psychological assessment (Finn, 2002). Here I use the word intersubjectivity in a different sense—as a type of human interpersonal experience in which one person "[mind reads]...another's thoughts, feelings, or intentions" (Stern, 2004, p. xvi). This is not a mystical process, although it is wondrous; it is well established that the human capacity for intersubjectivity is based in our innate ability to notice subtle facial expressions, body movements, and posture, to hear minute variations in tone of voice, and to infer intentions based on the context of another's behavior. Stern (2004), Trevarthen (1993), Tronick (1998) and others have written about "one-way intersubjectivity," which can be described as "I know what you are feeling." A more complicated experience is two-way intersubjectivity, best captured by the phrase: "I know that you know what I am feeling, and vice versa." Similarly, Siegel (1999) has written about the powerful experience of one person "feeling felt" by another.

Mirror Neurons

Recent advances in neurobiology have made it clear that the capacity for intersubjectivity is "wired into" our brains. One major advance was the discovery of mirror neurons by Rizzolatti and his colleagues at the University of Parma (Rizzolatti et al., 1996). To summarize, mirror neurons sit next to motor neurons in the brain. They fire when we are doing nothing other than watching another person behave (e.g., scratching her nose). And the pattern of neural firing mimics the exact pattern that would happen if we were scratching our own nose. It is now widely agreed that mirror neurons extend beyond simple motor behavior to help explain shared emotional experiences. To quote Stern (2004):

> Mirror neurons ... [permit] us to directly participate in another's actions without having to imitate them. We experience the other as if we were executing the same action, feeling the same emotion, making the same vocalization, or being touched as they are being touched ... This "participation" in another's mental life creates a sense of feeling/sharing with/understanding the person, in particular the person's intentions and feelings.
>
> (p.79)

Clearly mirror neurons are one of the important mechanisms underlying empathy and intersubjectivity, and they help explain why (with some individual differences) these phenomena are ubiquitous in humans, except perhaps in cases of brain disorders such as autism.

Intersubjectivity as a Basic Human Motivation

In a book published over 20 years ago, Stern (2004) advanced the hypothesis that we humans not only are innately *capable* of intersubjective experiences, but that we ardently desire them and seek them out. Stern posited that intersubjectivity is a basic human motivational system, such as the attachment system and the sexual system, and in fact, that the intersubjectivity system is more basic than the attachment system because attachment cannot take place without the ability of child and caregiver to read each other's cues and coordinate their emotional and behavioral responses. Also, Stern believed that intersubjectivity confers an evolutionary advantage, in allowing the nonverbal coordination of complex group activity (such as hunting together a dangerous wild animal), the establishment of family and group identity or cohesion (which contributes to survival in many ways), and the development of morality. Regarding the latter, the basic idea is that we might not experience guilt about hurting others except for the fact that we can feel what they are feeling.

If intersubjectivity is a basic human motivation, then it must activate goal-directed behaviors and be experienced by the individual as a need or longing. Stern (2004) details two instances where we feel this desire: (1) We all experience the need to read the intentions or feelings of people around us and will be anxious in groups or dyads if we are not able to do this. (As a thought experiment, imagine being put in a room full of strangers and being prevented from either seeing or hearing them!) (2) We all have a need to define, maintain, or reestablish self-identity and self-cohesion—to "know who we are." And we need the eyes and reactions of others to be able to do this. None of us can "figure out who we are" without "feeling felt" by others—although as Marion (the 50-year-old woman in my fourth scenario found out) there is also a danger in having our self-definition be totally determined by how others view us.

Because these two needs are part of an innate motivational system, they exist across the life span. We *never* outgrow our desire to be seen, accepted, and known by others—to be reflected in another's eyes and mind—and to get information in this way about who we are. Also, these needs can never be completely satiated; we are always on the lookout for new experiences of intersubjectivity.

Implications for Psychological Assessment

So, if people generally have an intense, innate longing to be known, understood, and accepted, what are the implications for our work as psychological assessors? I can think of five important points.

1) *We have a great deal to learn about the "micro-processes" involved in psychological assessment and psychotherapy, and research is greatly needed in this area.*

Clearly our work as assessors crucially depends on the "mutual penetration of minds" (Stern, 2004) that occurs between client and assessor, and we know little at this point about how this occurs on a minute-to-minute level during assessment sessions and what role our tests play in helping clients feel felt. I propose that what is appropriate here are detailed analyses of videotaped client-assessor interactions, perhaps paired with electropysiologic measures, much as Tronick (1998), Trevarthen (1993) and others have used to investigate parent-infant intersubjectivity. I suspect that such research could teach us more than we can possibly imagine about the process of psychological assessment.

2) *The intense experience of mirroring and acceptance that we offer people who participate in a psychological assessment has a high intrinsic value.*

Just think of all the money that is spent and made in our country on those lay personality tests that my client Marion found in her women's magazines, and you get a sense of how great the motivation to be known generally is. And of course, for some of our clients, feeling seen, understood, and accepted can be a matter of life and death.

I grasped this in a new way some years ago when I assessed a woman who had chronic, intermittent pelvic pain as the result of botched gynecological surgery. Although her pain was not particularly physically intense (e.g., it never got above a 4 on a scale of 1–10), the woman was in absolute despair about it, and neither her husband, her physicians, nor her psychotherapist seemed to understand why. Their lack of understanding made the woman feel worse, and as a result, she was quite suicidal when we began the psychological assessment. Through the assessment, and in part because of her Rorschach responses, I was able to help the woman put words to the extreme powerlessness she felt about the pain. She never knew when it would come or when it would go away. She could be in the middle of a good day, and suddenly it would return. And even on days when the pain was completely gone, she found it impossible to enjoy herself because she was worried that it would soon be back. After we talked about this powerlessness and how traumatizing it was for her, the client said that I was the first person who truly understood her anguish, and she stopped feeling acutely suicidal. (See Finn, 2012, for more on this TA.)

Another powerful experience was my assessment of a 30-year-old woman experiencing severe OCD symptoms. She could not leave the house to go to work without repeatedly returning to check that she had turned off the stove, locked the door, etc. When I asked her what frightened her the most, it was that she "would make a mistake and inadvertently hurt someone." Early in the assessment, I learned that she had recently had a miscarriage and was devastated by this loss, but her husband, family, and even her obstetrician could not empathize with her grief. They told her that she could get pregnant again and that she shouldn't focus on the lost fetus. She felt bad that she couldn't do this and worried that something was wrong with her. I sat with her in her grief, and during the assessment, we designed a ceremony she would use to dispose of the fetal cremains. Soon after this, her OCD symptoms disappeared.

3) *To get people to fully participate in a psychological assessment, we must "simply" activate the intersubjectivity motivational system.*

That is, if clients come to believe—prior to or in the beginning stages of an assessment—that the process is likely to lead to their feeling known, understood, and accepted, they will be eager to cooperate with us in any way. Also, if clients begin to learn things about themselves and feel accurately mirrored and respected as the assessment proceeds, their energy and motivation to continue should only increase. I believe this understanding gives new support for the procedures of collaborative psychological assessment, which are grounded in a phenomenological or intersubjective view of the assessment situation, and which have been proven to positively impact clients more than traditional assessment procedures.

4) *As we get better at knowing how to engage clients in psychological assessments, we must be rigorous about obtaining informed consent.*

If the longing to be seen, known, and understood by another is a basic human drive, and we learn even more about how to activate this motivational system to get people to reveal themselves to us in psychological assessment, we need to be extremely thoughtful about the potential consequences for clients, and we must inform them beforehand. I have been thinking about this a great deal recently following a psychological assessment a colleague and I did with a young, extremely bright, but troubled woman. This young woman posed several penetrating questions about herself at the beginning of the assessment, and—as the process continued—gradually came to know and understand many deeply disturbing things about her background growing up. Despite our best efforts to support the client emotionally, she sunk into a deep depression as the assessment unfolded, and fortunately, was able to begin seeing her psychotherapist three times a week immediately after the assessment ended. At her two-month follow-up session, the client told me she was glad she did the assessment, and that she would do it over again even as hard as it was, but that she also thought the "warning label on the Therapeutic Assessment can" needed to be written in bigger type. I have been thinking carefully about her comments.

5) *We must not underestimate people's appreciation for our work, and we must be wise about the termination phase of our assessments.*

As I think back on the assessments I have done, I realize that I can only fully understand the extent of clients' appreciation afterwards by positing that Therapeutic Assessment directly addresses a basic and crucial human need. Over the past 43 years, at the end of their assessments, various clients have:

(a) told me with tears in their eyes that they have never felt so understood, (b) offered to pay me more money than we had agreed upon for their assessments, (c) asked if they could refer their entire family for assessments (and in some cases, have actually done so), (d) sent me poems, cards, and photos for years after we completed our work, and (e) [this is true] asked if they could name their first child after me. Of course, I have been touched and honored by such gestures, while attempting not to take the clients' reactions entirely personally. (Again, conceiving of intersubjectivity as a basic human need helps me put these reactions in their appropriate context. I don't think they can be fully explained—as I have done previously—by positing a human drive for self-verification.) But I have also become much more sensitive and thoughtful about the termination phase of my assessments with clients. Some time ago, following the work of Diana Fosha (2000), I started spending much more time with clients at the end of their assessments, allowing them to process the experiences, express their appreciation, and say goodbye. Fosha found that this kind of "meta-therapeutic processing" helped psychotherapy clients consolidate their work and reach new states of integration. I totally agree.

References

Finn, S. E. (2002, March). *Challenges and lessons of intersubjectivity theory for psychological assessment.* Paper presented at the Society for Personality Assessment annual meeting, San Antonio, TX, as part of a symposium, "Concepts of the Self: Implications for Assessment," M. L. Silverstein, Chair. Reprinted as Chapter 17 in Finn, S. E. (2007). *In our clients' shoes: Theory and techniques of Therapeutic Assessment.* Erlbaum.

Finn, S. E. (2009). The many faces of empathy in experiential, person-centered, collaborative assessment. *Journal of Personality Assessment, 91*, 20–23.

Finn, S. E. (2012). Therapeutic Assessment with a couple in crisis: Undoing problematic projective identification via the Consensus Rorschach. In S. E. Finn, C. T. Fischer, & L. Handler (Eds.), *Collaborative/therapeutic assessment: A case book and guide* (pp. 379–400). Wiley.

Fosha, D. (2000). *The transforming power of affect: A model for accelerated change.* Basic Books.

Rizzolatti, G., Fadiga, L., Fogassi, L., & Gallese, V. (1996). Pre-motor cortex and the recognition of motor actions, *Cognitive Brain Research, 3*, 131–141.

Siegel, D. J. (1999). *The developing mind: Toward a neurobiology of interpersonal experience*. Guilford.

Stern, D. N. (2004). *The present moment in psychotherapy and everyday life*. Norton.

Trevarthen, C. (1993). The self born in intersubjectivity: An infant communicating. In U. Neisser (Ed.), *The perceived self* (pp. 121–173). Cambridge University Press.

Tronick, E. Z. (1998). Dyadically expanded states of consciousness and the process of therapeutic change. *Infant Mental Health Journal, 19*, 290–299.

Chapter 3

The Many Faces of Empathy in Experiential, Person-Centered, Collaborative Assessment*

In 2007, Barton Evans asked me to take part in a symposium at the annual meeting of the Society for Personality Assessment honoring Paul Lerner. I eagerly accepted the invitation because Paul Lerner was someone I greatly esteemed. When told the symposium title—"The Heart of Assessment"—I immediately associated to Lerner's heart-filled presence and to how I always saw him as a dynamic force at the center of SPA. I also remembered a quote from Lerner that had always stayed with me: "the heart of an experiential interpretive approach is the examiner's empathy"(Lerner, 1998, p. 186). Recalling this statement helped me realize that one thing I admired so much about Paul Lerner was his amazing empathy. In this chapter, I will write about various aspects and meanings of empathy, how many of these are evident in Lerner's published work, and how I have come to think about empathy in collaborative/therapeutic assessment.

Meanings of Empathy

Empathy as a Mode of Gathering Information

In various of his writings, Lerner made it clear that when he referred to empathy, he meant it in the sense that Kohut did in his seminal 1959 paper, "Introspection, Empathy, and Psychoanalysis." That is, Lerner often cited Kohut and stated that empathy was an "information-gathering activity." He elaborated, "the examiner uses the individual's entire [test] production—the response and the accompanying verbalizations—as a jumping-off point for attuning to the underlying subjective state" (1996, p. 47). Lerner also stated, "The examiner asks himself or herself, 'To have arrived at this response or used these phrases or words, what might the patient have been experiencing or trying to communicate at the moment?'" (1998, p. 187). Lerner made it clear that this empathic way of looking

* This chapter was previously published as an article in the *Journal of Personality Assessment, 91*(1), 20–23. The Many Faces of Empathy in Experiential, Person-Centered, Collaborative Assessment. Article DOI: 10.1080/00223890802483391 https://www.tandfonline.com/

DOI: 10.4324/9781003602231-3

at test materials could be applied not only to the content of Rorschach responses, but also to the scoring. I think he would have agreed also that empathy is useful in interpreting other kinds of psychological data besides the Rorschach. For example, we might ask ourselves, "What is it like to be a person with a WAIS-III Verbal IQ of 130 and a Performance IQ of 85?" or "What kind of person would copy the Bender Gestalt figures so that he needed 3 sheets of paper for his drawings?"

Lerner saw this way of interpreting psychological testing as directly in line with Mayman's (1964) "clinical-intuitive" approach, as well as Schachtel's (1966) "experiential" approach. At times, he also adopted Mayman's term "person-centered" for this method and contrasted it with a "test-centered" way of looking at assessment materials; Lerner also used the terms "clinical-humanistic" and "phenomenological" in some of his writings. One of our best examples of how he himself applied this strategy comes from the Appendix of Lerner's wonderful (2005b) article, "Red Beavers and Building Bridges Between Assessment and Treatment," in which he described the assessment and subsequent treatment of a 34-year-old woman (Table 3.1).

In this table, Lerner shows what he called his "first-order inferences" from the client's Rorschach. He posited that it was in this step of Rorschach interpretation that empathy was most involved. For example, in italics we see Lerner's notations that the client's request for structure and direction at the beginning of the Rorschach might indicate that she "looks to the outside" and "seeks external direction." As I mentioned, you can see that Lerner drew inferences not only

Table 3.1 Patient's Rorschach

I.	*seeks external direction* ^1. I see a bat Is that what you want?	*blackness* (Bat?) It's black, the wings, like it's on display *passivity, sense of being examined*	WFoC' AP
	Tentative Possible false-self features ^2. Perhaps a mask	(Mask?) Two white areas are eyes and it has the shape of a face.	W(s)Fo Mask *space response*
	Looks to the outside Should I continue? (Up to you)		
	^3. An x-ray, perhaps the pelvis *Again, being examined*	(X-ray?) Looks like the bone structure and the shades of grey and black	WFC' X-ray w+
II.	^1. Area in the middle looks like a lamp	(Lamp?) The shape of it	DSF + Obj *space response, emptiness*

Note: Excerpt from Appendix B in Lerner (2005b). The Rorschach scores are based on the system developed by Rapaport, Gill, and Schafer (1945).

from the Rorschach content, but also from the scoring. For example, after scoring the second white space response on Card II, Lerner notes that the client might be experiencing "emptiness." In the next step of the interpretive process, which Lerner called "transformation," these "first-order inferences" are examined, assembled, and integrated into higher-order inferences. Lerner described this process as follows: "bits and pieces start to fit together and the model takes shape; it comes to the forefront of one's mind and later material serves to correct, refine, and expand the model" (Lerner, 2004, p. 157).

As you can see, this way of approaching psychological testing is highly similar to what Fischer (2000) called the hermeneutic tradition underlying her collaborative, individualized assessment. To quote her (Fischer, 2000, p. 13), the assessor develops:

> his or her understanding by circling repeatedly from an observation back to context or to larger prior comprehensions, then back again to observation ... the hermeneutic quest moves repeatedly among the presented issue, the client in front of the assessor, theories of development and personality, research studies, statistical norms, the client's history, diagnostic traditions, previous clients, and the assessor's own life....Eventually the assessor—and in collaborative assessment, the assessor and the client—reaches useful, coherent understandings of the presented material.

I present this quote to highlight how collaborative psychological assessment extends the Mayman-Schachtel-Lerner tradition of test interpretation to include one more element—the involvement of the client in fine-tuning the assessor's empathy. This leads me to discuss another way of thinking of empathy, as an intersubjective process involving both client and assessor.

Empathy as a Two-Person Process

If we think of empathy as a two-person process, rather than as an activity of the clinician alone, I believe we achieve a richer understanding of the assessment process that helps explain otherwise puzzling events. For example, in the article I mentioned earlier, "Red Beavers and Building Bridges." Lerner described the young woman's approach to the assessment sessions as follows:

> She was highly cooperative in the sense of fulfilling all that was asked of her but initiated little. My feeling was one of having a dance partner who faithfully followed my lead but had minimal interest in whom she was dancing with.
>
> (Lerner, 2005b, p. 272)

Nevertheless, Lerner later commented,

> Despite her insulated and aloof manner, the patient produced a rich and revealing [Rorschach] record, one filled with considerable pain and dysphoric affect. I understood this discrepancy between presentation and test record as her desire, at some level, to tell her story and be listened to.
> (p. 272)

Could it be that Lerner's ability to understand this woman's inner world came not only from his ability to "feel into" her subjective world through her test responses, but also from her underlying desire to be understood and to communicate to him through symbolic language and images? If so, shouldn't her efforts also be recognized as furthering the process of empathy? This conceptualization of empathy as an intersubjective phenomenon has helped me understand something I've observed in Therapeutic Assessment. At the beginning of an evaluation, I gather questions from clients that they hope to answer from our work together (Finn, 2007). It has long struck me that after these questions are agreed upon and put in writing, clients then seem to go out of their way to provide me with the information I need to help answer them.

For example, recently a woman asked for help understanding why she always worried that her husband would leave her, although there were no indications that he ever thought about this. In the next session, without my bidding, she brought a small scrapbook to show me of photographs from her childhood and adolescence. As we looked at pictures from her teenage years, I learned that she had been deeply in love with her first boyfriend at age 15, but that he had been killed suddenly in a car accident when she was 16. I commented on how painful this must have been for her, and she surprised herself by breaking down in tears over something, she told me, she thought she had "gotten over years ago." It didn't take us long to consider whether there was a connection between her boyfriend's death and her fears of losing her husband, a theory she assured me that she did not have consciously in mind when she decided to bring the scrapbook to show me.

The interpersonal process of empathic understanding is even more evident in collaborative assessment—as Fischer alluded—when one discusses "first-order inferences" from testing with clients. For example, the following interchange took place between me and a 15-year-old girl regarding her first response to Card I of the Rorschach, "a cat's face." You should know that the girl's parents had asked, "Why doesn't Amy come to us when she's in trouble? Why won't she let us help her?"

Steve: Do cats have any special meaning for you?
Amy: Yes. I'm a cat inside
SF: In what way?
A: I'm really self-sufficient and aloof. And I only relate to people when I want to, not when they want.

SF: Is that because you distrust people?

A: Not really. I just don't need them. Cats aren't like dogs—they don't seek constant affection and praise. They just need you to feed them, and not even that if they can go outside and catch birds ... My cat Buster is like that, although sometimes he likes to sit in my lap, especially when it's cold.

SF: And do you occasionally like some affection too?

A: Yes, but only on my own terms. My mother always wants to hug me, but it's really to make her *feel better. It doesn't really have anything to do with me. So, I usually push her away.*

You can see through this interchange how I was using my empathy to try to "get in Amy's shoes," and she was at the same time tracking me and giving me information to help me understand her inner world better. I believe that recognizing the interpersonal aspects of such a process lets us be less anxious about our role as an assessor. It is no longer our sole job to understand clients' test productions in isolation; we can count on them also to contribute to our empathic understandings.

Empathy as a Healing Element in Human Interactions

Finally, I return to Kohut in discussing a final view of empathy—that is, as a powerful healing element in human interactions. Kohut spent 25 years stressing that empathy was "an information-collecting, data-gathering activity" that could be "right or wrong, in the service of compassion or hostility, pursued slowly and ploddingly or 'intuitively'" and is "never by itself supportive or therapeutic" (Kohut, 1982, p. 397). He did this, I believe, to distinguish his scientific use of the word empathy from our lay use of the term, where we often mean it as a synonym for "sympathy" or "compassion." What is lesser known, however, is that in the final paper he would write, and which was delivered posthumously by his son. Kohut (1982, p. 397) stated:

> Even though everything I have said up to now remains fully valid … I must now, unfortunately, add that empathy per se, the mere presence of empathy, has also a beneficial, in a broad sense, a therapeutic effect—both in the clinical setting and in human life, in general.

Kohut went on to detail specific evidence for this assertion, including his observation that it is the "empathic milieu" in which most of us live that keeps us "psychologically alive." He contrasted this to the "impersonal, dehumanized extermination" experienced by prisoners in Nazi concentration camps, saying this was much more psychologically destructive than an experience of "impassioned, hate-motivated killing" would have been (p. 398).

As evidence of the healing power of empathy, I'd like to quote from another published case of Lerner's, entitled "On Developing a Clinical Sense of Self" (2005a). In this paper, Lerner tells us about his assessment and later treatment of a 20-year-old man who was the son of one of Lerner's favorite psychoanalytic teachers. The young man was intelligent but lacked direction in his life, which concerned his parents. Although gratified that an esteemed and much-loved mentor had referred a son to him for treatment, Lerner soon found that he could not stop thinking during therapy sessions about how his teacher would evaluate his various interventions. Recognizing that this was hampering his work, and that he had to do something about it, Lerner also had an empathic insight that his own experience might be close to that of his patient:

> In an empathic, yet straightforward way, I said to the patient that I, not he, had unwittingly allowed his father into the treatment setting and that it was affecting our relationship and my capacity to be with him. I then wondered if he too had permitted his father's shadow to enter into too many aspects of his life.
>
> The patient leaped out of his chair, rushed over to me, shook my hand, and then returned and sat back down. With a passion and intensity he had never displayed with me previously, he blurted out, "Way to go Doc, you finally got it." He went on to explain that his inability to get away from, or least quiet his internal father had been a problem for him throughout his life. As he experienced it, his beliefs, values, and aspirations, his choices, were never fully his own. In words that were remarkably close to my own experience, he described his ever present need to secure his dad's approval, his attempts to live to his father's standards, and his feeling obliged to fulfill his father's dreams for him.
>
> (Lerner, 2005a, p. 22).

Lerner tells us that after this event, the treatment "literally took off," and that in the ensuing months both he and the client developed a firmer sense of self. Surely this is an example of what Kohut meant in his last paper, that in the context of Lerner's powerful empathy, this young man flourished and found direction, and at the same time, Lerner found his own analytic voice. In his discussion of the case, Lerner told us one of the things he learned: "interpretation had been held up as the most basic and most essential analytic tool. Yet, for me, what felt even more basic and more essential was empathy" (p. 23).

This idea, that empathy itself has healing potential, is one of the principles underlying my own work on Therapeutic Assessment. I have long believed that we all have a longing to be seen, deeply understood, and accepted for who we are. When we as clinicians are able to provide this kind of experience to our assessment clients, they, as well as we, benefit immensely. Over the years, numerous clients have told me how life-changing it was for them that I "got in their shoes" during a Therapeutic Assessment. Also, as in the instance of the young man Lerner treated, I have witnessed many of these individuals go on to take developmental leaps following such an experience.

Finally, I have written elsewhere about the ways I have grown as a person by being able to share, in a deep way, clients' inner worlds (Finn, 2005). I continue to believe that when clients are vulnerable with us during a psychological assessment, thereby allowing us to "feel our way into" what it is like to be them, they give us an amazing gift. In this way, we get a chance to "live many lives," discover aspects of ourselves we might otherwise never have encountered, and deepen our compassion. In Lerner's case, his work with his teacher's son helped him solidify his identity as an analyst and discover what he thought was healing in clinical interactions (as opposed to what he had been taught). In my own assessment work, I have had to confront aspects of my own defensive operations and see similarities between myself and various groups of individuals who make me "flinch." In doing so, I have learned experientially the truth of Sullivan's (1953) elegant postulate that we are all "much more simply human than otherwise" (p. 32).

Summary and Conclusion

In summary, I have outlined three related definitions of empathy in psychological assessment: (1) Empathy is a tool for gathering information and understanding the subjective world of our clients; (2) Empathy is an intersubjective process in which clients and assessors help each other name and verbalize important aspects of the clients' experience, and (3) Empathy is a healing element in human interactions that keeps us psychologically alive and growing.

All three aspects of empathy were strongly present in Paul Lerner, the man, and are clearly evident—as I have shown—in his written work. Lerner was an extraordinary clinician, thinker, teacher, and colleague, and his amazing capacity for empathy was part of what made him so special. I feel lucky to have benefited personally from Lerner's empathy; I consulted with him on more than one occasion about difficult assessment cases, and he was instrumental in my understanding of one Therapeutic Assessment that failed (Finn, 2004). Paul Lerner affected me and my work profoundly and helped me find my own heart. I will be forever grateful to have known him.

References

Finn, S. E. (2004, March). *"But I was only trying to help!": Therapeutic Assessment and Karpman's triangle*. Paper presented at the Society for Personality Assessment annual meeting, Miami, FL, as part of a symposium, "What Can We Learn from Failed Assessments?" S. E. Finn, Chair. Reprinted as Chapter 13 in S. E. Finn, (2007), *In our clients' shoes: Theory and techniques of Therapeutic Assessment.*

Finn, S. E. (2005). How psychological assessment taught me compassion and firmness. *Journal of Personality Assessment, 84*, 27–30.

Finn, S. E. (2007). *In our clients' shoes: Theory and techniques of Therapeutic Assessment*. Erlbaum.

Fischer, C. T. (2000). Collaborative, individualized assessment. *Journal of Personality Assessment, 74*, 2–14.

Kohut, H. (1959). Introspection, empathy, and psychoanalysis: An examination of the relationship between mode of observation and theory. *Journal of the American Psychoanalytic Association, 7*, 459–483.

Kohut, H. (1982). Introspection, empathy, and the semi-circle of mental health. *International Journal of Psychoanalysis, 63*, 395–407.

Lerner, P. M. (1996). The interpretive process in Rorschach testing. *Journal of Personality Assessment, 67*, 494–500.

Lerner, P. M. (1998). Schachtel and experiential Rorschach assessment. *Journal of Personality Assessment, 71*, 182–188.

Lerner, P. M. (2004). Further thoughts on an experiential psychoanalytic approach to the Rorschach. *Bulletin of the Menninger Clinic, 68*, 152–163.

Lerner, P. M. (2005a). On developing a clinical sense of self. *Journal of Personality Assessment, 84*, 21–24.

Lerner, P. M. (2005b). Red beavers and building bridges between assessment and treatment. *Journal of Personality Assessment, 85*, 271–279.

Mayman, M. (1964). *Some general propositions implicit in the clinical application of psychological tests*. Unpublished manuscript, The Menninger Foundation.

Rapaport, D., Gill, M., & Schafer, R. (1946). *Diagnostic psychological testing: The theory, statistical application, and and diagnostic application of a battery of tests: Vol. 2.* Year Book Publishers.

Schachtel, E. (1966). *Experiential foundations of Rorschach's test*. Basic Books.

Sullivan, H. S. (1953). *The interpersonal theory of psychiatry*. W. W. Norton & Co.

Chapter 4

Journeys through the Valley of Death

Multimethod Psychological Assessment and Personality Transformation in Long-Term Psychotherapy*

This chapter was written for a special issue of the *Journal of Personality Assessment* on the *Psychodynamic Diagnostic Manual* (*PDM;* PDM Task Force, 2006). I illustrate how multimethod psychological assessment can play a useful—if not essential—role in long-term psychotherapy when the goal is to facilitate profound shifts in how clients view themselves and relate to others. Although psychological assessment can be helpful in almost all long-term treatments, I focus in this chapter on its utility with one particular type of client who, in my experience, even excellent psychotherapists often find puzzling and challenging. These are talented and highly successful clients who often do not present with significant symptomatology on Axis I of the *Diagnostic and Statistical Manual of Mental Disorders* (4th ed. [*DSM–IV*]; American Psychiatric Association, 2001), but who have long-standing difficulties establishing and maintaining intimate relationships. My experience with these clients is consistent with the philosophy reflected in the *PDM*; that is, that their most important characteristics reside in a pattern of underlying emotional, personality, and interpersonal patterns rather than in overt symptoms or behaviors. As you will see, these clients also show a recognizable pattern of test scores in a multimethod personality assessment.

My insight into this class of clients has come about in two ways: (1) through assessment-based consultations I have conducted over many years to psychotherapists who find themselves confused and worried about certain clients in the middle of long-term therapies, and (2) through my own experiences assessing and treating clients in long-term interpersonally oriented psychotherapy. Therefore, I first briefly summarize an assessment consultation I did that fits the pattern I came to notice. Then I present a detailed case study of the assessment and treatment of one of my own clients.

* This chapter is based on an article previously published in 2011 in the *Journal of Personality Assessment*, 93(2), 123–141. Journeys Through the Valley of Death: Multimethod Psychological Assessment and Personality Transformation in Long-Term Psychotherapy. Article DOI: 10.1080/00223891.2010.542533 https://www.tandfonline.com/

DOI: 10.4324/9781003602231-4

Assessment Consultation in the Middle of a Long-term Treatment

In November 1993, shortly after I founded the Center for Therapeutic Assessment, I received a call from a colleague whose therapy and assessment work I greatly respected. She asked me whether I would do a psychological assessment with one of her clients, a middle-aged man I will call Bob, whom she had seen in psychotherapy for almost three years. As we talked, the following story emerged: Bob was an unmarried, highly successful businessman who had initially sought help for "relationship difficulties." The therapist had given Bob the Minnesota Multiphasic Personality Inventory–2 (MMPI–2; Butcher, Dahlstrom, Graham, Tellegen, & Kaemmer, 1989) at the beginning of the therapy, and she told me that his profile was "unremarkable" except for signs of mild depression (Scale 2 = 63*T*). Thus, she had confidently embarked on what she anticipated would be a straightforward course of therapy with a relatively mentally healthy man.

At first, the therapy had gone rather slowly, in part because Bob traveled frequently for his business and was not able to meet weekly. My colleague saw this pattern as possibly related to his difficulties with intimacy and asked Bob if he was titrating his closeness to her with his busy schedule. He granted that this might be the case, and eventually, they agreed to phone sessions whenever he was away from Austin. My colleague said that subsequently, about 18 months into the therapy, she had felt a deepening in Bob's attachment to her. At that point, Bob had some difficulties with a boss that were quite disorganizing to him, as he had always been successful and popular at work. The therapist had allowed Bob to call her several times between sessions to discuss important meetings, and he found these calls to be extremely helpful. Then Bob, of his own initiative, began coming to therapy two times a week. Shortly after that change, Bob became more depressed, and my colleague at first attributed this to the stresses of his job situation. However, over the ensuing months Bob's depression had worsened steadily, several courses of antidepressant medication had proven largely ineffective, he was having difficulty meeting work obligations, and was struggling—at the time of the assessment referral—with intense suicidal urges. My colleague was concerned, scared, and puzzled. She asked me: "What is going on with Bob? Did I misjudge his resiliency at the beginning of therapy? What is the source of all this depression? Am I doing something wrong? It's almost as if therapy has made Bob worse!"

An Important Lesson about the MMPI-2 and Rorschach

When I tested Bob, and many other clients like him in the years following this referral, his psychological test scores fit a pattern that I eventually wrote about in an article concerning how to give assessment feedback to clients based on different configurations of MMPI–2 and Rorschach scores (Finn, 1996). Figure 4.1

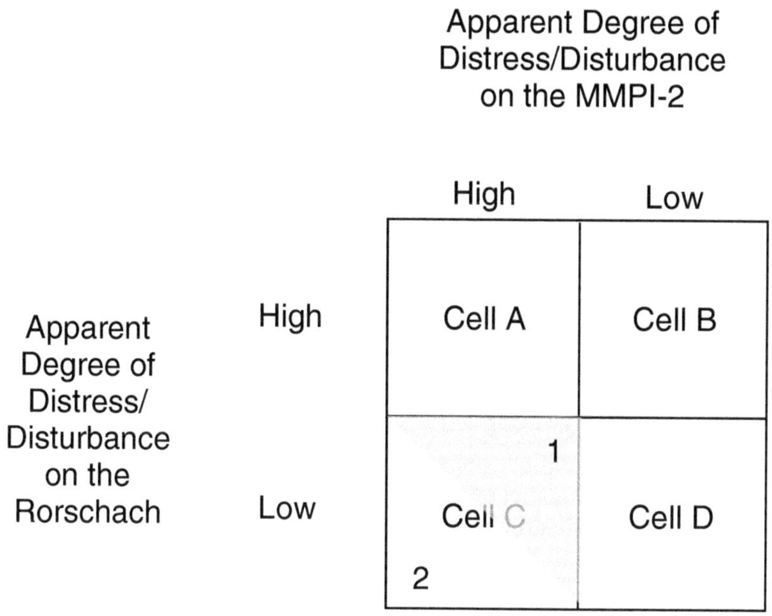

Figure 4.1 Patterns of MMPI-2 and Rorschach results.

Notes: Five configurations of MMPI–2 and Rorschach findings can be formed by examining the overall levels of distress, disturbance, or both revealed in the test protocols. Subtypes 1 and 2 in Cell C are differentiated by how engaged the client was, with protocols in Subtype 2 showing low R, high Lambda, low Affective Ratio, and/or low Weighted Sum of Color. This figure is adapted from Finn (1996) and each cell is discussed in detail in the original article.

shows a version of the main table from that article. Bob's testing fell squarely within Cell B of the table, in that his MMPI–2 (done by my colleague) looked relatively healthy, whereas his Rorschach (collected by me) suggested a great deal of distress and disturbance. (See Finn, 1996, for a full exposition of this table.)

In outpatient settings, Cell B represents the most frequent kind of discrepancy between the MMPI–2 and the Rorschach, and it is typically associated with clients who are not in immediate crisis when they present for mental health services. They might come as part of a couple wanting relationship counseling, they might be parents of a child with difficulties, or they might seek therapy puzzling over some relatively circumscribed difficulty they have not been able to resolve in spite of their otherwise successful lives. Often, as in the case of Bob, such clients' intractable struggles are in the area of intimate relationships. And, I have come to understand that both their MMPI–2 profiles and their Rorschachs contain important information about such clients' situations and dilemmas of change.

The relatively good MMPI–2, in these instances, accurately reflects the excellent coping mechanisms and general high level of functioning of these clients. These individuals typically do best in structured, impersonal, familiar situations, and—because they tend to order their lives accordingly—their MMPI–2 profiles capture how they will be seen by coworkers, acquaintances, and most people who do not know them extremely well. The Rorschach, in contrast, reveals underlying difficulties, affective states, and pathology that are "split off" or dissociated, but that emerge in emotionally arousing, regressive, interpersonal situations—such as long-term psychotherapy. If one takes a careful, detailed history from these clients, one might turn up events in their past that do not fit their typical presentation, such as instances of acting out, addictions, or difficulties with the law. Many of these individuals unconsciously avoid sustained close relationships, because they begin to feel and act "crazy" when such affiliations become more intense. As is well known, emotional and especially sexual intimacy has a way of opening up Pandora's box in everyone and bringing up unresolved wounds, conflicts, and struggles (where, in the best of situations, they can be worked on and healed). The clients in Cell B are very understandably terrified of intimacy because of the intensity of their unresolved wounds. They are typically unaware of this fear, however, and often come to therapy stating that they sincerely desire a close relationship.

Since I wrote about these clients in 1996, new developments in research, theory, and psychological assessment have helped me gain further understanding of their central dilemma. In recent years, I have frequently administered the Adult Attachment Projective Picture System (AAP; George & West, 2001, 2012; George, West, & Pettem, 1999) to clients along with the MMPI–2 and Rorschach, and I have discovered that many clients in Cell B are classified as having insecure-dismissing attachment status on the AAP. Dismissing individuals are known to have had early childhood experiences of being left alone with painful affect states; as a result, they learned to split off such emotions and to use a defense mechanism called "deactivation" (Bowlby, 1980; George & Solomon, 1989, 2008; George & West, 2012) in which achievement, status, and intellect are prioritized over intimacy (Slade, 2000). The literature on dismissing attachments helps us understand why Cell B clients are often so successful in their work, but are unsuccessful in forming lasting intimate relationships. First, work is generally an expression of the "exploratory system," which is prioritized in these clients over the attachment system (George & West, 2012). Second, work and other deactivation strategies—such as reading, watching television, and sleeping—help these individuals avoid underlying painful affect states related to early developmental traumas (George & West, 2012; Tatkin, 2003).

I believe the work of A. N. Schore (2001, 2005, 2009; J. R. Schore & Schore, 2008) sheds light on why the distress and disturbance evident in these clients' Rorschachs is generally not in their conscious awareness. Schore has amassed an impressive body of evidence that the negative affect states and implicit models of self and other resulting from insecure attachment experiences and early developmental trauma are primarily stored in the right hemisphere of the brain. The right hemisphere has dense reciprocal connections to limbic regions and subcortical areas of the brain, which have fewer direct connections to the left hemisphere. Thus, such material is often unconscious and inaccessible via language, although it shows up in dreams or in the transferences that develop in long-term psychotherapy (Bromberg, 2006). Furthermore, evidence is accruing from functional magnetic resonance imaging (fMRI) studies of the Rorschach (Asari et al., 2010a, 2010b) and of other performance-based personality tests such as the AAP (Bucheim et al., 2005) that performance-based tests are particularly sensitive to limbic area functioning and to right-hemisphere disorganization. I have posited that such tests are therefore more sensitive to the sequelae of insecure attachment and early trauma, whereas self-report tests like the MMPI–3, Beck Depression Inventory (BDI; Beck, Ward, Mendelson, Mock, & Erbaugh, 1961), and Symptom Checklist 90 (SCL–90; Derogatis, Lipman, & Covi, 1973)—which utilize more left-hemisphere cortical functions because of their verbal format—are more sensitive to *explicit* models of self and other and to conscious affects (Finn, 2009).

Back to Bob and my colleague's consternation, all of this has direct implications for therapists embarking on a course of treatment with clients whose testing fits the pattern shown in Cell B. I now tell them that they are working with a strong, talented individual who has survived circumstances that would have rendered many people unable to function. Instead, this person has used an array of coping mechanisms to carry on (including dissociation of affect), but this strategy had "side effects" currently expressed in the client's inability to form close relationships. There are several ways clients can "resolve" these difficulties, including having the luck to marry someone who is healthier emotionally and who patiently helps them overcome their terror about intimacy. However, in most instances, the client will need to enter into a dependent intimate relationship with a willing, wise, and sturdy psychotherapist, which will result in a semi-controlled disintegration experience through which the client will gain access to his or her split-off negative affective states. With hard work, perseverance, and an ineffable factor I call "grace," this process can result in a major shift in the client's (and to some extent, the therapist's) personality structure. However, this process will be difficult; the client actually will seem worse in the middle of it, and not every client who fits the Cell B pattern will or should attempt the work.

In the next section of the chapter, I write about a treatment I conducted with one client with the Cell B MMPI–Rorschach pattern. The client I present is not typical of most clients I have treated with the Cell B configuration; however, I chose this example because it is a dramatic illustration of the utility of multimethod psychological assessment for clients and therapists engaged in long-term psychotherapy. Also, one of my goals is to depict what it is like to work as a therapist in long-term treatment with a client from Cell B. Hence, I write about my subjective experience as well as the unfolding events in the therapy with my client.

Case Example

Initial Phase of Therapy

Thomas and I first met when he was 23, and he applied to join a psychotherapy group I was forming to help gay men develop and maintain intimate relationships. At the time, Thomas was a teacher in a private high school, having graduated from college the previous year. He was an accomplished musician and a straight-A student, was contemplating several different career paths, and had chosen to work before deciding what kind of graduate program he would enter. Thomas explained in our initial session that he had long known that he was gay, but never dated in high school or after, although at least one man had been quite interested in him in college. He said he had "fled" from that relationship, ending his friendship with the man in question, but could not explain why, except to say that he had been terrified, in spite of finding the man attractive. He had seen a therapist briefly in elementary school because his parents were concerned that he had only a few friends. He said he found the experience "pleasant enough" but not "earth shattering." He hoped group therapy would be a richer experience for him.

When I asked Thomas what he thought got in the way of his having sexual relationships, he said that he did not feel attractive, although people had told him that he "looked fine." I asked a bit about his family situation growing up. His father was a teacher, and his mother was a successful research scientist. He alluded briefly to some medical difficulties in his childhood, which had kept him from playing sports in school, but he did not volunteer more information at the time, and I did not ask. In retrospect, this might have been an error, but I sensed I needed to be sensitive about intruding in areas that might produce shame or anxiety before Thomas and I had developed a trusting relationship. I liked Thomas immediately and accepted him into the group. Also, early on he completed an MMPI–2 and met with me for feedback, an experience I offered to all members of my psychotherapy groups. Thomas's MMPI–2 profile from that first year in the psychotherapy group is shown in Figure 4.2.

As is evident, the profile is quite open and unguarded, and the only significant elevation is on Scale 8 (70*T*).[1] Examination of the Harris-Lingoes subscales showed that this elevation was almost completely accounted for by items

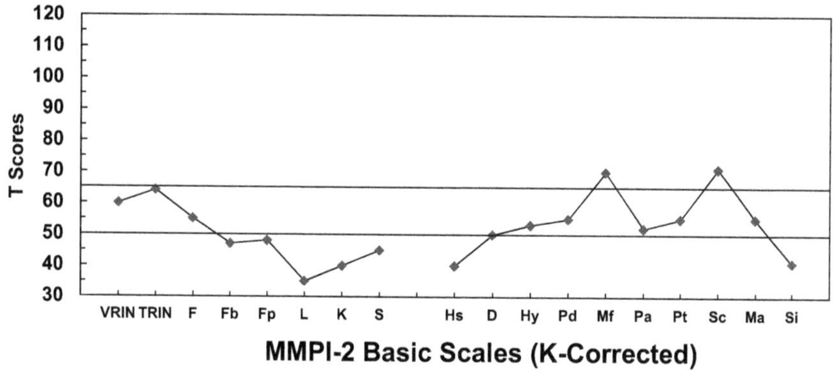

Figure 4.2 Thomas's MMPI–2 profile at the beginning of therapy.

Note: VRIN = Variable Response Inconsistency scale; TRIN = True-Response Inconsistency scale; F = Infrequency; Fb = Back F; Fp = Infrequency Psychopathology; L = Lie; K = Defensiveness; S = Superlative Self-Presentation; Hs = Scale 1, Hypochondriasis; D = Scale 2, Depression; Hy = Scale 3, Hysteria; Pd = Scale 4, Psychopathic Deviate; Mf = Scale 5, Masculinity-Femininity; Pa = Scale 6, Paranoia; Pt = Scale 7, Psychasthenia; Sc = Scale 8, Schizophrenia; Ma = Scale 9, Hypomania; Si = Scale 0, Social Introversion. Minnesota Multiphasic Personality Inventory-2 (MMPI-2) Profile for Basic Scales.

related to Social Alienation (Sc1 = 72*T*). Thomas felt different from other people and had never had an experience of "fitting in" well with a peer group. This was made more painful by the fact that he was a fairly sociable individual who longed for deeper connection, as can be seen from his low score on Scale 0 (42*T*). The reader will note that there are no significant indications of depression or anxiety in the profile.

As I watched Thomas in the therapy group, I could see some of the ways he struggled with intimacy. He seemed fairly formal at times, and although friendly, came off as a bit intimidating. I attributed some of this style to his having been raised in an upper-middle-class family that focused a great deal on appearances. I remember one day a group member asked Thomas if he was originally from Great Britain. When Thomas said "No," and asked why, several members agreed that his style seemed almost stereotypically British—reserved, polite, and slightly superior. Thomas also had a tendency to look bored and inattentive when the group focused on other members and to only fully engage when he was the center of attention. I saw this as an example of his intense need for mirroring, but the group members understandably found it off-putting. Thomas tried to gain their affection the way he had with adults in his life, by showing his extensive knowledge and talents, and even inviting group members, at one point, to attend one of his music recitals. Several did go and complimented Thomas in group about his considerable talent, but it seemed clear to me that although Thomas was respected in group, the other men did not feel particularly close to him.

As the therapy progressed, Thomas confessed to me in one of our periodic individual sessions that he was falling in love with the most physically attractive man in the group. I was surprised and told him that I thought no one could tell this, because if anything he was more formal and polite with him than with any of the other group members. We worked on his being able to say something in the group about his feelings for the man, but he never achieved this, and one day—after about a year—he announced that he had decided to move to another city to pursue a degree in broadcast journalism. He told me that he had a fantasy of being an anchor on the evening news of a major TV station, which I again attributed to his desire to be seen, attended to, and idealized. By then I had come to see Thomas as having a fragile self that was prone to fragmentation, and that his efforts to be mirrored were an attempt to provide a sense of self-cohesion. I received a card from Thomas shortly after he moved but did not hear from him again until about a year later.

A Crisis

At that point, Thomas called in crisis, and we had several phone sessions. I referred him to a therapist I knew in his area, but he did not find the experience very useful. To my ear, he clearly was in the middle of a major depression and seemed traumatized by a series of events. In the large city to which he had moved, Thomas felt completely lost and even more isolated than he had previously. He had had difficulty finding an affordable apartment and eventually ended up living in a tenement with a roommate who took advantage of him financially. Hampered by his cautious politeness, unable to set limits with his roommate, and depressed by the miserable conditions in his apartment, Thomas had tried his old strategy of throwing himself into his studies. But he did not find journalism as satisfying as he had imagined it would be, and he longed to be back in familiar territory. His sense of self was clearly fragmenting. So, after finishing his degree, he headed back to Austin.

Second Phase of Therapy

Thomas asked to rejoin his old therapy group and to begin weekly individual sessions with me. I sensed that he felt more connected to me because of the help I had provided while he was away, and I agreed to his proposed treatment plan. Thomas immediately entered a doctoral program in music, where he was quickly successful and appreciated by his professors. After several months of treatment, I felt we were at a junction where we might "deepen" our work. Thus, I suggested to Thomas that he and I do more psychological testing together. He agreed and posed the following questions for the assessment: "What are the major things that keep me from developing intimacy (to the extent of partnership) with a man?" "What keeps me from being more direct with my anger?" (This was an issue that came up relative to his roommate at his previous apartment and also in the psychotherapy group.) "How can I constructively handle my jealousy about other people's success at relationships?" "How do I not say to myself, 'What's wrong with you? Why can't you get it together?'"

First, Thomas and I repeated the MMPI–2 (Figure 4.3). The profile resembled the MMPI–2 from two years earlier, but the score on Scale 8 (56*T*) was now in the normal range. Thomas and I agreed that this change reflected the fact that he now felt more connected to me, his therapy group, and several friends, and this was confirmed by the drop on Sc1 from 72*T* to 59*T*. His score on Scale 6 (61*T*) was also higher than on the previous MMPI–2, but as Thomas commented, his recent experiences had driven home the point that not everyone was trustworthy, and it was reasonable that he should feel more cautious and guarded. Once again, there were no significant signs of psychological distress or disturbance. I

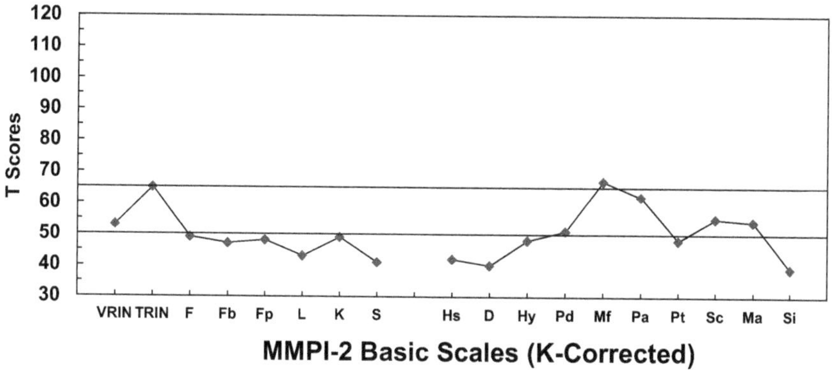

Figure 4.3 Thomas's MMPI–2 profile when he returned to therapy.

Notes: VRIN = Variable Response Inconsistency scale; TRIN = True-Response Inconsistency scale; F = Infrequency; Fb = Back F; Fp = Infrequency Psychopathology; L = Lie; K = Defensiveness; S = Superlative Self-Presentation; Hs = Scale 1, Hypochondriasis; D = Scale 2, Depression; Hy = Scale 3, Hysteria; Pd = Scale 4, Psychopathic Deviate; Mf = Scale 5, Masculinity-Femininity; Pa = Scale 6, Paranoia; Pt = Scale 7, Psychasthenia; Sc = Scale 8, Schizophrenia; Ma = Scale 9, Hypomania; Si = Scale 0, Social Introversion. Minnesota Multiphasic Personality Inventory-2 (MMPI-2) Profile for Basic Scales.

told Thomas that I couldn't say much from the MMPI–2 about the questions he had posed, and I suggested that we do the Rorschach.

A Mid-Therapy Rorschach Experience

As I have written about elsewhere (Finn, 1994), I had a fair amount of experience by that time giving the Rorschach to my own clients mid-therapy. I knew that some people cautioned against this practice, and that clients generally give more open, unguarded Rorschach responses to their own therapists than they do to an unknown assessor (Exner, Armbruster, & Mittman, 1978). Thus, one had to be cautious about interpreting certain Rorschach scores or one could over-pathologize the client. I was confident that I could adjust for such factors in interpreting Thomas's Rorschach and that his scores would prove to be a valid representation of his internal world. My previous experiences had also taught me that giving the Rorschach to my own therapy client could be an incredibly intense experience that sometimes mobilized powerful transference and counter-transference feelings. Still, I think neither Thomas nor I was prepared for what happened when we met to do the Rorschach.

The first important result was that the administration took 2.5 hours. In fact, I was not able to talk much with Thomas immediately afterward, as I had another meeting I had to attend. I considered asking Thomas to come back the next day to discuss his experience, but I did not want to be intrusive, given what he had disclosed in the testing. Also, both Thomas and I were completely exhausted after the initial session. The images Thomas saw and described were raw, powerful, overwhelming, and disturbing. I felt numb and "fuzzy" after the meeting, and it took me some time to come back to myself after the experience. Thomas later told me that the same was true for him.

Here are selected responses from the response phase of Thomas's Rorschach:[2]

Card I, R1: I see the outline of a human pelvis, actually a skeleton. The leg bones have been torn off and the torso and rib cage also. It's like an anatomical exhibit in a medical school for a course in urology. This helps students learn about the body.

R2: I'm also seeing a bug ... with large multipatterned wings, like under glass. It's been anesthetized with chloroform, but it's reaching toward the light. It's dark, maybe night, but it's flapping hard, reaching out, reaching toward the light.

R3: This looks like a cutout from an impressionist painting. Here are the trees, forest, lake line, and reflection. Someone cut that out from a larger painting.

Card II, R5: Two Japanese kabuki theater people. The red part is a swirl of hair done up with a wooden hairpin. They're looking at each other, in the middle of a long formal dance routine. They're wearing long flowing kimonos with spots of red. Their hands are together.

R6: This one is a scene from a slaughterhouse. The body of a sheep with the head and tail cut off, dark warm blood oozing on a stainless-steel table. I see death, coldness, violence here. It's really been torn and hurt or ripped. It's not a clean death. It's a scene from an abattoir. It's a daily occurrence.

Card III, R8: This looks to me like an animal that's being dissected, I imagine in biology class. There are pins stuck to the flesh here and here. Maybe it's a frog. It's opened up, the eyes have been plucked out of the sockets, the heart is split in two, and it's splayed open. There are two kidneys that have been excised and this is the ureter leading down to the genital area. This is an animal you learn from, something you stare at. There's a smell to this one too—of chloroform or whatever you preserve people, I mean animals with. These are the folds of the skin and the creases in the face.

Card IV, R9: This is sort of a Star Wars-esque space creature. We're down at the feet looking up. The body tapers up because of the perspective. It's a picture taken from the ground. The face looks like a vagina almost. I don't know if this is what he talks out of. He is somehow deformed, his arms didn't sprout as they should have—a Thalidomide Star Wars creature. He's viewed as defective. It almost looks like he's jumping down on you—almost like we've caught him mid-air.

R10: This is again a section from a painting—a lake. It's great. It follows the rule of thirds. There are strong diagonals. We see a big cedar tree or something here. It's just a very peaceful lake.

As these responses illustrate, Thomas had many incredibly morbid responses, interspersed with reflections and nature and landscape responses. His responses to the last three colored cards struck me as different from those that preceded them, and I assume that this was because Thomas was coping with the increased emotional arousal of those cards. Some responses to these cards were short, and almost constricted, whereas others were longer, more intellectualized, and more fantastic. The following is one of the latter responses, from Card X:

R29: These are Siamese twins, chic artistic Siamese twins dressed in Oscar de la Renta blood red gowns with sequins, with Bobby hats on like English policemen have. They are attached at the head; this is a device that keeps them alive. They're on a glamorous bed, holding a bra between them, having a joke with the photographer. They think the picture is only for their private consumption and no one else. All these colors make them happy, soothe them. They're in their early 30s. They have had a hard life, but they prevail. This is an Elephant Man-esque moment, like John Merrick tidying up to see the aristocrats. These women are well bred; they live in Paris, among the elite. They're off to a ball at the Hôtel de Crillon at the Place de la Concorde. This picture is being taken before they go out. They're horsing around. The photographer is their mother; she's saying "Smile." They're elegant and about to be taken outside to this ball at this incredible Parisian hotel. They're very excited, distracted from their station in life, from being attached at the head—sort of like Audrey Hepburn in My Fair Lady. *They have elegant thin necks. This is a picture of elegance in the midst of horrifying sadness. This is the nobility of "I will not do as Joe Kennedy did and lobotomize my defective daughter. I will dress them up and give them the chance to interact with society." There's dignity here. It reminds me of a phrase from William Faulkner's Nobel Prize speech: "I hope man prevails." These people prevail over circumstances.*

I did have the presence of mind to tell Thomas that day that I knew something very important had happened, and that he had "really told me a lot" about himself. I urged him to call if he needed to touch base before our next regular therapy session, but I was not surprised, given his characteristic reserve, that he did not.

It took me several weeks to score the protocol, and I also sought consultation from my colleagues at the Center for Therapeutic Assessment, in part because I needed help "holding" the content of the protocol. We jointly concluded that this Rorschach was in part a "transference test" (Weiss, 1993) of me on the part of Thomas, and that he was unconsciously asking, "Can you handle me, or will I overwhelm you as I have others in the past?" I was determined to rise to the challenge.

This Rorschach, in combination with the MMPI–2 done several weeks earlier, placed Thomas squarely in Cell B of Figure 4.1. It is important to keep in mind the possible effects on Thomas's scores of doing the Rorschach with his own therapist. The definitive study, by Exner et al. (1978) suggests that one should expect more Blends, slightly more color and human movement responses, somewhat lower form qualities, fewer Populars, and more sex responses. Exner et al. found these differences were not extreme, however, and they therefore do not explain away the level of difficulties shown in Thomas's Structural Summary. Other clinicians have also reported that it was useful to give the Rorschach to their own clients and that this procedure yielded interpretable profiles (e.g., Keddy & Erdberg, 2010).[3]

As shown in Table 4.1, Thomas's Rorschach depicts severe emotional distress and disturbance, including depression (DEPI= 5), thought disorder (WSum6 = 101), problems with affective regulation (FC: CF + C = 6:8), and major impairment in the area of attachment and intimate relationships [T = 0; Isolate/R = .34, H: (H) + Hd + (Hd) = 4:8]. There also were signs evident in the response content that Thomas felt extremely defective and damaged deep down (MOR = 8; V = 2), although his scores suggested he covered this up with intellectualization [2AB + (Art + Ay) = 29] and by going "one-up" (Fr + rF = 10). On Armstrong

Table 4.1 The lower portion of the Structural Summary of Thomas's Rorschach

Ratios, Percentages, and Derivations										
R		= 32	L		= .03		FC:CF+C	= 6:8	COP = 3	AG = 2
							Pure C	= 1	Food	= 1
EB	= 14	:11.5	EA	= 25.5	EBPer	= 1.2	SumC':WSumC	= 3:11.5	Isolate/R	= 0.34
eb	= 14	:6	es	= 20	D	= +2	Afr	= 0.78	H:(H)+Hd+(Hd)	= 4:8
			Adj es	= 13	Adj D	= +4	S	= 6	(H)+(Hd):(A)+(Ad)	= 7:4
							Blends:R	= 20:32	H+A:Hd+Ad	= 21:3
FM	= 6		SumC'	= 3	SumT	= 0	CP	= 1		
m	= 8		SumV	= 2	SumY	= 1				
a:p	= 20:8		Sum6	= 23	P	= 5	Zf	= 28	3r+(2)/R	= 1.1
Ma:Mp	= 11:3		Lv2	= 8	X+%	= .59	Zd	= +13.0	Fr+rF	= 10
2AB+Art+Ay	= 29		WSum6	= 101	F+%	= 1.0	W:D:Dd	= 31:1:0	FD	= 2
M	= 1		M none	= 0	X-%	= .16	W:M	= 31:14	An+Xy	= 4
					S-%	= 0	DQ+	= 20	MOR	= 8
					Xu%	= .25	DQv	= 4	TCI	= .59
SCZI = 2		DEPI = 5			CDI = 1		S-CON = 7		HVI = Yes	OBS = No

This is the 4th edition of the Structural Summary because that is what was current at the time I tested Thomas. TCI = Trauma Content Index (Armstrong & Loewenstein, 1990).

and Loewenstein's (1990) Trauma Content Index, Thomas scored .59, in the range of clients who have been severely traumatized and who have dissociative disorders (Kamphuis, Kugeares, & Finn, 2000). Armstrong and Loewenstein theorized that traumatized individuals have mini-"flashbacks" as they look at the Rorschach cards, which leads them to report responses with aggressive, morbid, anatomy, sex, and blood content. Even as I recorded Thomas's responses, I was sure that something like this was happening for him (and, as I wrote earlier, I also was sent somewhat into shock).

On close examination, another remarkable thing about Thomas's Structural Summary is that it showed the incredible psychological resources at his disposal, including intelligence and creativity (EA = 25.5, DQ + = 20), emotional sensitivity (WSumC = 11.5, Afr = .78), and a keen awareness of social rules (COP = 3, P = 5). The protocol also showed the variety of psychological defenses Thomas used to manage his severe underlying distress, including those mentioned earlier of intellectualization (2AB + Aft + Ay = 29) and grandiosity (Fr + rF = 10, 3r + (2)/r = 1.1, W/M = 31/14), as well as dissociation (DQv = 4), denial (CP = 1), and schizoid withdrawal (Isolate/R = .34). The end result was that Thomas's D and Adjusted D scores were + 2 and + 4, respectively, suggesting that Thomas's ego resources were generally enough to keep him protected from the immense amount of pain he carried inside. This ego strength is also evident in Thomas's ability to produce a normal range MMPI–2 profile. Without this result, it would be difficult to believe that a person with some of Thomas's Rorschach scores (e.g., WSum6 = 101, DEPI = 5, S-CON = 7) was not hospitalized. Instead, he was functioning quite well in the world. However, Thomas paid a cost in that his characterological defenses greatly interfered with his ability to form and maintain close relationships. Also, he was at risk of "falling through the ice" into an underlying pool of depression and self-hate, much as he had experienced when he went away to school.

I knew I could now address Thomas's main question for the assessment: "What are the major things that keep me from developing intimacy (to the extent of partnership) with a man?" I also thought I understood the function of his "one-up" interpersonal stance and his tendency to target himself about his inability to form deep relationships. (His third question was this: "How can I not say to myself, 'What's wrong with you? Why can't you get it together?'") As you see from Thomas's 10 reflection responses and his W/M ratio, the Rorschach suggested he acted "better than others" to stay out of intense shame and self-hate. If one—as a thought experiment—removed those reflection responses, and recalculated the Egocentricity Index, Thomas's score would be .19, which along with his 2 Vista, 8 Morbid, and 2 Color-Shading Blend responses, suggested that he felt very badly about himself deep down. His apparent reserve and grandiosity were an attempt to shore up a fragile sense of self, which began to fragment under various kinds of stress.

Therapy after the Psychological Assessment

Thomas and I began to discuss the assessment results and his questions over the ensuing months of therapy. He was extremely open to my thoughts about the meaning of the discrepancy between his MMPI–2 and Rorschach, and as recommended with clients in Cell B (Finn, 1996), I praised his considerable coping skills and talked about the risk of his "opening up Pandora's box" if he got too intimate with someone. He responded by saying he very much wanted to work on his underlying depression so that he could have a sexual relationship with a man. We also began to discuss the content of his Rorschach responses, which opened up a whole line of history that I knew only a bit about at the time, and that Thomas himself was only partly aware of. I have thought long and hard about whether I should have rigorously pursued this history earlier in my work with Thomas, and although I cannot know for sure what result this would have brought, I am aware of three things that speak against this: (a) I hypothesize that Thomas and I were both unconsciously waiting until it was the right time for us to discuss this traumatic material. In my initial interview when he alluded to his early medical history, I had a strong sense that it would shame him if I asked more at the time. (b) I am reminded of A. N. Schore's (2009) insistence that this kind of material is typically not in conscious awareness, and Thomas has assured me that he himself did not connect his early history to his difficulties in relationships. (c) I have come to believe in the power of the Rorschach to tap into and elucidate traumatic images and affect states and to bring this material out in the open where it can be discussed.

Here is what emerged at that time: Thomas was born full term, the first of his parents' three sons. He breathed and cried right away, but it was quickly noticed he had an imperforate anus and other abnormalities in his genito-urinary system. Basically, Thomas's body was able to extract nutrients but was unable to excrete waste products, and he was rushed when he was 12 hours old to another large city in Texas, where he had a series of emergency surgeries over the next month. As best we could later determine from the medical records we gathered, between 1 day and 12 years of age, Thomas had 27 surgeries focused on the midsection of his body. These included a colostomy and two ureterostomies, which made openings for feces and urine to leave Thomas's body. Eventually, he had a pull-through procedure that brought his rectum to the surface, and his ureters were connected to his urethra. However, he had no anal sphincter control at all because that muscle simply was not there.

Thomas's mother went to extraordinary lengths to get him the best medical care in the country, and she coordinated his highly complex schedule of surgeries and postoperative care. It is no exaggeration to say that she saved Thomas's life, and that his survival was a medical miracle at the time. One physician we later talked to said frankly that if Thomas had been born 10 years earlier, he would have died. We also learned that Thomas's condition was such an anomaly that many of his major surgeries took place in amphitheater operating rooms of large teaching hospitals, with medical students and other physicians observing. This helped explain the dissected and slaughtered animals in his Rorschach percepts, and Thomas's hunger to be seen as a person rather than as an object of study.

At one point, Thomas and I invited his parents in for a session to discuss all these events, for I was sure that they could provide information that would be helpful to Thomas. It was at that point that I began to understand another aspect of Thomas's early life. In part because of her personality, and I believe because of the role she was thrust into as Thomas's medical manager, Thomas's mother seemed completely out of touch with the emotional import of what Thomas had been through. Thomas's father deferred to his wife and had also been unable to respond sufficiently to Thomas's emotional needs. In fact, as Thomas later told me, his surgeries were never really discussed before or after they happened, and 15 years after the last of these, his whole family now seemed to act as if they had never taken place. Thomas still had some major medical challenges (e.g., fecal incontinence and a tendency toward kidney stones) that needed to be monitored. His mother was available for problem solving regarding these issues. However, no one talked about the heartbreak and difficulties the family had been through when Thomas was younger, and when I gently asked about this during the conjoint session, Thomas's mother curtly brushed my question aside, saying, "One does what one has to do." The result of this silence was that Thomas felt like a ghost or a phantom, he said, who people "looked right through." His early trauma had not been appropriately mirrored, with the result that his self lacked coherence and vitality.

Again, to give his mother credit, Thomas's resilience seemed to have facilitated her not focusing on his emotions. As I read the medical records from when he was a child, I saw that numerous physicians described him as bright, active, curious, and seemingly unfazed by his medical condition. We must also remember that pediatric medicine was in its infancy when Thomas was being treated, and at the time very few people paid attention to the emotional needs of children undergoing invasive medical treatments. Now there are whole therapies developed for such children that are sometimes conducted in the hospitals, where children "operate on" teddy bears and talk about their feelings (e.g., Knudsen, 1975). Still, Thomas's family's way of coping with an exceptionally overwhelming and painful experience—which involved functional problem solving, silence, and a focus on his considerable strengths and talents—set Thomas up, I believe, to have massive shame and to feel that his medical difficulties were not to be talked about with others.

As Thomas and I began to explore these matters in our sessions, I found that we had to move very slowly. First, it became clear that Thomas was easily overwhelmed by emotions and he would dissociate very quickly once we moved from facts to feelings. Once, after we spent a session looking at some of his medical records, he was in a daze for hours afterward. I remembered his Rorschach results, and we learned to pay close attention to when Thomas would start to go into shock and to back off and slow down. Second, we went slowly because Thomas was very protective of his parents, especially his mother, to whom he was grateful for having saved his life. Thus, initially he was reluctant to dwell on anything that could be construed as criticism of them. I learned to keep my tone extremely neutral and simply to talk about what I thought he might have needed as a child and what would be helpful from his parents now (i.e., some acknowledgment that some aspects of his life continued to be difficult).

In part because of the shame that showed up on his Rorschach, I also gave Thomas wide latitude as to what he shared with his therapy group. For a long while, he told them nothing about his medical history and current struggles. Gradually, with my coaching, he shared a little and was encouraged by the acceptance and compassion he received. The other men began to understand him more; he was more vulnerable with them, and I began to sense a deeper attachment forming. This paralleled the growing affection I felt for Thomas. I had always liked him, identified with him some, and admired his brilliance. As we worked on his medical trauma, though, I began to feel more protective, more connected and caring, and more fatherly toward him.

A Therapy-Induced Crisis

As our work unfolded, Thomas began coming to therapy twice a week. I believe this gave him the added support he needed to go deeper. Thomas began to talk about a subject he had never discussed with anyone: his intense body shame. I learned that he had numerous surgical scars crisscrossing his torso and that he kept a shirt on even when swimming. He said that he hated even looking at himself in a mirror. He also revealed the difficulties he had with his kidneys and his bowel functioning, and he told me of his conviction that no man would ever want to be sexual with him in part because of this. I encouraged him to visit a specialist to see if anything could be done to help; as a result, he started taking a new medication, and his daily bowel functioning got considerably better. He talked in the therapy group about the scars on his body, and the group reacted well. He even experimented with taking his shirt off at a local swimming hole and was encouraged when no one reacted negatively.

It was about this time—when Thomas began to have a bit of hope—that he suddenly plunged into a period of intense despair. He became suicidal, and in several poignant individual sessions sobbed as he talked about how completely worthless and deformed he felt. My heart ached for him, and his despair was difficult to sit with. At one point I even considered suggesting hospitalization. During one session, Thomas described himself as being in the "Valley of Death,"[4] and I guess I went there with him to some extent. I was quite scared and worried that I was taking the wrong approach in his treatment, and that I had made things worse for him. (The reader might remember that these were the exact same feelings reported by my colleague who worked with "Bob.") I had one or more sleepless nights after Thomas called me at home in the evening, desperate and in anguish. I got support from my colleagues and comforted myself by remembering my own "dark nights of the soul" in psychotherapy—from which I eventually emerged better than ever. I did not know exactly how to help Thomas, but I was determined that I would be as present as I could be with his pain, so that he would not have to experience it alone. Then one day, perhaps in part to soothe myself, I asked Thomas if he would complete another MMPI–2. He was willing; the resulting profile is shown in Figure 4.4.

Thomas's MMPI–2 from this time was highly distressed and disturbed, and it resembled the profile typical for trauma survivors or people with borderline level personality organization. Strange as it might seem, however, I found the MMPI–2 comforting and helpful. It was comforting because it gave me a rubric for understanding the emotional place Thomas was in. This profile is almost an exact representation on the MMPI–2 of the difficulties that had shown up earlier on Thomas's Rorschach: depression, confused thinking, problems with emotion management, and severe alienation and isolation from others. This profile was very different from the earlier ones from Thomas, and I realized that through our work, he and I had gotten beneath his sturdy defenses, and what was an

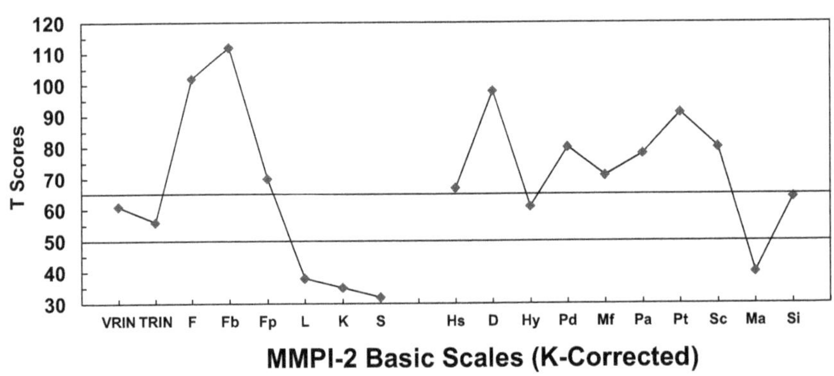

Figure 4.4 Thomas's MMPI–2 profile when he was in crisis mid-therapy.

Notes: VRIN = Variable Response Inconsistency scale; TRIN = True-Response Inconsistency scale; F = Infrequency; Fb = Back F; Fp = Infrequency Psychopathology; L = Lie; K = Defensiveness; S = Superlative Self-Presentation; Hs = Scale 1, Hypochondriasis; D = Scale 2, Depression; Hy = Scale 3, Hysteria; Pd = Scale 4, Psychopathic Deviate; Mf = Scale 5, Masculinity-Femininity; Pa = Scale 6, Paranoia; Pt = Scale 7, Psychasthenia; Sc = Scale 8, Schizophrenia; Ma = Scale 9, Hypomania; Si = Scale 0, Social Introversion. Minnesota Multiphasic Personality Inventory-2 (MMPI-2) Profile for Basic Scales.

underlying disturbance previously was now out on the surface. In effect, Thomas had moved from Cell B to Cell A on the MMPI–Rorschach table (cf. Table 4.1), and he was in a therapy-facilitated period of extreme pain. I still worried about whether he could survive the process intact, but the MMPI–2 also gave me an idea about how to proceed.

In examining his test scores, I also realized that Thomas was struggling with a great deal of rage, which had yet to be expressed. The highest code type, 2–7–8—which is associated with depression, anxiety, shame, and suicidal ideation—was just slightly above a lesser-elevated 4–6 code type. This latter pattern often indicates anger, vindictiveness, and sadistic tendencies. I also remembered that on his Rorschach, Thomas had an elevated number of white space (S = 6), and aggressive movement responses (AG = 2). I hypothesized that Thomas's hope had begun to mobilize another part of his grief process—his fury toward his family and the physicians who operated on him. However, this anger was severely blocked, in part because he had to split it off growing up, and also because he continued to be quite involved with his family. I wondered if Thomas's urges to kill himself were a reaction formation against his desire to murder his "saviors."

I did not interpret this directly to Thomas at the time, but I began to listen for, ask about, and support any signs of anger that I heard. Within 9 to 10 months, Thomas was talking in individual sessions about his fantasies of torturing and humiliating the surgeons who had operated on him. He also got a great deal of support from the other men as he brought this material into his therapy group. As time went on, Thomas accessed anger at his parents for being so emotionally unavailable to him, and for not having really "seen him" for who he was. We then had a series of individual sessions in which he raged about his parents' decision to keep him alive rather than let him die as an infant. As he did this work, his depression began to abate and he seemed more peaceful. Then one day, he announced that he had firmly decided he was better off alive than dead, and that he was glad—in spite of all he had been through—for the medical interventions that had saved his life. We both wept, and I knew that he had turned a crucial corner.

Final Stages of Treatment

Thomas continued in individual treatment with me for another five years after that session (making eight years in total), but rather than continuing with my detailed account, I briefly summarize the latter half of our work. I ended my therapy group, and Thomas joined another run by an excellent therapist I knew. Thomas did a number of Eye Movement Desensitization and Reprocessing (EMDR) sessions with a colleague, which he found extremely useful. He also began taking Lexapro and Buspar, which he felt helped transform his personality and gave him access to a wide range of experiences he would otherwise never have had. Of course there were more periods of depression, but none as severe as the one I have described. Then, at one point, Thomas went off to Europe for a year to pursue his music. We kept in contact during that period, and it was there that he had his first significant sexual relationship with a man. His heart was broken when the relationship ended, but Thomas realized that it had nothing to do with his body, and soon he began to date another man. He came back to the United States, finished his graduate degree, and continued to see me in therapy once or twice weekly. We spent a great deal of time talking about his dating, with his gradually becoming more discerning about the partners he chose. After his graduation, he obtained an excellent position in a large city elsewhere in the state. We had six to seven months to talk about our therapy ending, and he was eloquent in his appreciation of me and of our work. We also did another MMPI–2 and Rorschach about a year before we ended.

The MMPI–2 profile was not as good in some ways as Thomas's initial profile, in that it showed a bit of depression, some anxiety, and some struggles with self-esteem. In many ways, however, it seemed a much more realistic profile for someone with Thomas's history than what he had first produced before getting deep into therapy. The second Rorschach was quite complex, like the first one (see Table 4.2 for the Structural Summary). It still showed a great deal of painful affect and disturbing ideation, but the object relations were better. The HVI was no longer positive, the number of reflection responses had dropped from 10 to 3, the Isolate/R was .20 (as opposed to .35), Thomas now had a Texture response and 11 Pure H responses, and the H balance was better (11:2 instead of 4:8). There were signs that Thomas felt better about himself; for example, there were no Vista responses and the Morbids had dropped from eight to six. The Trauma Content Index (Armstrong & Loewenstein, 1990) had also dropped from .59 to .38. In summary, Thomas seemed to feel somewhat better about himself, less alienated and isolated, and had achieved some resolution of his past trauma, with the result that he was using fewer narcissistic defenses. His perceptual accuracy on the second Rorschach was slightly worse (X + % = .48 vs. .59), but this appeared partly due to his being less distanced from his feelings.

The full response phase is presented in the Appendix. Some of the responses were still quite disturbing and traumatic (e.g., Response 6), but there were also a number of responses that contained content (absent from the first Rorschach) related to nurturance, transformation, and exploration. Here are excerpts of some of these responses:

Card I, R3 (inverted): These are two hummingbirds with oversized heads, both feeding from the same food source, honey or some sort of container. These are the beaks up here receiving sustenance. They have oversized heads, but everything else is in proportion. Their wings are beating. They're content as they feed ...

Table 4.2 Lower portion of the Structural Summary of Thomas's second Rorschach

Ratios, Percentages, and Derivations

R		= 40	L	= .14			FC:CF + C	= 4:12	COP = 7	AG = 2
EB	= 15	:14.5	EA	= 29.5	EBPer	= NA	Pure C	= 1	Food	= 4
							SumC':WSumC	= 2:14.5	Isolate/R	= 0.20
eb	= 24	:3	es	= 27	D	= 0	Afr	= 0.43	H:(H) + Hd + (Hd)	= 11:2
			Adj es	= 13	Adj D	= +4	S	= 1	(H) + (Hd):(A) + (Ad)	= 2:3
							Blends:R	= 20:40	H + A:Hd + Ad	= 33:3
FM	= 14		SumC'	= 2	SumT	= 1	CP	= 1		
m	= 10		SumV	= 0	SumY	= 0				
a:p	= 20:19		Sum6	= 30	P	= 10	Zf	= 38	3r + (2)/R	= .63
Ma:Mp	= 7:8		Lv2	= 12	X + %	= .48	Zd	= +13.0	Fr + rF	= 3
2AB + Art + Ay	= 27		WSum6	= 123	F + %	= .40	W:D:Dd	= 32:4:4	FD	= 3
M	= 3		M none	= 0	X-%	= .23	W:M	= 32:15	An + Xy	= 1
					S-%	= .11	DQ +	= 33	MOR	= 6
					Xu%	= .30	DQv	= 2	TCI	= .38
SCZI = 4		DEPI = 5		CDI = 2			S-CON = 8		HVI = No	OBS = No

This is the 4th edition of the Structural Summary because that is what was current at the time I tested Thomas. TCI = Trauma Content Index (Armstrong & Loewenstein, 1990).

Card III, R12 (<): A long skinny fish floating over a bigger fish who's malformed and stuck to a food source. Perhaps it's an underdeveloped fish that develops outside. It's waiting to be a big fish. It's not done with the food source. It's gone a long way, but probably has another couple of weeks. It's still tethered to the food source and will die if separated. It has to stay and be content with the long skinny fish swimming around. But they're making friends. "When I get done, we'll play." This is a transition. It's hopeful, healthy, doing what it should. It's taking nurturing from the food system and getting ready to interact once he gets untethered. It's a hopeful, happy picture.

Card IV, R14 (>): This is the picture of where a land bomb has gone off. An explosion has lifted up the ground, intact. It takes the roots and trees intact and blows them off. It was a big messy bomb, but this was not about destruction or devastation. This is not an unhappy picture. It looks like barren land, but it will be fruitful. But it won't have that root system there. It'll start over.

R16 (<): This is just another view of two images ago. You can see a bit better the damage done to it. It's not been totally leveled. There's a good bit left, but the part that's been cut off is significant, the tallest part. There's quite a bit left, really dense green left. This operation meant to cut off just a bit. It's not a whole land bomb. The part that got blown off had just grown wild and gotten out of hand. There's solidity here, not devastation. It's like land surgery, major land surgery. But the core part is there. It's fine.

Card V, R17: I see a moth. I think I saw one last time. This vaguely reminds me of that image, but this moth is getting rid of its old legs. The middle part is the true moth growing out of it. This part on the side is the old part, molting—in the final stages of molt. Once it comes out, it will have a sleek firm body, which will allow more movement. The old appendages are about to fall off. It's coming out of its adolescence and the moth is ready. It's time to let go of the old, and this moth is ready to do it.

Card IX, R35 (inverted): All I see, it's hard to make out, are two Chinese goldfish, beautiful peach-colored goldfish in a pond, exploring under a plant searching for food. It's peaceful, soothing to look at. Beautiful pale orange fish underneath a gorgeous flower blooming, intense pink with green leaves. It's so pretty, soothing; there's a glorious light. There are so many hues of color. That's what I like. They're going to the depths, taking the plunge. I want to swim with them in the clear water. They're in the moment of descent, in a deep, rich, murky, nutrient-rich spot beneath the plant. It's nutrient-rich water. I can taste it. The fish will slurp it up. I want to go along, ride on their backs, go along with them. I love this hue of pink. It's so happy—the color of hydrangea—sweet, feminine, but it's got power. It's beautiful. I would want 15 vases of these flowers inside my house. It's a picture of life: blooming, feeding, thinking. Healthy fish going down to feed themselves. A flower at the peak of its time. What will the fish find? Where does the flower come from?

Overall, I found these responses comforting. I understood that the work Thomas and I had done had been extremely difficult, that his traumatic history would always be somewhat present with him, and that he feared he was not yet ready to separate from me. It was also apparent, however, that he had come through the therapy changed and renewed, and I believed he was almost ready to leave me and go out into the world. We worked for another year and then said goodbye. This was approximately seven years ago.

Thomas has visited me multiple times since he left town, and he is now doing quite well. He is well liked and appreciated at his work, has several good buddies, and most importantly, is now living with a partner, Gustavo, with whom he has been in a sexual relationship for several years. When Thomas and Gustavo were getting ready to move in together, he brought Gustavo in to meet me when they were in Austin together. I liked Gustavo immediately and am very happy that the relationship is succeeding. When Thomas visits, he says that he still misses me, and I still think about him often and am very grateful for the experience of working with him.

Recently, Thomas and I have had more contact because he reviewed this manuscript, corrected several errors in the history, and gave me permission to publish the article. I had initially omitted details about Thomas's medical condition to protect his confidentiality, but it was his opinion, and I came to agree, that this level of information is necessary for readers to get an accurate sense of his experience. Finally, at my invitation, Thomas wrote a short piece about his experience of the events I relate, which I append here.[5]

A Comment from Thomas

> The way of love is not a subtle argument.
> The door there is devastation.
> Birds make great sky-circles of their freedom.
> How do they learn it? They fall, and falling, they're given wings.
>
> —*Jalāl al-Dīn Muḥammad Rūmī, 13th-century Sufi poet*

Steve Finn shared this poem with me sometime in the summer of 1998, when we were in the deep throes of my psychological testing and my response to it. As I studied and absorbed its wisdom, the poem soon became the perfect summation of my psychological path, and as I came to learn, my spiritual path, too.

There was nothing subtle at all for me about the results of my psychological testing.

The metaphors—succinct and dead on—that the two Rorschach tests and the MMPI–2 profiles provided me spoke to a pain before and beyond words that I had always carried. Until the testing, I had indeed worked hard in therapy, but it was rather like snorkeling: I descended, held my breath for a while, surveyed the underwater landscape, and then returned for air. Therapy after the testing was like an extended visit to the Mariana Trench. I had no idea as I completed the tests the rich and painful bounty they would yield. The world opened to me through psychological testing was totally foreign, treacherous, full of chasms and pools of quicksand. The testing cut through like a razor to my core beliefs, attitudes, assumptions, and patterns that were totally unconscious to me yet that shrouded every part of my experience. Working with the issues and experiences they brought to my consciousness has been the most important part of my growth as a human.

As Steve recounts, this work was long, exceedingly difficult at times, and did not yield immediately rewarding results.

Lucky for me, though, Steve's hand (as were the hands of the other therapists in Austin with whom I worked) was steady and sure.

After my psychological testing, I was Rumi's bird, falling at what seemed like a million miles an hour toward the ground, unsure what was ahead other than certain annihilation. Very, very slowly, my descent slowed and I began to grow wings—wings that have enabled me to say a clear and unambiguous "yes" to life and its complications; wings that finally allowed me to heal from 30-year-old scars; wings that helped me enter intimately instead of terrified into relationships with my family, my friends, and my lover.

Thanks to Steve's expert guidance and to my own work, I now have my wings—born of devastation and of love.

Summary and Conclusions

In closing, there are several points I wish to stress.

1. It is a rigorous process to do long-term psychotherapy with clients who effectively use coping mechanisms to deal with underlying states of depression, shame, emptiness, and anger. Clearly this work is not for everyone! As I tried to illustrate with the case of Thomas, it can be quite frightening, destabilizing, and overwhelming—for both client and therapist—to form the kind of attachment that exposes clients' underlying pain and difficulties. My experience is that often clients "check out" therapists unconsciously before really starting this work; silently asking them, "Will you be there with me if we open this up?" and "Do you really believe I can get through this pain to another place?" And perhaps therapists are also deciding, inside themselves, "Am I ready to take this journey again?" and "Is this a person I can commit to?" I think this kind of mutual sizing up is essential, because once the uncovering process is begun, it might be impossible to stop it and put the lid back on Pandora's box.

I also want to emphasize that there is no shame for either client or therapist in deciding not to pursue such a lengthy or rigorous course of treatment, and that timing is important. Clients who do not have the energy, resources, or will for this type of psychotherapy are really better off doing something briefer and less intense. Therapists who do not have the time, desire, or emotional energy to engage in this type of work are better off referring the client to someone else or offering to help them in other ways. I know from experience that there are many things one can work on and address with clients without engaging in long-term intense psychotherapy. I also acknowledge the reality that many clients are not in the financial situation to undertake this kind of work, and that long-term psychotherapy is not easily available to people who cannot pay for it themselves.

2. Multimethod psychological assessment can be enormously helpful in the process of long-term psychotherapy by identifying those clients who could benefit from it, helping therapists gain more empathy for their clients' dilemmas of change, providing guideposts and reassurance for clients and therapists as they walk through the Valley of Death, to use Thomas's term, and tracking changes in clients as therapy progresses. To return to the case of Bob from the beginning of this chapter, I was able to use the client's assessment results to explain to my colleague that she had not done anything wrong, that she had been partially right about Bob's good ego strength, and that I thought that she and he could get through the difficult period they were in. At a follow-up three months after the assessment, Bob was still depressed, but not suicidal, and my colleague was no longer scared and confused about what was happening in the treatment.

In that instance, psychological testing was useful in giving new information to the client and therapist and making sense of a confusing and frightening experience that was occurring. However, I agree with Appelbaum (1990), the famous assessment psychologist, who asserted that an assessment could be invaluable even if it were only to confirm what a therapist already thought he or she knew about a client. Appelbaum commented that in the middle of long-term psychotherapy it is easy to lose one's bearings and that he would often have given his eye teeth just to have independent support for his working hypotheses and treatment plan. Assessment can provide such independent confirmation.

To return to a point emphasized in the *Psychodynamic Diagnostic Manual* (PDM Task Force, 2006), the type of assessment that is necessary in such situations is one that documents the overt symptoms and behaviors of the client, but that also goes beyond them to focus on the client's internal experience and to illuminate the client's as-yet unvoiced emotional dilemmas. In my experience, this kind of assessment requires a multimethod approach that utilizes interviews, self-report instruments, and performance-based personality tests such as the Rorschach and AAP.

3. When a client and therapist are ready to deepen their work, psychological assessment can help them do so. As is evident in the case of Thomas, the mid-therapy Rorschach and MMPI–2 profiles not only gave me a road map for what Thomas was going through, but they also spurred our transition into the deeper work in the first place. Again, I believe this catalytic effect is more profound when the therapist conducts the psychological assessment himself or herself with the client. Sometimes I like to play both roles—of therapist and assessor—to create this kind of intensity in the treatment. Other times, for example, with clients I find personally challenging, I ask one of my colleagues to do the assessment so they can serve as an outside support and advisor for my work with the client. I have been helped with my own clients by my experience being the outside consultant for therapists working in long-term therapy with clients in Cell B.

Getting training and experience in psychological assessment and long-term psychotherapy will help you get better at both. Doing long-term psychotherapy with Thomas and other clients has taught me, on a visceral level, what certain MMPI–2 and Rorschach scores most likely mean for clients and their treatment. This experience has helped me find convincing clear language with which to give assessment feedback to clients and referring therapists. It has also assisted me in making more realistic treatment recommendations; I do not tell clients in Cell B that they can probably resolve their intimacy problems with a year or two of psychotherapy. Conversely, by studying clients' assessment protocols, I have become more attentive to certain processes in psychotherapy. I am more aware now when clients are defending against painful affect in sessions, and of what certain psychological defenses look like in real life. This allows me to make more fine-tuned interpretations, which are better timed and more mirroring of clients' experience. I strongly believe there are numerous benefits in getting well trained in both assessment and psychotherapy.

4. Last, our profession suffers when we make too big of a distinction between assessment and psychotherapy. Although each type of work does require certain special skills and training, I believe we hamper ourselves when we insist on seeing assessment and psychotherapy as completely separate enterprises. I have built my career on the belief that many forms of psychological assessment have powerful therapeutic potential. I also firmly believe that high-quality psychotherapy requires a process of constant assessment and reevaluation, whether one achieves this through formal psychological assessment or in some other way. This leads me to recommend that we reexamine long-standing rules of thumb that, for example, therapists should never test their own clients, or that clinicians should never accept clients for psychotherapy whom they have previously assessed. These old guidelines

do alert us to potential challenges that occur when we combine assessment and psychotherapy. However, if we adhere to such rules inflexibly, we miss out on incredible opportunities to help our clients grow and to further our own development as psychologists and as people.

Notes

1 The elevation on Scale 5 (69T) is not at all unusual for a gay man with an interest in the arts (Martin & Finn, 2010).

2 To see these responses in the context of the entire Rorschach, see the Appendix.

3 I do not mean to imply that the fact that Thomas was given the Rorschach by his own therapist had no effect on his responses. In fact, I am sure many of his responses were unconscious communications to me of material he wanted to deal with in the therapy. However, I do believe that the scores on his Structural Summary cannot be explained by his taking the Rorschach with me rather than with an unknown assessor.

4 I am sure Thomas was referring to the "Valley of the Shadow of Death" from Psalm 23, which he knew well. I found his slight error significant and even more descriptive of the process we were undergoing than the original phrase.

5 I made the decision to include the added information only after careful deliberation and after consulting with numerous colleagues and several ethics experts. In the end, it was clear to me that Thomas's urge to tell his story "as it really was" reflected his having overcome great shame about the things revealed in this chapter and not some pathological form of exhibitionism. I also felt it would be hypocritical and antitherapeutic on my part to urge more secrecy than Thomas wanted. Thomas and I thoroughly discussed the possibility that a motivated person could determine his identity and thereby link him to the highly personal information revealed here. He did not dismiss this eventuality but said it did not worry him and would not cause him harm if it happened. In a series of discussions, Thomas and I also talked about the relational and psychological meaning of my having chosen to write about him and our work. Once again, I was impressed by his openness, level-headedness, and psychological awareness. I became convinced that our work on this chapter had in fact reinforced some of the gains Thomas made in therapy. Finally, I acknowledge that it is not commonplace to ask a client to contribute a comment to a published case history, but such an action fits well into the humanistic and phenomenological model of collaborative/therapeutic assessment that I use in my work (Finn, 2007; Fischer, 1985/1994), and also is encouraged by this journal for cases submitted for publication (Meyer, Nichols, & Handler, 2005).

References

American Psychiatric Association. (2001). *Diagnostic and statistical manual of mental disorders* (4th ed.). Author.

Appelbaum, S. A. (1990). The relationship between assessment and psychotherapy. *Journal of Personality Assessment*, *54*, 791–801.

Armstrong, J. G., & Loewenstein, R. J. (1990). Characteristics of patients with multiple personality and dissociative disorders on psychological testing. *The Journal of Nervous and Mental Disease*, *178*, 448–454.

Asari, T., Konishi, S., Jimura, K., Chkazoe, J., Nakamura, N., & Miyashita, Y. (2010a). Amygdalar enlargement associated with unique perception. *Cortex, 46*, 94–99.
Asari, T., Konishi, S., Jimura, K., Chkazoe, J., Nakamura, N., & Miyashita, Y. (2010b). Amygdalar modulation of frontotemporal activity during the inkblot test. *Psychiatry Research: Neuroimaging, 182*, 103–110.
Beck, A. T., Ward, C. H., Mendelson, M., Mock, J., & Erbaugh, J. (1961). An inventory for measuring depression. *Archives of General Psychiatry, 4*, 561–571.
Bowlby, J. (1980). *Attachment and loss: Vol. 3. Loss: Sadness and depression*. Basic Books.
Bromberg, P. M. (2006). *Awakening the dreamer: Clinical journeys*. Analytic Press.
Bucheim, A., Erk, S., George, C., Kachele, H., Ruchsow, M., Spitzer, M., & Walter, H. (2005). Measuring attachment representation in an fMRI environment: A pilot study. *Psychopathology, 589*, 1–9.
Butcher, J. N., Dahlstrom, W. G., Graham, J. R., Tellegen, A., & Kaemmer, B. (1989). *MMPI–2: Minnesota Multiphasic Personality Inventory–2: Manual for administration and scoring*. University of Minnesota Press.
Derogatis, L. R., Lipman, R. S., & Covi, L. (1973). SCL–90: An outpatient psychiatric rating scale—preliminary report. *Psychopharmacological Bulletin, 9*, 13–28.
Exner, J. E., Jr., Armbruster, G., & Mittman, B. (1978). The Rorschach response process. *Journal of Personality Assessment, 42*, 27–38. https://doi.org/10.1207/s15327752jpa42014
Finn, S. E. (1994, April). *Testing one's own clients mid-therapy with the Rorschach*. Paper presented at the Society for Personality Assessment annual meeting, Chicago, IL.
Finn, S. E. (1996). Assessment feedback integrating MMPI–2 and Rorschach findings. *Journal of Personality Assessment, 67*, 543–557. https://doi.org/10.1207/s15327752jpa670310
Finn, S. E. (2007). *In our clients' shoes: Theory and techniques of Therapeutic Assessment*. Erlbaum.
Finn, S. E. (2009, August). *Recent advances in Therapeutic Assessment: Integrating insights from neuropsychiatry into psychological assessment*. Paper presented at the annual meeting of the American Psychological Association, Toronto, ON, Canada.
Fischer, C. T. (1994). *Individualizing psychological assessment*. Erlbaum. (Original work published 1985).
George, C., & Solomon, J. (1989). Internal working models of caregiving and security of attachment at age six. *Infant Mental Health Journal, 10*, 222–237.
George, C., & Solomon, J. (2008). The caregiving system: A behavioral systems approach to parenting. In CassidyJ. & P. R. Shaver (Eds.), *Handbook of attachment: Theory, research, and clinical applications* (2nd ed., pp. 833–856). Guilford.
George, C., & West, M. (2001). The development and preliminary validation of a new measure of adult attachment: The Adult Attachment Projective. *Attachment and Human Development, 3*, 30–61.
George, C., & West, M. (2012). *The Adult Attachment Projective Picture System*. Guilford.
George, C., West, M., & Pettem, O. (1999). The Adult Attachment Projective: Disorganization of adult attachment at the level of representation. In J. Solomon & C. George (Eds.), *Attachment disorganization* (pp. 462–507). Guilford.

Kamphuis, J. H., Kugeares, S. L., & Finn, S. E. (2000). Rorschach correlates of sexual abuse: Trauma content and aggression indices. *Journal of Personality Assessment, 75*, 212–224.
Keddy, P., & Erdberg, P. (2010). Changes in the Rorschach and MMPI–2 after electroconvulsive therapy (ECT): A collaborative assessment case study. *Journal of Personality Assessment, 92*, 279–295.
Knudsen, K. (1975). Play therapy: Preparing the young child for surgery. *Nursing Clinics of North America, 10*, 679–686.
Martin, E., & Finn, S. E. (2010). *Masculinity and femininity in the MMPI–2 and MMPI–A*. University of Minnesota Press.
Meyer, G. J., Nichols, D. S., & Handler, L. (2005). A call for case submissions. *Journal of Personality Assessment, 84*, 1–2.
PDM Task Force. (2006). *Psychodynamic diagnostic manual*. Silver Spring, MD: Alliance of Psychoanalytic Organizations.
Schore, A. N. (2001). The effects of relational trauma on right brain development, affect regulation, and infant mental health. *Infant Mental Health Journal, 22*, 201–269.
Schore, A. N. (2005). Attachment, affect regulation, and the developing right brain: Linking developmental neuroscience to pediatrics. *Pediatrics in Review, 26*, 204–212.
Schore, A. N. (2009). Right brain affect regulation: An essential mechanism of development, trauma, dissociation, and psychotherapy. In D. Fosha, M. Solomon, & D. Siegel (Eds.), *The healing power of emotions: Integrating relationships, body, and mind. A dialogue among scientists and clinicians* (pp. 112–144). Norton.
Schore, J. R., & Schore, A. N. (2008). Modern attachment theory: The central role of affect regulation in development and treatment. *Clinical Social Work Journal, 36*, 9–20.
Slade, A. (2000). The development and organization of attachment: Implications for psychoanalysis. *Journal of the American Psychoanalytic Association, 48*, 1147–1174.
Tatkin, S. (2003). Marital therapy and the psychobiology of turning toward and turning away—Part 1. *The Therapist, 15*, 75–78.
Weiss, J. (1993). *How psychotherapy works*. Guilford.

Appendix

Response Phase of Thomas's Two Rorschachs

Thomas's First Rorschach

Card I, R1: I see the outline of a human pelvis, actually a skeleton. The leg bones have been torn off and the torso and rib cage also. It's like an anatomical exhibit in a medical school for a course in urology. This helps students learn about the body.

R2: I'm also seeing a bug, this creature thing, with large multipatterned wings, like under glass. It's been anesthetized with chloroform, but it's reaching toward the light. It's dark, maybe night, but it's flapping hard, reaching out, reaching toward the light. Should I say more? *[SF: It's up to you.]* Can I turn it? *[SF: It's up to you.]*

> R3: This looks like a cutout from an impressionist painting. Here are the trees, forest, lake line, and reflection. Someone cut that out from a larger painting.

I can keep talking, but don't want to keep going if it's too much. *[SF: It's up to you.]*

V R4: This almost looks like a football mascot. Here are the eyes. An angry creature reaching out for the ball. A mascot à la Texas Tech Red Raiders.

Card II, R5: Two Japanese kabuki theater people. The red part is a swirl of hair done up with a wooden hairpin. They're looking at each other, in the middle of a long formal dance routine. They're wearing long flowing kimonos with spots of red. Their hands are together.

> R6: This one is a scene from a slaughterhouse. The body of a sheep with the head and tail cut off, dark warm blood oozing on a stainless-steel table. I see death, coldness, violence here. It's really been torn and hurt or ripped. It's not a clean death. It's a scene from an abattoir. It's a daily occurrence.

I think that's all I see.

Card III, R7: I see two people, two women, with breasts here, their back, rear end, feet. I don't know what kind of position that is. I thought it was two women, but this looks like a penis. It's almost like their fucking something. I don't know. There's a butterfly in between them, and almost like little Christmas tree ornaments hanging down from above. We're in the Eden place where all you can do is fuck and look at butterflies. They're holding what they are fucking and these angels are singing.

V R8: This looks to me like an animal that's being dissected, I imagine in biology class. There are pins stuck to the flesh here and here. Maybe it's a frog. It's opened up, the eyes have been plucked out of the sockets, the heart is split in two, and it's splayed open. There are two kidneys that have been excised and this is the ureter leading down to the genital area. This is an animal you learn from, something you stare at. There's a smell to this one too—of chloroform or whatever you preserve people, I mean animals with. These are the folds of the skin and the creases in the face. < Nothing else comes to mind with that one.

Card IV, R9: This is sort of a Star Wars-esque space creature. We're down at the feet looking up. The body tapers up because of the perspective. It's a picture taken from the ground. The face looks like a vagina almost. I don't know if this is what he talks out of. He is somehow deformed, his arms didn't sprout as they should have—a Thalidomide Star Wars creature. He's viewed as defective. It almost looks like he's jumping down on you—almost like we've caught him midair.

> R10: This is again a section from a painting—a lake. It's great. It follows the rule of thirds. There are strong diagonals. We see a big cedar tree or something here. It's just a very peaceful lake.

V R11: This way it's of a horse-like, goat-like creature ... a Merlin, a sorcerer. Here is the crown, the eyes, and the horse-like face, with webbed limp things. It's casting a spell and welcoming me in, sitting on a throne, about to embrace me. He's regal. This is an aristocrat, elegant, almost like from a family crest. He's noble, king-like, powerful, reserved.

< R12: I see this man's head coming out of a swan's body. The swan is looking backwards. This pastiche of animals ... a dog-pig raising its head here in this background. It could be cover art for a William Faulkner novel. And again, the reflection in the water.

Card V, R13: I see a butterfly, a moth, not a very interesting one ... a run-of-the-mill moth splayed out that would get caught in a light bulb in the porch outside. Nothing more to say about that one. *(Turns card.)* I just keep seeing the same thing.

Card VI, R14: I see this Indian goddess in this really terrific fabric gown, something on top of something, with long flowing black hair and her arms outstretched. Her daughter is in front. They're in an Indian holy place. We're only seeing the back of them. I don't know what they're on top of. It's some nondescript place. I don't know what this is. There's some shaft going on, it leads to a light place. Maybe they're saying a prayer for this too. I don't know.

V **R15**: This is a mother here and her mirror image and a machine gun of some sort. She's protecting her child, who is being attacked by someone. She's not firing, just threatening to, saying, "I will use the gun." Her son is here. There's fire here, smoke, it's like a hologram of a giant burning fire. Out of it comes this image. She's dressed almost Marian-like, the Virgin Mary, Middle Eastern. "No one will harm me or my son." She was left by her husband and only has her son and herself and the gun and the people who are after her or him. It's definitely in Jerusalem or someplace in the Middle East. There's lots of sand on the ground and it's very hot. She has dark black eyes, and olive skin, and she's not afraid to kill and will do so if provoked.

< **R16:** I'm seeing this tugboat, steamboat thing going along a river. It's leaving behind this Oz-like place with Gaudi sculpture, a funky Pee-wee's Playhouse, like the Cathedral of the Sagrada Familia in Barcelona. Things are melting, but not in a bad way. It's a playful steamboat; it set sail from this fantastic city, this fairy tale land. It's cartoon-esque. The ship talks. Here's an eye. It could be out of Dr. Seuss land. The ship's name is Morton. It just goes along, doing what a tugboat does. It grew up as a young tugboat. Now it does what a middle-aged tugboat does. It's not a superhero, or a guardian angel. It doesn't carry a gun. If pirates came along it would be toast. This is a happy fairy tale with no marauding ships. But if there were any he'd be stepped upon. He's heading home. My goodness!

Card VII, R17: Two women from the 1950s who are staring at each other. No, almost like the red-headed character from the *Flintstones.* Thelma? She's looking at herself in a mirror. Her ponytail is flipped up, her hands splayed out in back, grinning to herself. But the aesthetic is from the 1960s. The hair, the skirt is long, the prim and proper blouse. I can imagine pearls being here. She has a very thin waist. She has taken heed of what the culture has told her to please her husband. She diets, smokes Lucky Strike cigarettes—short without filters—to keep her weight down. She takes pride in her small waist and will insist her 7- or 8-year-old daughters will conform also. She doesn't love easily. She's a very insecure woman. Her husband is a bit of an ass. These people aren't terribly high, just middle-class people in the late 50s, early 60s. She will ignore *The Feminine Mystique* when it is written in the early 1960s and keep doing the same thing. Her daughters don't like her. She's a very, very sad woman.

V R18: It's almost this doll from *The Nutcracker*—a Chinese variation of the doll from *The Nutcracker.* It has a big head and it's doing a Cossack dance, with legs splayed out, lined up with other people with its arms outstretched, wearing a bright-colored military outfit—blue with brass buttons. It has a stolid, inexpressive face with a moustache—a figure from prerevolutionary Russia. He's pompous, full of shit. Yet there's something comforting about it. He's dumb. He's a soldier in real life. He's not sharp enough to see that he's being manipulated and will be sent to die. The officers are watching in the audience and know these enlisted men will be sent out to die. It's like from *Life* magazine—Maxim entertaining the officers at the commissary—full of joy. This is the human side of war. Then we go to the next section two or three pages later. Maxim gets bumped off in the Siberian tundra, wearing the same jacket. We are meant to see this as ... it comes from a photo essay on the horrors of war. Maxim—not very bright, but committed to the cause—dies. His mother and brother have come from Novosibirsk to watch the show. Another picture shows mom and son watching this happy performance. The caption says, "Little did mom and little Vladimir know that soon Maxim would be dead." That's how this fits in the narrative. *(Looks on the back of the card, sighs, rubs his face.)*

Card VIII, R19: I don't know what the hell this is. I see two bears climbing up something. It reminds me of two bears climbing up a uterus—these sperm-like bears climbing up this uterus.

R20: Maybe to me it resembles a Georgia O'Keefe painting, vaguely resembling a bright flower, but it looks very vaginal to me.

R21: This comes from a medical textbook. It has to do with men's or women's genitalia, illustrated by Netter. It's muted clamshell gray. I don't know what this part of the body is or does. But it's a very important part of the urinary system or sexual system. I don't know what it is and I'm not getting help understanding what it is. Here are little vessels or veins. The text is written very coldly, sparsely, with no emotion in it. It's simply an exhibit—one colored image, excising it from the body—this organ and coloring it these artificial colors. It exists without the body—without the human. The blue part has a rubbery feel, like a lung. This has a synaptic feel—gray, long, and sticky. There is blood flowing through here. It's receiving life from the red space. I'm afraid of this picture, of this blue part. It just seems very objectified. I know I have one of whatever these are, but I don't want ... I'm interested to know I have one and what it looks like, but I don't know what it is.

> R22: This view is another lake view, with bison. It's in Arizona or California. Here are outcroppings of red stone. These aren't true colors; they've been tinted. The bison are in mid-motion, bigger than life. This is a picture from an Indian mythology book, the wild god Bison, stepping up to the sun. It's an illustration from an Indian children's book about the sanctity of nature, that bison are divine, and that the great god Bison is up in the sky. This is the Indian equivalent of Christ's resurrection. Creation has won an earthly battle and is about to take its place on high. It's steeping on the giant stone creature. It's not fierce, more like the Indian equivalent of Aslam, stepping up to take his place on high with the sun god. It's joyful, the end of the Indian children's myth. This is Little Orphan Annie singing "The Sun Will Rise Tomorrow." This is a picture from a storybook Indian mothers read to their children. The caption says: "The great god Bison took his place on earth." The child is filled with comfort. There's order in the world. The mother shuts the book and kisses the child. It's a perfect ending. There's hope. It's like an altarpiece with Christ writhing inside with pain and then panels with technicolor Jesus, a picture of total glory. This is that equivalent for me for Indians. *(Sighs loudly)*

V R23: I just see a pretty design, this is a flower of sorts, the leaves, the root system. It's a pleasing, somewhat abstract design of a flower for a tacky piece of wallpaper. Someone saw this design and thought it would look good in someone's dining room, so they replicated it 1,000 times. But it's ugly times 5,000 on someone's wall.

Card IX, R24: Two witch-like characters, drinking, playing jazz, having a good time. It's Halloween, they're dressed up in an outfit, drinking of alcohol of some sort, maybe champagne, spraying something back and forth to each other. This is a scene from a Disney musical about Halloween. There's an orchestra playing the background, singing *Hal- loween Rock,* some kind of Leonard Bernstein number. It's not a new cartoon. It's from the 1940s when they had imagination. These are genies from Iran or Iraq at the graveyard—genies summoned out of bottles by two sorcerers, singing a song, smiling. They had been unable to get out of their bottles. There's a smoky feel and there's dancing in the background. These are two contented dead souls and every October 31st they party. The evening starts out very happy. I imagine they're in New Orleans. There are black harmonies, jazz harmonies, and orchestra of black men on Charles Street in the French Quarter. They are happy to see each other again, to be risen from the dead. But sadness pervades the end of the evening because they must go back until next year. This is the very beginning of the evening. The party has just started. These people are dancing, the dance of the dead, but with the genies. They're not out to grant wishes, just doing their dancing thing. It reminds me of *Fantasia,* a 1950s hip version of *Fantasia.*

> R25: This way I see a tree. God has sent down a lightning bolt. He's pissed at someone. He's started a flame. These are tongues of fire, or ...

R26: These are flames of the Holy Spirit descending on the earth, coming down en masse, flame lapping up in the air. This is a picture of salvation, of damnation. It's not a burning tree. It's about to stretch towards all humanity and take in an embrace. This is salvation. This is a sophisticated picture. Here are the tongues of fire. "And the Spirit dwelt among us." It's done quietly, with no fanfare, a silent descent. This is Pentecost. V I don't see anything with that one.

> R27: I see the belly of a goldfish rising up to meet the water line. There's a bubble of oxygen, and a plant here. It's very soothing—the dark green and the beautiful orange. It's like a tiger fish in a Chinese restaurant, with glorious glowing fins, and a wonderful shimmer. *(Makes swimming motions with his hand.)* It's coming up to drink. We have a wonderful moment of seeing it spread out coming to drink.

Card X, R28: Immediately I see Paris, the Eiffel Tower, images of excitement. The shapes don't represent things; they are excitement. All of the colors accent the wonder of the Eiffel Tower. Only this structure represents something real. All the rest is Paris. "Ooo la la, c'est Paris! C'est jaune. C'est bleu. C'est vert." It's from the 60s, although the blue is a 50s color.

R29: These are Siamese twins, chic artistic Siamese twins dressed in Oscar de la Renta blood red gowns with sequins, with Bobby hats on like English policemen have. They are attached at the head; this is a device that keeps them alive. They're on a glamorous bed, holding a bra between them, having a joke with the photographer. They think the picture is only for their private consumption and no one else. All these colors make them happy, soothe them. They're in their early 30's. They have had a hard life, but they prevail. This is an Elephant Man-esque moment, like John Merrick tidying up to see the aristocrats. These women are well bred; they live in Paris, among the elite. They're off to a ball at the Hôtel de Crillon at the Place de la Concorde. This picture is being taken before they go out. They're horsing around. The photographer is their mother; she's saying "Smile." They're elegant and about to be taken outside to this ball at this incredible Parisian hotel. They're very excited, distracted from their station in life, from being attached at the head—sort of like Audrey Hepburn in *My Fair Lady.*

They have elegant thin necks. This is a picture of elegance in the midst of horrifying sadness. This is the nobility of "I will not do as Joe Kennedy did and lobotomize my defective daughter. I will dress them up and give them the chance to interact with society." There's dignity here. It reminds me of a phrase from William Faulkner's Nobel Prize speech: "I hope man prevails." These people prevail over circumstances.

R30: In this view I see a Salvador Dali-esque free association of forms and colors that don't make sense. It's bizarre, fanciful. The blue is a crab character and also a flower of the same hue. What the hell are they called? The brown thing is chicken. There's a Texas yellow rose about to bloom. Here's a wild turkey that's been beaten up, stripped of its plumes. He just got out of a fight. It's a pleasing La La Land. Pretty, but what the hell is it?

V R31: In this I see a Pee-Wee Herman-esque figure—two eyes, a nose, mouth. No! It's like that Dutch painter who makes portraits of people out of fruits and vegetables. The flowers are ears. This sprig of leaf is the brow. This is what I see. It's just a very pleasant, but a bit strange picture. The person who made it was on acid. Yes, a person's pleasant acid trip. He did it after he dropped, put it on the walls and liked it, and then put it in his notebook with other photos and drawings. And they say, "This is what the 60s were like." This is my image of what drug culture was like at my own high school—pleasant, but also terrifying—with no real-world reference—charming but also fucked up. Grow up! I feel frustrated with this person. He's a loser, a drug addict. Maybe he keeps this in his album, but this pleasant acid trip fried his brain and fucked him up for good. *The Electric Kool-Aid Acid Test.* Like Ken Kesey. It's art from a poster—San Francisco—The Doors—art from Berkeley in 1968 advertising an acid party, a Kool- Aid acid party. I see people coming up to it. "Yeah man. Let's go do that!" San Francisco 1968. This is lost youth. This is indulgence. This is hedonism. This is excess. Under this smile is the terror of what drugs did to this person's mind who drew this. *(Sigh.)*

< R32: In the last scene here, I see creatures in suspended animation. Here is a brontosaurus, again a mirror image. This is a caterpillar that used to exist then. Here are some amoebas, and a sea creature; who the hell knows what it was! A plant. This is a picture from a children's science book. It brings together creatures who lived at the time. They would never actually be together. This might be found on a museum wall, the Natural History Museum in New York on Central Park. It's fanciful, but boring. The artists think they're doing hot stuff, but it's boring. They spend so much time with colors and designs, but it's totally boring. Even as a child I found this kind of thing boring, and now I come back to the museum again and again and find it boring. But there's part of me that is fascinated too. Because this is the only representation I have of what the world was like at that time. *(Looks at back of card and sighs.)*

Thomas's Second Rorschach

Card I, R1: I think I remember some of what I said last time—a moth. I still see that now too, with it being a mirror image of itself. It has hands protruding, reaching for something. A bug or moth in flight, wings extended, and flakes of its wings are sloughing off. It's reaching out for its child, its baby moth. It's rushing towards home, going home quickly. It has a pretty pattern. A happy moth going about its daily routine, going home after work. *(Long pause.) [SF: If you keep looking, you'll see something else also.]*

Can I manipulate the image? *[SF: It's up to you.]*

> R2: An elephant, a Dumbo sort of creature, on a lake. It's just been hit in the behind. It's going forward, a bit in motion. There are hills and valleys in the background. It's young, an adolescent elephant with big ears.

V R3: These are two hummingbirds with oversized heads, both feeding from the same food source, honey or some sort of container. These are the beaks up here receiving sustenance. They have oversized heads, but everything else is in proportion. Their wings are beating. They're content as they feed. They remind me a bit of Big Bird from *Sesame Street.*

< R4: I see more or less the opposite of the second image, except this time it's Piglet, really big, dinosaur-sized, stomping through a forest on a mission, maybe to find food. He really dominates over the landscape. He has lots of forward momentum.

Card II, R5: These are two Chinese women with hair done up this way, like a frosty cone from Dairy Queen. They're sisters, engaged in a ritual from a temple, kneeling, heads pressed together. You can't see the faces because of the light. They have black gowns. It seems mystical and there's probably smoke and incense in the room with them. There are red spots on their dresses in a pattern. This might be something out of *The King and I,* perhaps not Chinese, but Thai. They are exotic, youthful, and innocent women, unmarried, 18 or 19. They're doing this ritual for their father, who is seated above them. They're doing it to please him. It's part of the custom of coming of age. They have to do this when they're 19, have to do this to please their father. They want to do it; they've practiced it a lot and see it as a gift to their father. This is something that's been in the family for 700 years. They're perpetuating dance, ritual, whatever it is. Their gowns are not really black. The colors are obscured, but they're azure, aquamarine, with blues and reds. This picture obscures what's really there, almost like a black-and-white photo, something out of *National Geographic.* It's a picture taken in 1920. It's something that's no longer done—a curiosity and a quaint thing.

R6: This looks to be an animal, decapitated, newly killed, cut off right below the neck and the head has been taken to be processed somewhere, maybe in butcher plant, an abattoir. There's blood smearing on the white tile. It's cold, messy; the fur is still on the animal. I don't know what kind it is. It doesn't look like a sheep or cow. The hind feet have been cut off also. It's bleeding. There's blood smeared over the carcass. It's been left alone. The killer is in the other room delivering the heart and feet to the other person who deals with them. It's just sitting there. It has no spirit, no life in it. It's just a piece of meat. It's dead. It's lost its sentient powers, its thinking, feeling, and it's dead. Someone cut off the tail or something. Its rectum seems to be on the outside, sticking out. There's been mutilation of its hindquarters also, but there's no blood to show it like with the head and feet. This might have been a dog that looked up to its killer with expectant eyes and had no idea what was about to befall him. Again, the color doesn't represent what's there. Perhaps it's a black and white photo. It's probably a yellow lab or a border collie. Someone loved this pet, but he had to be killed for some reason, maybe because he was old. Rather than disposing of the body, the family took him to the butcher. He's being hacked up to be used for I don't know what. His name is Rex, and after the head is taken off, he'll be cremated. They'll throw his body onto a pile of other similarly disfigured dogs to be cremated. It's almost like the head was taken off to be stuffed for the family and mounted on the wall with a plaque: "Rex:

Loving friend for 15 years." The rest is about to fed into the incinerator. The family will come for the ashes and keep them in a little container under the stuffed head. This is a bloody death, just death and mutilation so that the family can have what it wants. Out of this disfiguring of the whole dog comes this prettified head, stuffed, washed, given plastic eyeballs, a fake tongue, on a faux wood panel for a conversation piece in the living room. But the family never comes to see this piece, just drops off the dog, writes the check, signs the paper, and says "See you in 2 weeks." They're oblivious about what it takes to get Rex mountable for their wall. They'll never consider it. This is a part of Rex they don't want to see. This is hard and real, and they don't want to see it. They just want the head.

V R7: These are two guys in a ... two Sumo wrestlers in a musical, with elaborate capes on, long dresses on. This is a PR photo. It shows them in action, doing a wild dance number in imitation of each other. It's joyful—two guys you'd not think would be dancing in a musical—arms in the air in flight. The red area between is a special effect. They bring their hands together and something detonates between them—a special effect. This is a PR photo to get people to come. It's the highlight of the show. "Come see Akaito Sumo dancers from Kyoto—a whole new world of experience!" It's almost like a delicate ballet—precise. They are big guys, but they have great control of their bodies. They're very precise in spite of their largesse, their bigness.

< R8: This is a penis-dog and the penis has been cut off from the body and is laying. That's what he does, this dog who has a penis for a head, how he communicates with the world. It's cut off, falling to the ground with drops of blood falling off of it. It's newly harvested. Again, it's a picture of cruelty, maybe necessary cruelty because it was going to die or was dead. Out of the picture is the sharp stainless-steel knife. To touch it would draw blood. It takes no power or effort from the man holding the knife, just bearing down hard. Simultaneously the penis dog is falling on his back legs. The nervous system contained in the head realized what's been happening but can't do anything about it. Again, it's a moment of death. He has a momentary awareness but can't do anything. Like at the guillotine people can talk for 3 seconds. His head was cut off 2 seconds again and is falling to the floor. He's heavy. It's an animal dying, legs buckling under, no brain to control the body. He will fall in a heap with the penis head next to him. We don't see in the background, what's not in the picture is the man with the knife. It's quick. He'll go do 50 more today. I don't know why, but he's numb to it. He's just going to do the next one. Someone else comes to pick up the pieces. He doesn't clean up. His job is just to cut. And there's just about to be an incredible amount of blood all over the floor. It will bleed and bleed and bleed. They will get the hose and push it away with an industrial broom—get out the hose and wash the tile and bring the next one in. It's pretty mechanical really—cut, go, wash. This is the picture of what happens—stopping the action of what happens in 3 seconds—a picture of death and agony so we can consider it.

Card III, R9: These are two women, men, I can't tell. They have breasts, but also an erect penis. They're on an island, like Tahiti. Like the other image they're engaged in a dance. It' a happy time, exotic, maybe it's Hawaii. There's a butterfly in between them. They're doing some kind of fertility dance. Maybe that's why they're sexually ambiguous. It's some dance for the fertility of humans. It's measured, but happy, a springtime ritual imploring the gods to let us reproduce. I think they are women. They have women-like faces, make-up, fine features. They're wearing this penis adornment that is part of their outfit. They're gathered, dipping into something, but it's happy.

R10: This is a long skinny fish darting around an aquarium. This one sees this bit of entrails of something that's been put in the fish tank—part of a frog heart with the artery going to it. This little fish is darting over this other creature to go get these entrails first. It's really intent and will just go right over this creature.

V R11: This is a beetle from some kind of ad campaign to stop killing beetles. It's cutsie, from PR materials, with sunglasses and a bow. "The beetle is not your enemy." It's stupid, from some magazine, anthropomorphizing the beetle, giving it an outfit, hands up. It's stupid because it's gross. It's a fucking beetle—give me a break.

< R12: Again, I see some sort of fish tank scene—a long skinny fish floating over a bigger fish who's malformed and stuck to a food source. Perhaps it's an underdeveloped fish that develops outside. It's waiting to be a big fish. It's not done with the food source. It's gone a long way but probably has another couple of weeks. It's still tethered to the food source and will die if separated. It has to stay and be content with the long skinny fish swimming around. But they're making friends. "When I get done, we'll play." This is a transition. It's hopeful, healthy, doing what it should. It's taking nurturing from the food system and getting ready to interact once he gets untethered. It's a hopeful, happy picture.

Card IV, R13: This is a picture of a lamb in an outrageous get-up. It's a funny picture of a sweet little lamb, four or five years old, sweet, in an enormous costume. He's standing on a stool, inside, with the outrageous costume draped over him. It's like the Wegman portraits of dogs. The irony is, it's just a little lamb who has no idea why they're doing it. It's for the viewer, for humans. No one is considering what the lamb is experiencing. It's funny or supposed to be funny anyway. There's this enormous costume, with tendrils for hands. It's a Sci-Fi fantasy. The little lamb is bleating, not unhappily, but bleating. It's by some weird photographer who puts animals in costumes. It's a sweet lamb, that's why it was picked for it, just bleating away. There's irony. It's such an ugly, hideous costume covering the sweet little lamb who was minding his own business outside. He has nothing to do with the inside. It's sort of funny, but not really. *(Laughs.)* But it is kind of funny.

> R14: This is the picture of where a land bomb has gone off. An explosion has lifted up the ground, intact. It takes the roots and trees intact and blows them off. A big, fucking bomb. It just blew it off. There's lots of air, it's a stormy scene. Big shit happened here. This little piece of land has had the foundation taken away. The outer layer was ripped off at the source. It was a big messy bomb, but this was not about destruction or devastation. This is not an unhappy picture. It takes and roots and all and just blows it off. This is a little ship or car or something, exploring to make sure everything got taken off, inspecting to make sure. "Did we get it all?" It's reporting back to the explosives department, a ways away. This stiff is effectively dead that's been blown off, but it doesn't know it yet—like a dead animal with its eyes open. It's suspended by wires and an elaborate system of pulleys that held it up. And this car/inspector is making sure he got it all. It's a big piece of land, big. He's probing around to make sure he got it. It's right by water too. The tree, grasses, earth had grown up by the water. It just blew the shit out of it. When the inspector car is satisfied, they'll take dump trucks, release the cables, let it go, haul it off. It looks like barren land, but it will be fruitful. But it won't have that root system there. It'll start over.

V R15: Again, some silly little Sci-Fi image from the cover of a dumb Sci-Fi book. This is some imperial wizard type, probably Chinese, with arms outstretched, slanty eyes, trying to scare us. It's a poor fantasy of some earth creature. Neither gives fright. I would take this book and say, "Can't you do better? Give me a break!" The artist tried to be scary, but it doesn't work. This doesn't scare me. It's just silly.

< R16: This is just another view of two images ago. There were 5 or 10 photographers out to capture this moment. This is a view from outside. You can see a bit better the damage done to it. It's not been totally leveled. There's a good bit left, but the part that's been cut off is significant, the tallest part. There's quite a bit left, really dense green left. This operation meant to cut off just a bit. It's not a whole land bomb. The part that got blown off had just grown wild and gotten out of hand. The inspector vehicle is spaceship-like. There's solidity here, not devastation. It's like land surgery, major land surgery. But the core part is there. It's fine.

Card V, R17: I see a moth. I think I saw one last time. This vaguely reminds me of that image, but this moth is getting rid of its old legs. The middle part is the true moth growing out of it. Its features are useful, just compact. This part on the side is the old part, molting—in the final stages of molt. Once it comes out, it will have a sleek firm body, which will allow more movement. The old appendages are about to fall off. It's coming out of its adolescence and the moth is ready. It's time to let go of the old, and this moth is ready to do it.

> R18: This is a picture of a bird that is dead. It crashed head-first and its head is buried in the ground. It's an ostrich or some tall thin bird. It's dead, has been here for several days, and a fox or something has come and ate one leg, leaving bones. The fox got full. Soon vultures will be along and eat it—dead meat, a dead bird with its head in the sand. It's kind of funny in a way. A dead bird crashed and buried with its head in the sand, being eaten by whoever walks by, with feathers on, brown feathers. It looks like a Captain Hook peg leg, but it's not, a skinny, sharp leg. He'll probably come by tomorrow and eat a second leg. A silly little dead bird with its head in the ground.

V R19: This is an elaborate party costume—a clip-on moustache. The top part fits in the nose. The bottom part you press and it opens and you put it in the nose. An elaborate moustache like an Italian ethnic person from New York in the 1920s. It's an early costume, from before adhesive was invented. It's uncomfortable to wear. A moustache relic, made with big, thick buffalo fur. It's uncomfortable to the skin. It itches. But it's what you'd wear dressing up as a male flapper. It hurts. "When can I take this costume off?" It's like in a museum. A little placard talks about its history.

< R20: This picture is of a horse on water skis. It's an old horse. He has his head up. He's praying. His front leg legs are really thin, deformed. He can only get around on motorized water skis. He has his head up, imploring God for I don't know what. A disabled horse on a safety wheelchair thing, zipping along, doing his morning prayers. This picture doesn't show his beauty because the contraption covers that up. Underneath he has a beautiful body. His legs are deformed. But underneath are beautiful rippling muscles. He can't get around otherwise. He just gins along, but nobody can see. He's making it the best he can, with his head high, not embarrassed by his stick legs. He just placidly motors around the pool where he lives, visits friends, on his daily morning rounds. He just goes and talks from this contraption because he can't get around otherwise. But he's content, just zipping around town.

Card VI, R21: This is some weird kitschy thing from a tacky gift shop in Taos for White middle-class people who want just a little taste of an Indian thing to put on their wall. These Navajo women and bear rug equal the American Indian experience. Weird. But it's something you'd see on the shelf at the Taos airport or downtown. It's trashy, kitsch, dumb. It's meant to evoke something that's not there. It's made in China. She's supposed to be an intensely spiritual woman in touch with all the forces attached to the manly bear, an American Indian spiritual being. It's to go on some paneled wall. They're trying to buy some spiritually pure piece of American, but it's fake, stupid, whatever.

> R22: This is like a boat, a tugboat or something, pulling away from Funland. It's a kid's picture, leaving the Pee-Wee Herman fun house after a day's outing. It's something Gaudi would make. There are no edges all around. It looks like the Sagrada Familia. It's the journey home from 10-year-old boy and girl whacked out fun. It's boring and banal but the kids like it. It's like fun house mirrors at carnivals. Most adults don't go. They're just being taken home to the parking lot across the lake.

V R23: *(long pause)* I think this is ... it reminds me of what I said last time. I still see a mother protecting her child with a gun, but it's different. It's almost like Han Solo in *The Empire Strikes Back* who gets frozen and comes back. She's that way, frozen, or freeze-dried, a waxed figure. But it's a real gun. I don't know if the kid's there anymore. She's in light blue. She's a sentry. But she's not real, not animated. No one is there. It's like a wax figure in museum, in Madame Tussaud's. People come and look at the image. A wax figure of a woman dressed in blue like the Virgin Mary, with a wax Uzi. She's in there with Winston Churchill and the Pope. It's an exhibit of women. This is in a moment of intense fighting. She's angry, disturbed, frightened. It's not animated. It's an exhibit in a museum with the tag, "Woman protecting son, fending off soldiers." This is something to be observed. It's not real. It's life-like. You can walk up and take a picture. She looks real in the picture, but she's not. She's a relic, an object.

< R24: This is just the opposite of the second image—Tugboat Willy taking home kids from the fun house. The fun house reminds me of the *Starry Night* Van Gogh painting. It has the same energy to it. It was christened Tugboat Willy by Minnie Mouse. A woman came out and broke a bottle of Coke on its side, in Orlando, Florida. The kids love it and clamor for it and here comes big ol' Tugboat Willy, just going back and forth doing his job with happy kids on board and tired parents.

Card VII, R25: These are two women from the 1950s. They have on poodle skirts and ponytails. They have 1950s bangs, thin waists, and are doing a dance at the sock hop in front of a crowd of people. They're having fun, dancing back and forth with lots of energy.

R26: This is a weird picture. Pieces of fried shrimp and chicken from Long John Silver's. Breaded fish filets, breaded chicken, breaded shrimp. I don't get it.

V R27: In this picture you've got a couple of young ladies with big hair doing a dance routine for older men. They are sex kittens, with big boobs and thin waists. They are prostitutes or girls—smutty looking. They have big shocks of red hair. They are hoping they'll be taken home. They're wriggling their bottoms around.

< R28: I see the opposite of what I saw in the second frame—pieces of shrimp, filet of fish, just sitting there.

Card VIII, R29: I see two polar bears climbing up I'm not sure what. It's like a weird art collage by Frank Netter who does medical drawings. I can only identify the bears. The gray thing looks like a synapse. I can't identify the green thing. I'm drawn to the textures. The bottom part looks like a flower. The polar bears are climbing up the synapse and the green thing from the body. It's just a collage. It doesn't make sense. The polar bears want to be on top. It's like something a weird artistic medical student would do. It's a piece called "Pandora's Box" by a medical student from Houston—a collage of disparate elements that only means something to the artist.

R30: Hmmm ... still the polar bear climbing. The red thing and green thing are a rock. And the white thing is a branch. He's crossing over from point A to point B. It's a red polar bear, not real, just a representation. It's boring. The only interesting thing is the colors. A polar bear going to an icy isle somewhere in search of food or something, just going somewhere.

V R31: This is again a weird kind of collage from the psychedelic 60s. The body is a flower. It blooms bright orange, with green leaves. These are Barnum and Bailey Circus elephants on their hind legs lifting something up to the flower. It's a 1960 ad for Barnum and Bailey Circus in Berkeley, California. The sun is coming out. It's fantastic, a fantasy. Love and circus and flowers. It's a circus advertisement.

< R32: I simply see the polar bears going in opposite directions, or maybe a fox. Some four-legged mammal. I don't know why the colors are there. It just some fantasy. Just walking.

Card IX, R33: This looks like a scene from *Fantasia,* or *Witches.* I hear Disney orchestral music in the background. It's the dance of the dead. The witches are doing a dance around the brew pot. Below, Aladdin's come out and is singing a song, "In the Middle of the Night." Aladdin's come out and is doing a routine. It's an animated Disney film—a *Fantasia* kind of thing. They're all harmless. The witches can't hurt anybody. It's just a cartoon.

R34: I see an old man in the green, slumped over a writing table in the orange. He's picking up a pen thinking about what he'll write next. I don't know why he's colored that way. Just sitting at a writing desk thinking, an old guy, with white hair. He's content, writing away for no one in particular, enjoying it, trying to think about what to write next.

V R35: All I see, it's hard to make out, are two Chinese goldfish, beautiful peach-colored goldfish in a pond, exploring under a plant searching for food. "Maybe we can eat the plant's roots or find minnows." It's peaceful, soothing to look at. Beautiful pale orange fish underneath a gorgeous flower blooming, intense pink with green leaves. It's almost an idealized picture from Monet. The way fish are supposed to look, like in some pond in Giverny, under a lily pad, calmly trolling the water. It's so pretty, soothing; there's a glorious light. There are so many hues of color. That's what I like. They're going to the depths, taking the plunge. I want to swim with them in the clear water. They're in the moment of descent, in a deep, rich, murky, nutrient-rich spot beneath the plant. I don't know where the plant springs from, but the fish will check it out. It's nutrient-rich water. I can taste it. The fish will slurp it up. I want to go along, ride on their backs, go along with them. I love this hue of pink. It's so happy—the color of hydrangea—sweet, feminine, but it's got power. It's beautiful. I would want 15 vases of these flowers inside my house. It's a picture of life: blooming, feeding, thinking. Healthy fish going down to feed themselves. A flower at the peak of its time. It's exciting, the unknown in this. What will the fish find? Where does the flower come from?

< R36: This is another fantastic picture of like this fire descending, coming down, putting itself in a bit of trees, shooting for the heart of the trees. It's huge—50 to 100 feet long. The trees are huge. The fire is hot, has been burning long, is hitting the tree but not burning it. I don't know if it will. I don't know what the pink is. It's a swift, quick fire that came of nowhere that's going straight to the heart of what it runs into, about to envelop it. If the tree does burn, we're seeing the moment before it catches fire—glorious, beautiful—the raw force of nature from on high. It will envelop this green thing and become this ball of fire. This pink seems to me almost to be a little toddler with a big head watching it. He has no words, just watching, sitting on his rear end watching this incredible fire consume this tree in the peak of life. There are color gradations. The brown is the part of the tree starting to burn. The kid is watching, content, with nothing to say. But a beautiful sight is about to happen. It's gonna be a glorious fire.

Card X, R37: Hmmm ... ah yes, I remember this one. These are two women decked out in elegant finery going to a ball. They are sisters or friends. They contrived to get a contraption together to get the two hats to come together to form the Eiffel Tower. They are going to a fancy party at Maxims or Harrods. They are all done up. But it's like a painting or a picture of them, fantastical. It's not a photo. They're just doing weird stuff, having fun with the contraption on their hat. They agreed to look like one arm of a crab, with the leaf on it, and there are seahorses in between. One of the girls, named Janice—this is a painting of how she feels about her relationship with Diane. All the symbols have secret meaning to her. The red gown is from a fancy ball where they were presented as debutantes at the Plaza. The hat is their trip to Paris. The crabs are their trip fishing with one of their fathers. The blue bra is about the date with one guy who tried to get into one of their bras. It's part of their shared history. The sea horses are when they were members of some club off Nantucket. This is Janice's pictorial representation of her relationship with Diane. She gives it to her in private. Their shared past is in the symbols. They are 35 to 40 now, only see each other every 1 to 2 years. They have gone their separate ways, gone to other lives, but have shared lives. Janice is in New York, Diane in California. Janice presents her with this painting, a reminiscence of shared times together. "We went to the ocean, to Paris together." It's a happy, heart-filled memento. She writes on the bottom, "Friends forever. I'll always be here with you." This is a celebration of friendship.

> R38: This is like a piece, a collection of weird animals, a brontosaurus, crab, olive green heron. It's a Rauschenberg collage, with weird, fun, fantastical beasts. It references the past, 500 million years of nature, all on one card. A weird celebration, pleasant, pretty. You don't expect to find them all together in one place.

V R39: The central image I see as being two nuns, two young nuns, in prayer, facing each other, leaning back. They have a veil on, a habit on, they're really thin, sickly looking. They look really bored. All they do is sit around and pray. The whole world is exploding around them in greens, yellows, blues, and the excitement is bursting forth. They are ignoring it or can't engage with it. Color! These are two mid-20s nuns sitting there praying. They can't engage with the color, the excitement. They are sitting in their monochromatic robes. They can't mirror, engage with their surroundings. There is so much they are missing because they are in this prayer, and I don't like them. They're idiots. They don't get it. They're not with it. They don't see what's around them. They just do their holy pious prayer. Behind are two beautiful blues, life, rose, beautiful leaves, all going on around them. And I'll leave them and I want blue and yellow and green. I want them—that color, energy. I don't want them, the nuns.

< R40: This is like some dinosaur creature, no scary-looking T-Rex. A brontosaurus who has his head in his ass, giving a rim job or something. The pink creature is ecstatic, something in the water. The brontosaurus is giving a rim job. He's into it. The blue is excitement. Here's a creature who stands on one foot in the water, eats plants, gets a rim job, and fireworks go off in the sky. It's joy. It's not a dirty scene. One animal gives another pleasure, like the part where guys are farting and flowers come out their ass. They are weird creatures, funny to look at, pleasant to look at. And why is this brontosaurus giving this one a rim job? It's like an animal in the *Garden of Delights*. Happy, really happy.

Chapter 5

Implications of Recent Research in Neurobiology for Psychological Assessment*

I find this an exciting time to be a clinical psychologist. My enthusiasm is partly because in recent years, a convergence has developed between research and theory in the areas of attachment, infant development, neurobiology, psychopathology, and psychotherapy that is revolutionizing the way we think about and interact with the clients who seek our services. Such writers, researchers, and thinkers as Allan Schore (1997, 2002, 2003a, 2003b, 2003c, 2009, 2010), Daniel Siegel (1999), Daniel Stern (2004), Ed Tronick (1998), Antonio Damasio (1999), Diana Fosha (2000), and Beatrice Beebe (2000) have fostered a climate of interdisciplinary collaboration that is yielding rich rewards for many areas of psychology. My goal in this paper is to extend this bounty to the area of psychological assessment, which, as of yet, has not fully participated in this cross-fertilization. In particular, I will discuss how my study of attachment, neurobiology, and new developments in psychotherapy has given me new insights into psychological assessment and its potential power as a clinical intervention in my own work in Therapeutic Assessment.

The Consensus That Is Emerging from Neuropsychiatry

I wish to highlight three widely accepted findings that are emerging from neuropsychiatry and developmental neurobiology.

Attachment Failures and Early Trauma Are Related to Many Forms of Psychopathology

First, it is now generally understood that secure attachment experiences during critical periods of infant development are essential for the development of such

* This chapter was previously published as an article in the *Journal of Personality Assessment*, 2012, 94(5), 440–449. Implications of Recent Research in Neurobiology for Psychological Assessment. Article DOI: 10.1080/00223891.2012.700665 https://www.tandfonline.com/

DOI: 10.4324/9781003602231-5

important psychological functions as emotion regulation, empathy, behavioral control, moral development, and social relatedness (Cicchetti, 1994; Schore, 1997, 2003c). Conversely, insecure attachment and developmental trauma are implicated in many different forms of psychopathology, including severe personality disorders, addictions, affective disorders, dissociative disorders, and psychosomatic illnesses. Clearly, many of these conditions have genetic or innate biological components to them. But it is also now evident that a powerful environmental factor is the extent to which individuals experienced early caretaking characterized by empathic attunement, collaborative communication, and repair of disruptions—the hallmarks of secure attachment relationships (Stern, 2004). Schore (2003a, 2003b) and others have done an impressive job of delineating the specific mechanisms through which early attachment experiences influence critical areas of brain development. Let me now summarize one important aspect of Schore's work.

The Importance of the Right Hemisphere

One of Schore's major points, for which he has assembled an impressive array of evidence, is that the right hemisphere of the brain—because of its dense reciprocal connections to limbic regions and subcortical areas—is dominant for the processing of attachment and affective experiences (Schore, 2002, 2009). In successful mother-infant[1] interactions there is a complex interplay (in sensorily intact mothers and infants) between eye contact, vocalizations, facial expressions, hand gestures and movements of the arm and head—all coming together to express interpersonal awareness and emotions (Aitken & Trevarthen, 1997). It has been shown that the coordination of such signals occurs primarily outside of the mother's awareness and is governed primarily by the right hemisphere, which excels at interpreting this host of subtle signals. Schore makes the point that such communications occur from "right-hemisphere-to-right hemisphere" (of mother to infant and back again). One implication of this is that insecure attachment experiences and their negative emotional sequelae have their greatest effect on right hemisphere functioning and therefore are frequently unconscious and not readily accessible through language (Schore, 2009).

Schore (2009), Bromberg (2006), and others have eloquently explained how such negative affect states—and accompanying implicit models of self and other—become dissociated, perhaps to show up in dreams or to be enacted in the transference that develops in a long-term psychotherapy. They and other experts also make a convincing case that successful psychotherapies of individuals with significant developmental trauma rest upon the capacity of the clinician to form a secure attachment relationship with the client and then, in Schore's terms, to nonverbally relate to the client—"right-hemispheret-to-right-hemisphere"—and thereby regulate the client's negative affect states and help the client reorganize his or her right hemisphere (Schore, 2003b).

The Importance of Emotion in Psychological Treatment

All this work has led to a paradigm shift in psychological treatment (Schore, 2009), in which there is more focus than ever before on the real, affect-regulating functions of the therapist-client relationship and on the importance of dealing with emotion in psychotherapy. In fact, a recent important meta-analysis by Diener, Hilsenroth, and Weinberger (2007) examined existing studies of psychodynamic psychotherapy and looked at outcome as a relationship of how much the therapies specifically focused on affect. Affect focus was defined at the therapist making comments like, "I noticed that your voice changed a bit when we were talking about your relationship, and I wonder what you are feeling right now" and "In order to make these feelings more clear, it might help to try and focus in on exactly what you're experiencing right now, at this moment." The overall correlation of affect focus and outcome across treatments was $r = .30$, and therapist facilitation of affective experience/expression increased patient success rates from 35% to 65%. This effect was greater than the well-known association between therapist-patient alliance and therapy outcome, which has been estimated at $r = .22$ (Martin, Garske, & Davis, 2000). In short, the results of this meta-analysis suggest that the more therapists facilitate emotional experience and expression in psychodynamic psychotherapy, the more clients change in positive ways, and that a powerful predictor of therapeutic success is the extent to which therapists facilitate affect (Diener et al., 2007). In my opinion, this finding suggests that purely cognitive approaches that rely heavily on the processing of verbal communication are not enough for many clients, and that successful therapists help their clients access emotions and then use empathic attunement and a host of nonverbal processes to help the clients regulate those negative affect states. Many newer, relational psychotherapies rely heavily on these principles in working with clients with severe personality disorders and trauma. Among my favorites are those therapeutic approaches developed by Diana Fosha (2000) and Leigh McCullough Valliant (1997).

Applications to Psychological Assessment

There are numerous implications of these new understandings for the practice of psychological assessment. Let me highlight three.

The Importance of the Assessor–Client Relationship

First, I believe that in traditional psychological assessment we have grossly underestimated the importance of the assessor–client relationship, as if participating in psychological testing was no more complex for a client than taking a blood test. In my own training, my assessment professor talked to us graduate students about the importance of "establishing rapport" with our "examinees," but there was little in-depth conceptualization of what this meant or how it was to be achieved. I believe this practice is still more the norm than the exception in most graduate training programs. As many of you know, in my own model of Therapeutic Assessment, we begin every assessment with in-depth discussions with clients about the personal questions they wish to explore through the assessment, and very early on we discovered that this technique led to active client participation in our assessments and less guarded test protocols (Finn, 2007). However, it took me some years to realize that my success in framing questions with clients was largely due to my ability to make them feel safe, attended to, and respected in a relatively short period of time. I then came to understand that in some cases, I had to explicitly teach empathic listening, mirroring, and other relational skills to individuals wanting to practice Therapeutic Assessment.

Currently I would say that my main goal in the initial session with a client is to demonstrate those relational qualities that will promote the client's seeing me as a potential secure attachment figure: emotional attunement, collaborative communication, and repair of disruptions. In keeping with Schore's model, I believe much of this interaction occurs on a nonverbal level. As the client talks about problems and difficulties she is most likely ashamed of, she sees me listening intently with a non-judgmental, open, curious attitude. I share a sense of what I am hearing and invite the client to confirm or modify what I say. My questions reflect my goal of understanding her particular experience and of finding the right words to describe it. And if I misstep and one of my questions provokes shame or intense anxiety in the client, I take note of her reaction and either apologize or simply correct my stance, noting a place of sensitivity that will guide my subsequent comments and questions. My experience is that assessment sessions approached in this way leave clients feeling calmer, accepted, less ashamed, curious about themselves, and more hopeful, and that they set the stage for powerful therapeutic changes to occur in the assessment.

The Importance of Performance-Based Personality Tests

A second major topic in assessment that is illuminated by recent research in neuropsychiatry is that of projective, or as they are now increasingly called, performance-based personality tests. An area of intense debate in recent years has been the relatively frequent lack of concordance between measurements of certain constructs via self-report tests, interviews, or observer ratings and estimations of those same constructs via performance-based personality tests like the Rorschach. The fact is that many seemingly well-functioning individuals have Rorschachs that suggest a great deal of psychopathology (Finn, 1996, 2011b). This lack of concordance has led some critics to assert that performance-based personality tests are invalid, over-pathologize, and are little better than reading tea leaves (Wood, Nezworski, & Lillienfeld, 2003). I (Finn, 1996, 2011b) and others (Bornstein, 2004; Meyer, 1997) have attempted to explain such discrepancies and discuss how they are useful clinically, and there is an array of research that supports the validity of performance-based personality tests. But the work of Schore (2009) and others now sets the stage for even more useful discussions.

Basically, I propose that tests like the Rorschach, TAT, AAP, and others—because of their visual, emotionally arousing stimulus properties and the emotionally arousing aspects of their administration procedures—tap into material that is more reflective of right-hemisphere and subcortical functioning. Other tests like the MMPI-2, BDI, SCL-90, etc. utilize more left-hemisphere cortical functions because of their verbal format and non-emotionally arousing administration. (I don't want to overly simplify—obviously, both types of tests utilize both hemispheres to some degree.) What this means is that the Rorschach and similar tests tap into more implicit (to use Schore's word) schemas about self and other, which in some individuals (e.g., those with dismissing attachment status) are quite discrepant from their explicit, conscious conceptions. Also, because these procedures tap into right-hemisphere functioning more directly, they also allow us to see how people behave when presented with stimuli that can be quite emotionally arousing. Because many of our clients struggle with emotional regulation, performance-based tests give an idea of how they function when they are emotionally aroused. And with those clients whose problems in living are due to insecure attachment or developmental trauma, these tests often provide a window—that is not readily available otherwise—into their right-hemisphere disorganization and subcortical dysregulation.

Research in this area is just beginning, but now there are multiple studies examining how performance-based personality tests are processed in the brain, and their results seem to support my theory. Several studies concerned a relatively new performance-based personality test, the Adult Attachment Projective Picture System (AAP; George & West, 2012). The AAP is a validated measure of adult attachment representation (status) and shows a high degree of concordance with the Adult Attachment Interview (George, Kaplan, & Main, 1984/1985/1996). It consists of seven cards with line drawings, each of which was chosen to arouse the attachment system. As one goes through the set, the cards are generally progressively emotionally arousing, and as I have written about before (Finn, 2011), many clients have intense emotional reactions when taking the test. Some of the cards show figures that are alone; others show dyads. The stories are rigorously coded, and the codes are used to assign clients to one of the four major attachment status classifications: Secure, Dismissing, Preoccupied, and Unresolved.

In a pioneering study, George and her colleagues in Germany administered the AAP to a group of 16 non-patient women while they were scanned in an fMRI machine (Erk, S., George, Kächele, Ruchsow, Spitzer, Kircher, & Walter, 2005). Five of the women had excessive head movement, leaving 11 women's scans to be analyzed. Afterwards, the women's stories were coded and the women were classified into two groups, those with organized attachment status (secure, dismissing, or preoccupied; N = 6) and another with unresolved/disorganized attachment status (=5). You will remember that unresolved attachment is particularly associated in research with past trauma and with various forms of psychopathology.

Women with unresolved attachment showed significantly more activation in their limbic areas than did women with resolved/organized attachment. This activation was centered mainly in the right amygdala and the hippocampus, which are associated with perception of fear and autobiographical memory, respectively. From the fMRI results, it appeared that the AAP may have reactivated "unresolved" traumatic or negative autobiographical memories among the women with unresolved attachment, especially the last cards of the AAP, which often elicit stories about traumatic situations. In short, the different AAP results reflected significant differences in how these pictures were processed in the brains of the two groups of women.

A second study examined the AAP performance and brain activation of 11 women diagnosed with Borderline Personality Disorder (BPD) compared to 17 mentally healthy female volunteers (Buchheim, Erk, George, Kächele, Kircher, Martius et al., 2008). Because of their well-known sensitivity to abandonment, it was predicted that the women with BPD would show a greater number of traumatic marker codes in their stories to the alone cards of the AAP, and that those same women would show increased activation of brain regions associated with fear and pain during such times. Both hypotheses were confirmed. The fMRI results indicated that when viewing the alone pictures, women with BPD showed more activation of limbic regions associated with pain and fear, namely the dorsal anterior cingulate cortex, than did the healthy volunteers.

Other fMRI studies have centered on the Rorschach. For example, in one study, individuals with lower form-quality scores on the Rorschach had larger amygdalas—known to be a sign of their amygdalas being activated more often (Asari, Knoishi, Jimura, Chikazoe, Nakamura, & Miyashita, 2008). This suggests that emotional activation greatly influences the extent to which one distorts reality. Also, one study looked at Rorschach scores of individuals receiving positive and negative feedback about their performance on a frustrating simple motor prediction test. When listening to negative feedback, those individuals with more achromatic color (C') scores showed more activation of the posterior medial prefrontal cortex (r = .34), an area of the brain known to be implicated in the processing of negative emotions (Jimura, Konoshi, Asari, & Miyashita, 2009). It seems that individuals with higher C' scores reacted more strongly to the negative feedback than those without much C'. This finding has implications, I believe, for giving feedback to clients with high C' scores about their psychological assessment results.

In summary, I believe that evidence will continue to accrue that performance-based personality tests have a very important place in our psychological assessment batteries, because these tests allow us to access parts of the brain that are difficult to reach with other methods, and because they are extremely useful in measuring different aspects of emotional and interpersonal functioning that are not well captured by other assessment procedures.[2] Some 70+ years after Bruno Klopfer began publishing his influential work on the Rorschach (Klopfer & Kelley, 1942), we are closer than ever to being able to explain why the Rorschach and similar tests work and how to interpret their results and use them to inform subsequent treatment.

Therapeutic Benefits of Providing Emotional Experiences to Clients during Psychological Assessment

Last, I would like to propose that just as successful psychotherapies arouse and help clients deal with an array of affect states, the same is true of psychological assessment. That is, if we want to use our psychological assessments to help clients heal and change (as we aspire to in Therapeutic Assessment)—and not just as sources of information about clients' personalities and psychopathology—we need to learn to maximize the emotional impact of our assessments. This means changing our view of the feedback process in psychological assessment from that of a cognitive transmission of information to that of a highly emotional event that has the possibility of profoundly changing clients' views of themselves. We must also expand our view of the psychological assessor from that of an "objective" technician who is good with tests and numbers to that of a highly interpersonally skilled clinician who takes responsibility for helping clients deal with the potentially emotionally overwhelming information that can come out of an assessment. Last, if we want to maximize the therapeutic impact of our work, I believe we must learn to use emotionally arousing test materials for maximum benefit. To illustrate, let me now discuss a Therapeutic Assessment I did several years ago that demonstrates well how performance-based personality tests can be used to make potent therapeutic interventions.

Case Example

Referral

Ben was a 27-year-old gay man referred to me by John—a psychologist—who told me that he had been treating Ben for "sexual addiction" for over a year. I had not worked with John previously but knew that he had a specialty in treating sexual addiction. When he called, John shared that he was concerned and somewhat frustrated with Ben, because Ben continued to "act out" sexually in risky ways, despite regular individual and group therapy and participation in a 12-step program for sexual addiction. John said that Ben had a difficult time identifying specific emotional triggers for his sexual acting out and that he wondered if Ben might need to go to a residential treatment program for sex addicts. This option was a possibility in that Ben worked as a janitor in a national chain "Big Box" store and had excellent health insurance that would pay for such treatment.

Initial Sessions

A few days later, Ben called and scheduled an initial session. When I greeted him in the waiting room, I found a slight, dark-haired young man with a hangdog look. He spoke softly and rapidly without making much eye contact and ripped apart a facial tissue as we talked. Ben said his main questions for the assessment were: "Why do I keep on acting out sexually in dangerous ways, even though I know that it's really stupid?" "What am I going to have to do to stop acting out?" and "Why do I hate myself?" His shame as he gave these questions was palpable, and it took all my skill as a psychologist to create some moments of contact with Ben, in which he could see that I was not judging him. For example, I asked Ben what he liked or found positive about his sexual encounters, which seemed to startle him. I commented on his apparent surprise and Ben said no one had ever asked him that question before. He then made direct eye contact for the first time and said, "When I have sex with a good-looking man, I feel good and attractive myself. And I don't usually feel that way at all." Ben then went on to say that he saw himself as a "120-lb. weakling" and that he had never been good at sports. I asked more about his early years and found that Ben's mother was hospitalized for depression several times in his childhood and that Ben's father worked a great deal and was rarely home. However, Ben was very protective of his parents when relating this information and assured me that his parents loved him a great deal.

Test Results

The first test I gave Ben was the MMPI-2, and his profile was a clearly defined 4–7 code type. (See Figure 5.1.) This code type is associated with an alternating cycle of acting out followed by severe shame and self-recrimination. This pattern is generally very difficult to interrupt, and most experts agree that the major underlying dynamic with these individuals is severe shame, and that the acting out behavior gives temporary relief from this (e.g., Graham, 2011). As the reader can see, there were no indications of serious depression on Ben's MMPI-2.

In hopes of exploring Ben's question of why he hated himself, I asked him to fill out the first part of the Early Memory Procedure (Bruhn, 1990), in which clients journal about their earliest memories and then rate them for how positive vs. negative, and how clear vs. fuzzy they are. In Bruhn's interpretive framework, a person's clearest, most negatively rated memory is believed to be a metaphor

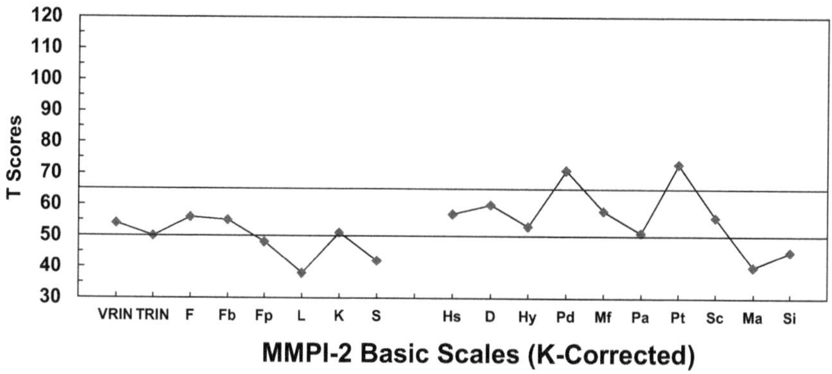

Figure 5.1 Ben's MMPI–2 profile.

Notes: VRIN = Variable Response Inconsistency scale; TRIN = True-Response Inconsistency scale; F = Infrequency; Fb = Back F; Fp = Infrequency Psychopathology; L = Lie; K = Defensiveness; S = Superlative Self-Presentation; Hs = Scale 1, Hypochondriasis; D = Scale 2, Depression; Hy = Scale 3, Hysteria; Pd = Scale 4, Psychopathic Deviate; Mf = Scale 5, Masculinity-Femininity; Pa = Scale 6, Paranoia; Pt = Scale 7, Psychasthenia; Sc = Scale 8, Schizophrenia; Ma = Scale 9, Hypomania; Si = Scale 0, Social Introversion. Minnesota Multiphasic Personality Inventory-2 (MMPI-2) Profile for Basic Scales. Copyright © 2001 the Regents of the University of Minnesota. All rights reserved. Used by permission of the University of Minnesota Press. "MMPI-2" and "Minnesota Multiphasic Personality Inventory-2" are trademarks owned by the University of Minnesota Press.

for his/her core unresolved issue. In Ben's case, his earliest memory—from age four—was:

> *Mom is in bed, where she has been all day, probably for weeks, and my brother and I are trying to get her up so she will eat something. My father told us when he left that morning to make sure she got up. We keep trying and trying but she won't get up. I start crying because I'm afraid my father will be mad at us. I think it was the very next day that the ambulance came and took her to the hospital, where she had shock treatments.*

Ben wrote that the strongest feeling in the memory was "feeling like a failure" because he and his brother hadn't been able to rouse his mother. When we talked about the memory, I asked if he thought there was any connection to his "hating himself" and he said no. He said that his mother had apologized many times for her depression and that he knew that she loved him.

In contrast to the MMPI-2, on the Rorschach (Exner, 2003), Ben's Depression Index was 6, suggesting a great deal of underlying painful affect (Table 4.1). Ben had 4 *Vista* responses—suggesting severe shame, a very low Egocentricity index (.12)—confirming how poorly he thought about himself, and his Suicide

Constellation score was 9—above the usual cut-off for significant suicidal impulses. Ben also had many White Space (*S* = 8) and Aggressive Content (*AgC* = 7) responses, which made me think that he was also dealing with a great deal of underlying anger. His large number of sex responses (*Sx* = 7) seemed to fit with his sexual acting out and preoccupation.

What I found most interesting, however, was the sequence of scores on Ben's Rorschach. He had five *Morbid* responses, spaced throughout the protocol, and I noticed that Ben reported overt sexual percepts immediately after many of the morbid contents or other markers of painful emotion. For example, on Card VI, Ben's responses were "A folded decaying leaf" (to the whole, earning both a *Morbid* and a *Vista* score) and then "An erect penis" (a *Sex* response) to D6. On Card IX, he saw "rotten food," again to the whole (earning both a *MOR* and a *Food* response), followed by "the muscular chest of a man, with erect nipples. He is aroused" (to the D6 area, scored *Hd* and *Sx*).

This sequence of scores gave further weight to a hypothesis I had started to develop when I saw the discrepancy between Ben's MMPI-2 and Rorschach. As I have previously discussed (Finn, 1996, 2011b), this pattern—where the MMPI shows much less distress or disturbance than the Rorschach—is common among individuals who use character defenses to protect themselves from painful split-off affect states. Ben's Rorschach, as I previously explained, gave a window into Ben's right-hemisphere disorganization and to the considerable grief, anger, and shame he was keeping at bay. The MMPI-2 gave a picture of the coping mechanisms Ben was using to avoid these painful affect states. And the sequence of his Rorschach responses strongly suggested that Ben's sexual preoccupations intensified whenever he began to get close to his underlying overwhelming negative emotions. No wonder he couldn't stop his sexual acting out! Finally, the Rorschach interpersonal and relational scores helped explain why Ben was unlikely to turn to other people as an alternative way of not being traumatized by his underlying depression. Although he had several Cooperative Movements (*COP* = 2), other scores suggested Ben did not view other people as helpful emotional supports (*Pure H* = 1, *Isolation Index* = .23, *GHR:PHR* = 1:5). This made sense, given that Ben's parents were probably not able to be steady and attuned emotional supports when he was growing up.

Assessment Intervention Session

Given this tentative understanding of Ben's situation, I then pondered how I could help Ben understand the important role his sexual thoughts and behavior were playing for him, so that he would have less shame and more compassion for himself. I also wanted to help John understand why it was not so easy for Ben to just stop his sexual behavior. I had tried to talk with Ben after the standard administration of the Rorschach about the pattern I noticed in his responses, but he seemed agitated and uncomfortable and said that he needed to leave. (I found out much later that he left the session and immediately went to a place where he met men for anonymous sex.) So, I decided to conduct what we in Therapeutic Assessment call an Assessment Intervention session (Finn, 2007). The purpose of such sessions is to elicit an *in vivo* analog of the client's main problem in living—as reflected in his/her assessment questions—and to engage the client in observing, analyzing, and reaching new understandings. Sometimes, the client and assessor also experiment with interventions that may ameliorate the problem behavior, with hopes that these may be generalized to life outside the assessment sessions.

At our next meeting, I began by telling Ben that we would be exploring his first question, of what led him to act out sexually. He said he was glad. I then asked Ben to rate—on a scale from 0 to 10—how sexually compulsive he felt at that moment in time. He said he was having a good day and was at about a "1" on the scale. I told him I would be checking in with him at various points during the session to see if that rating changed. I then showed Ben a series of cards from the TAT and gave him the standard instructions. I chose my first three cards because I thought they would be emotionally "neutral" for Ben, and it appeared I was right. For example, to a picture of a boat resting on a river bank (Card 12BG), Ben told a story about two brothers who went fishing on a hot summer's day. To a picture of a woman climbing a winding set of stairs (Card 13G), Ben told a story of a person riding an escalator while shopping in a department store. After these neutral cards, I asked Ben for another rating, and he said that he was still feeling at a 1 on the scale of sexual compulsivity. I then gave Ben three cards—3BM (a despondent figure kneeling on the ground), 3GF (a distressed woman standing in a doorway with her hand over her face), and 13B (a boy sitting in a doorway looking dejected)—that I believed would elicit his underlying painful affect. His three stories were very dysphoric. The first two stories concerned depressed women, and I suspected they depicted actual incidents involving his mother. This is the story he told to Card 13B:

> *He's left alone again. There's no one there for the boy. His parents are gone, his brothers and sisters are off somewhere, and he has no friends. He's tired of all this and is sitting there waiting for his...someone to come home. [SF: What is he thinking and feeling?] Awful. Alone. I mean I guess it's better off to be dead ...* (Ben started to cry) *since nobody cares and notices.*

I sat quietly with Ben for a few moments as he regained his composure. I said, "That one is pretty painful." He started crying again, averted his eyes, and said, "I guess that was me... that was me when I grew up. But I don't like to admit that." I asked Ben why he didn't like to admit that, and he explained, "Because...I mean...I had good parents...but they weren't good with kids. But I loved them anyway. I loved them." I said, "It's painful to think about how bleak it was back then, because then it's hard to think of them as good parents." Ben reiterated, "They were my parents and I loved them. They did their best. The boy did his best" (pointing to the TAT card).

I sympathized and then asked Ben to rate how sexually compulsive he was feeling at the moment. He paused and stopped crying, did a quick scan, looked surprised, and said, "A lot! Yeah, a 10! I guess I didn't realize how my feelings…I mean as I was telling the story I was thinking of all the ways of acting out and where I was going to go after this session!" He looked agitated, puzzled, and a bit ashamed. I jumped in, "So Ben, it looks to me that the sexual acting out is way to try to cope with these awful feelings." Ben said, "I guess you're right. I didn't realize how my childhood pushed me to do all these bad things." I elaborated, "I think there were a lot of feelings of emptiness and loneliness when you were growing up, and it's been hard for you to let yourself know that." Ben cautiously agreed, but then defended his parents again, "I mean I had a good childhood. My parents did their best. I guess I felt alone, but…" I tried to side-step Ben's ambivalence by returning to the less personal TAT card, "Ben, go with me here. When you would think about this little boy, what would he have done with these awful feelings?" Ben laughed nervously and looked away, "I didn't want to tell you this, but…the boy would go off to his room to masturbate…I didn't know what you were going to think about me…of him." I said I would tell him what I really thought and then waited until Ben made eye contact again. I said, "I think it was a pretty creative way to cope with his terrible feelings." Ben quickly asked, "It was?" I continued, "I think so. Because it's not like there was somebody else around to talk to, right?" Ben agreed, and from this point in the session he seemed to get lighter and his mood brightened considerably to the point that he started to smile. As I watched him relax and smile, I remember thinking, "He is really beautiful when he looks like this." We continued to talk about the self-soothing aspects of his sexual behavior, with Ben making more and more connections. Several times I emphasized, "Ben, I think these feelings are too big for you to feel alone. That's why you've had to use other ways to help yourself." Before Ben left, I expressed concern and asked him what else he could do after the session besides go hunting for sex. He said that he was going to a 12-step meeting and would be seeing John the next day. He also said that he felt less compulsive just from our talking together and gave himself a rating of 3 on the 10-point scale. I felt very satisfied by something he said toward the end of the session, "I never realized how talking to someone about this could help. I feel so much better."

Space limitations prevent me from describing the end of Ben's Therapeutic Assessment in detail.[3] I can report that the Assessment Intervention Session and the subsequent feedback session represented a major turning point for Ben (and for John), and one year after the assessment Ben was no longer engaging in risky sexual behavior.

Conclusion

In our current work in Therapeutic Assessment, we are using recent understandings from Shore (2010), Siegel (1999), Stern (2004), Fosha (2000), and others to become even more adept at arranging and making use of these types of emotionally arousing assessment events. This is leading to even more powerful healing experiences for many different types of clients, and I think we will continue learning more about how to conduct assessment-based interventions. Evidence continues to accrue that psychological assessment can be a powerful, brief intervention and that the methods of Therapeutic Assessment maximize such effects (e.g., Poston & Hanson, 2010). I reiterate how excited and privileged I feel to be a clinical psychologist, and particularly, an assessment psychologist, at this juncture in our history.

Notes

1 I refer to "mothers'" interactions throughout the chapter while recognizing that the primary caregiver for some infants may be a father, grandparent, aunt, or uncle.
2 As predicted, this research has continued to accrue. For example, Giromini et al. (2017) concluded: "looking at the Rorschach inkblots while thinking about what they might be activates areas of the brain that are implicated in the perception and processing of emotions and emotional memories" (p. 30).
3 A detailed account of the entire Therapeutic Assessment is published in a chapter by Finn and Chudzik (2010).

References

Aitken, K. J., & Trevarthen, C. (1997). Self-other organization in human psychological development. *Development and Psychopathology, 9*, 651–675.

Asari, T., Konishi, S., Jimura, K., Chkazoe, J., Nakamura, N., & Miyashita, Y. (2008). Amygdalar enlargement associated with unique perception. *Cortex, 30*, 1–6.

Beebe, B. (2000). Coconstructing mother-infant distress: The microsychrony of maternal impingement and infant avoidance in the face-to-face encounter. *Psychoanalytic Inquiry, 20*, 412–440.

Bornstein, R. F. (2004). A process dissociation approach to objective-projective test score interrelationships. *Journal of Personality Assessment, 78*, 47–68.

Bromberg, P. M. (2006). *Awakening the dreamer: Clinical journeys*. Analytic Press.

Bruhn, A. R. (1990). *Earliest childhood memories: Vol. 1. Theory and application to clinical practice*. Praeger.

Buchheim, A., Erk, S., George, C., Kächele, H., Ruchsow, M, Spitzer, M., Kircher, T., & Walter, H. (2005). Measuring attachment representation in an fMRI environment: A pilot study. *Psychopathology, 589*, 1–9.

Buchheim, A., Erk, S., George, C., Kächele, H., Kircher, T., Martius, P., Pokorny, D., Ruchsow, M., Spitzer, M., & Walter, H. (2008). Neural correlates of attachment dysregulation in borderline personality disorder using functional magnetic resonance imaging. *Psychiatry Research: Neuroimaging, 163*, 223–235.

Cicchetti, D. (1994). Integrating developmental risk factors: Perspectives from developmental psychopathology. In C. A. Nelson (Ed.), *Minnesota symposium on child psychology. Vol. 27, Threats to optimal development* (pp. 285–325). Erlbaum.

Damasio, A. (1999). *The feeling of what happens: Body and emotion in the making of consciousness*. Harcourt Brace.

Diener, M. J., Hilsenroth, M. J., & Weinberger, J. (2007). Therapist affect focus and patient outcomes in psychodynamic psychotherapy: A meta-analysis. *American Journal of Psychiatry, 164*, 936–941.

Exner, J. (2003). *The Rorschach: A comprehensive system* (4th ed.). Wiley.

Finn, S. E. (1996). Assessment feedback integrating MMPI-2 and Rorschach findings. *Journal of Personality Assessment, 67*, 543–557.

Finn, S. E. (2007). *In our clients' shoes: Theory and techniques of Therapeutic Assessment*. Earlbaum.

Finn, S. E. (2011a). Use of the Adult Attachment Projective Picture System (AAP) in the middle of a long-term psychotherapy. *Journal of Personality Assessment, 93*, 427–433.

Finn, S. E. (2011b). Journeys through the valley of death: Multimethod psychological assessment and personality transformation in long-term psychotherapy. *Journal of Personality Assessment, 93*, 123–141.

Finn, S. E., & Chudzik, L. (2010). L'Evaluation Thérapeutique: une intervention originale brève. In SultanS. & L. Chudzik (Eds.), *Du diagnostic au traitement: Rorschach et MMPI-2* (pp. 203–226). Mardaga.

Fosha, D. (2000). *The transforming power of affect: A model for accelerated change*. Basic Books.

George, C., Kaplan, N., & Main, M. (1984/1985/1996). *Attachment interview for adults*. Unpublished manuscript. University of California, Berkeley.

George, C., & West, M. (2012). *The Adult Attachment Projective Picture System: Attachment theory and assessment in adults*. Guilford.

Giromini, L., Viglione, D. J., Zannaro, A., & Cuada, F. (2017). Neural activation during production of Rorschach responses: An fMRI study. *Psychiatry Research: Neuroimaging, 262*, 25–31.

Graham, J. R. (2011). *MMPI-2: Assessing personality and psychopathology*. Oxford University Press.

Jimura, K., Konishi, S., Asari, T., & Miyashita, Y. (2009). Involvement of the medial prefrontal cortex in emotion during feedback presentation. *NeuroReport, 20*, 886–890.

Klopfer, B., & Kelley, D. M. (1942). *The Rorschach technique*. World Book Co.

Martin, D. J., Garske, J. P., & Davis, M. K. (2000). Relation of the therapeutic alliance with outcome and other variables: A meta-analytic review. *Journal of Consulting and Clinical Psychology, 68*, 438–450.

Valliant, L.Mccullough (1997). *Changing character: Short-term anxiety-regulating psychotherapy for restructuring defenses, affects, and attachment*. Basic Books.

Meyer, G. J. (1997). On the integration of personality assessment methods: The Rorschach and MMPI. *Journal of Personality Assessment, 68*, 297–330.

Poston, J. M., & Hanson, W. M. (2010). Meta-analysis of psychological assessment as a therapeutic intervention. *Psychological Assessment, 22*, 203–212.

Schore, A. N. (1997). Early organization of the nonlinear right brain and development of a predisposition to psychiatric disorders. *Development and Psychopathology, 9*, 595–631.

Schore, A. N. (2002). The right brain as the neurobiological substrate of Freud's dynamic unconscious. In D. Scharff (Ed.), *The psychoanalytic century: Freud's legacy for the future* (pp. 61–88). Other Press.

Schore, A. N. (2003a). *Affect dysregulation and disorders of the self.* Norton.

Schore, A. N. (2003b). *Affect regulation and repair of the self.* Norton.

Schore, A. N. (2003c). Early relational trauma, disorganized attachment, and the development of a predisposition to violence. In D. Siegel & M. Solomon (Eds.), *Healing trauma: Attachment, mind, body, and brain* (pp. 101–167). W. W. Norton.

Schore, A. N. (2009). Right brain affect regulation: An essential mechanism of development, trauma, dissociation, and psychotherapy. In D. Fosha, M. Solomon, & D. Siegel (Eds.), *The healing power of emotions: Integrating relationships, body, and mind. A dialogue among scientists and clinicians* (pp. 112–144). Norton.

Schore, A. N. (2010). Relational trauma and the developing right brain: The neurobiology of broken attachment bonds. In T. Baradon (Ed.), *Relational trauma in infancy* (pp. 19–47). Routledge.

Siegel, D. J. (1999). *The developing mind: How relationships and the brain interact to shape who we are*. Guilford.

Stern, D. N. (2004). *The present moment in psychotherapy and everyday life*. W. W. Norton.

Tronick, E. Z. (1998). Dyadically expanded states of consciousness and the process of therapeutic change. *Infant Mental Health Journal, 19*, 290–299.

Wood, J. M., Nezworski, T. M., & Lillienfeld, S. O. (2003). *What's wrong with the Rorschach?* Josey-Bass.

Chapter 6

"When I Found My Father"

A Rorschach-Evoked Trauma Flashback Helps a Client Heal*

Sally was a 35-year-old woman referred to me more than 20 years ago by Margaret, a close colleague who frequently sent difficult therapy clients for Therapeutic Assessment. Sally and Margaret had been working together for about 18 months at the time of the referral, focusing mainly on Sally's tendency (in her own words) to "hook up with psychopaths" as romantic partners. Sally had a long pattern of getting into relationships with highly narcissistic men, becoming entranced with them soon after knowing them, and then failing to heed signs that they were not the "Prince Charmings" she thought them to be. Sally had begun psychotherapy with Margaret after a particularly disastrous relationship, in which she had given an idealized fiancé $50,000 for a "new business venture," after which he had promptly disappeared.

Sally and Margaret both felt they had made progress in therapy before the assessment, and one insight they had come to concerned Sally's father. Sally had been very close to her father up until his death by suicide when she was eight years old. She and Margaret came to believe that Sally understandably still idealized her father since she had never known him as an older child or adult who might see his faults. His abrupt death led to an incomplete grief process, summarized by Sally as, "I'm still looking for that perfect father who went away when I was 8, and I keep trying to force the men I meet into that mold, even when they don't fit it." Although she could now define the problem, Sally still felt at risk of repeating her relationship pattern, and her main question for the TA was, "What do I need to do or feel to be able to choose a man who really cares for me?"

The early parts of the TA went well, and I found it easy to work with Sally and Margaret. I gave Sally the MMPI-2, and the most remarkable part of her profile was an elevation on Scale 3 and a low score on Scale 6. I discussed the profile with her before I collected other data, introducing the Therapeutic

* This chapter is adapted from a paper presented at the annual meeting of the Society for Personality Assessment, March 17, 2018, Washington, D.C., as part of a symposium "Singularity: Utility of Single Rorschach or Projective Responses in Personality Assessment," B. L. Smith (Chair)

DOI: 10.4324/9781003602231-6

Assessment concept of the "broken trust meter" that results when a person has to "trust people early on who were not trustworthy." Sally immediately talked about her mother, who was a volatile, chaotic woman who had periods of severe depression alternating with violent rages that were often directed at Sally's father. Sally and her older sister had witnessed some terrible scenes, and Sally and I speculated she had been emotionally traumatized by these events. We wondered if her poor judgment in romantic relationships might be connected to these attachment traumas.

The most significant event in the assessment occurred when Sally and I were doing the Rorschach; it is still extremely vivid in my memory. Sally fairly easily engaged with the test and easily gave responses as we went along. I had noted some traumatic contents on Cards II, III, VIII, and IX, perhaps elicited by the color, e.g., "Two people fighting (Card II) and a bleeding heart at the bottom showing the pain being created," or "An explosion (Card IX) with destruction all around it." When I got to Card X, I handed Sally the card, she looked at it, gave a loud grunt, and fell back violently in her seat. I couldn't figure out what was happening and turned to look at Sally. Her eyes were large, her face was white, and after a moment she said in a very small voice, "The blood splattered on the wall when I found my father." I was so unprepared for this and shocked that I asked, "What did you say?" and she repeated, "The brains and blood on the wall after my father shot himself. I found him." At that point, Sally looked like a deer in headlights and was clearly in a dissociated, frozen state. I took the card out of her hands and moved my chair across from her. She was blank. I talked to her gently and asked her to focus on my voice and on various features of the room. She began to come back to herself, seemed to remember what had just happened, and then dissociated again; I worked with her slowly to get grounded, and eventually she began to cry. I was also full of emotions, among which were horror at what I had heard, and awe and curiosity about what I had just witnessed with the Rorschach. To make it brief, that day I got Sally back enough to herself to leave (luckily, she lived very close) and with her permission I immediately called Margaret and told her what had happened.

As you might imagine, this Rorschach event was discussed many times in the ensuing assessment and psychotherapy, and this is what I learned: Sally had indeed been the one to find her father after he had committed suicide, and while she later claimed that she never actually "forgot" this fact, she said she had not thought about it for years, and clearly she had never mentioned it during her psychotherapy or the early sessions of the Therapeutic Assessment. Margaret, the therapist, later ended up meeting with Sally and her sister (seven years older) to discuss the events, and this is what the sister relayed. As already mentioned, their mother was a highly unstable woman. Sally's father, an architect, worked most days in a small office separated from the house, and routinely Sally would go there after school, have tea with her father, and they would go up to the main house together for dinner. The family pieced together from small comments and other facts that Sally's father had been concerned about his wife being the one to discover his suicide, so he had shot himself shortly before his 8-year-old daughter was due to arrive home from school, intending for Sally to find him when she came to have tea with him. The sister said Sally had run to a neighbor's house for help, and that things had been so chaotic for weeks afterwards that it was only much later that the family had put together how the father had arranged things. She also said that Sally never talked about this aspect of her father's death, so the family was not even sure what she had seen or remembered (and interestingly, no one ever asked). I'll tell you more of the story in a minute, but for now let us think scientifically about this astonishing Rorschach event.

Many of you are familiar with the Trauma Content Index (TCI) developed by Armstrong and Lowenstein in 1990: TCI = (Sx + An + Bl + MOR + AG)/R. Although originally developed to identify clients with Dissociative Identity Disorder, the TCI has been validated in multiple independent samples as a possible measure of trauma. For example, my colleagues and I demonstrated that the TCI was elevated compared to normal controls in a sample of women with verified histories of sexual abuse (Kamphuis, Kugeares, & Finn, 2000). Although the TCI was never integrated into the Comprehensive System, a very similar index (Critical Contents) is part of R-PAS (Meyer et al., 2011), and users are cautioned that high scores, besides possibly indicating trauma, may also be associated with conscious attempts at malingering or with severe psychological disturbance. What I find fascinating is Armstrong's and Loewenstein's original theory that in certain clients these types of Rorschach responses (i.e., with AG, MOR, Sx, Bl, and An codes) represent "dissociative and self-hypnotic attempts to defend against intrusion of traumatic memories into full conscious awareness" (p. 453). I interpret this sentence as meaning that when some clients give traumatic Rorschach responses they are "displacing" traumatic memories into Rorschach percepts in an attempt to keep them at bay. However, I am also convinced that at times the Rorschach stimuli are so potent that they can actually provoke traumatic flashbacks, as appears to have happened with Sally.

In my 2012 paper (see Chapter 5), "Implications of Recent Research in Neurobiology for Psychological Assessment," I summarized a number of fMRI studies of performance-based personality tests—including the Rorschach—and suggested that these procedures "tap into material that is more reflective of right-hemisphere and subcortical functioning" than do other assessment procedures, which is part of why they are uniquely helpful. I referenced a study by Asari and colleagues in 2008, showing brain activation proximal to the limbic system at the moment when a sample of Japanese respondees were seeing FQ- responses on the Rorschach. (By the way, "blood spattered on a wall" is an FQ- response for Card X in either the CS or R-PAS.) I still don't know whether Sally actually had an episodic memory of finding her father prior to our doing the Rorschach administration, but she had certainly acted as if she did not. My hypothesis was that seeing the Rorschach card created a small flashback that "kicked" a representation of that horrible moment into explicit memory. I also believe that this recall took place in a very special context, i.e., in the middle of a Therapeutic Assessment where Sally and I had engaged her curiosity, established a great deal of trust, and where she already had experienced emotional support. I believe that we created a safe context in which Sally could have her flashback, and then the Rorschach did its work. Some of you have heard me say before that when clients give us Assessment Questions at the beginning of a TA, they then proceed to consciously and unconsciously give us every piece of information needed to answer those questions. The Rorschach and our other tests are tools through which clients can communicate the information needed both to us and eventually, with our help, to themselves.

As may be evident, this alone does not guarantee that traumatic memories will be resolved. When the Rorschach has done its job by bringing up previously dissociated traumas, it then is contingent on the client and therapist to metaprocess this material and for the client to feel "mentalized" by the therapist and other people. In short, this means that others need to help "hold" and "mirror" the multiple emotions the client has about the traumatic event, so that they do not feel overwhelmed and alone with these emotions. It is this step that eventually leads to the traumatic event being integrated into the client's view of self and the world and for the symptom it has caused to cease.

Let me close by finishing the story of my work with Sally. Following the Rorschach "breakthrough" (Sally's word, again) and the ensuing discussions with me, Margaret, and her sister, Sally began to think of her father in a different way. She still loved him and grieved for his death, but she also realized he had not really held her best interests in mind in important ways, both in the manner he suicided, but also before that. Sally was able to feel anger at her father for not protecting her and her sister from their mother, and for how he frequently withdrew, leaving them to deal with her volatility on their own. Margaret told me about one particularly important therapy session three months after the assessment, in which Sally had been able to scream at her father (in an empty chair): "You coward! You took the easy way out and left us to deal with that crazy sick woman. I hate you for that." Margaret said that she saw a huge change in Sally after that session.

About a year after the assessment, I received an email from Sally thanking me again for the Therapeutic Assessment and telling me that she had just gotten engaged to a wonderful man. When I saw Margaret soon after, she told me that Sally had chosen really well this time and was marrying a generous, kind man who was also strong and who adored Sally. Of course, I was delighted, and I blew a mental kiss at my Rorschach cards. My work with Sally gave me a clearer idea of how the Rorschach could be used to help clients heal from unresolved trauma.

References

Armstrong, J. G., & Loewenstein, R. J. (1990). Characteristics of patients with multiple personality and dissociative disorders on psychological testing. *The Journal of Nervous and Mental Disease*, *178*, 448–454.

Asari, T., Konishi, S., Jimura, K., Chikazoe, J., Nakamura, N., & Miyashita, Y. (2008). Right temporopolar activation associated with unique perception. *NeuroImage*, *41*, 145–152.

Kamphuis, J. H., Kugeares, S. L., & Finn, S. E. (2000). Rorschach correlates of sexual abuse: Trauma content and aggression indices. *Journal of Personality Assessment*, *75*, 212–224. https://doi.org/10.1207/S15327752JPA75023

Meyer, G. J., Viglione, D. J., Mihura, J. L., Erard, R. E., & Erdberg, P. (2011). *The Rorschach Performance Assessment System (R-PAS)*. R-PAS.

Chapter 7

What Current Understandings of Shame Mean for Psychological Assessment*

Over the past 30 years, I have undertaken an in-depth study of the psychological literature on shame, in part because I became convinced that it was a very significant phenomenon among the clients I saw (and, I must add, in my own life). Since I am a product of my *Zeitgeist*, it is perhaps not coincidental that during this same period of time, shame has become increasingly recognized as an important human experience that has numerous clinical implications. Research and writings on shame have exploded in recent years, with notable contributions from Benau (2022), George (2025), Izard (1991), Kaufman (2004), Lewis (1987), Morrison (1996), Nathanson (1992), Schore (1994, 1998, 2003a, 2003b), Stern (1985), and Tomkins (1987), among others. Also, a host of newly formulated psychotherapies, such as those developed by Linehan (1993), Davanloo (1978), Fosha (2000), and McCullough Vaillant (1997) place great emphasis on excessive shame and its role in the development of different psychological disorders.

When we turn to the field of psychological assessment, until recently there has been considerably less attention devoted to shame, although five self-report inventories that aspire to measure dispositional shame have generated a number of research studies in clinical, social, and personality psychology: the Adapted Shame and Guilt Scale (ASGS; Hoblitzelle, 1987); the Dimensions of Conscience Questionnaire (DCQ; Johnson et al., 1987), the Test of Self-Conscious Affect (TOSCA; Tangney, Wagner, & Gramzow, 1989), the Personal Feelings Questionnaire-2 (PFQ-2; Harder & Zalma, 1990), and the Internalized Shame Scale (ISS; Cook, 1996). I am not aware of anyone who uses these tests in applied clinical work, and there is a problem with all these self-report tests: many people are not aware of the shame they carry and have potent defenses that prevent them from recognizing it. Thankfully, now there is an excellent performance-based personality test of shame, the Thurston Cradock Test of

* This chapter is adapted from a paper presented at the annual meeting of the Society for Personality Assessment, March 10, 2011, Boston, MA, as part of a symposium "Working with Shame in Psychological Assessment," S. E. Finn (Chair).

DOI: 10.4324/9781003602231-7

Shame (TCTS; Thurston & Cradock O'Leary, 2009), consisting of 10 picture story cards designed to elicit shame that are scored for shame themes and defenses against shame. There is a growing body of literature on the clinical use of the TCTS (Cradock O'Leary, 2017; Cradock O'Leary, Kelley, & Parrish, 2020; Cradock O'Leary, Nakamura, & Finn, 2020), and I myself have written about using the TCTS to great benefit in an Assessment Intervention Session (Finn, 2019). In addition, there is a recently developed shame coding system for clients' responses to the Adult Attachment Projective Picture System (AAP; George, 2025).

What is most striking in my mind is that there is little literature or research on how shame impacts the process of applied psychological assessment, although it is clear to me that it does. In this chapter, I will first present a general understanding of normal and pathological shame derived from the literature, and then I share my reflections on what this conceptualization means for applied clinical personality assessment.

A General Understanding of Normal and Pathological Shame

How Shame Develops

It is now generally believed that shame experiences originate in the second year of life when attachment figures begin to shift their role from being primarily caretakers to that of socialization agents. The rapid increase in cognitive, neuromuscular, and gross motor activity in the infant creates a new tension in her relationship with her parents, as they strive to keep her safe from the consequences of her unbridled joyful explorations. Imagine an infant who toddles away from the mother and looks back at her as she reaches toward something deemed disgusting or dangerous, such as the kitty litter box. (This is a real event that I witnessed years ago with a friend and her daughter.) From previous experience with a good-enough mother, the infant has come to anticipate a psycho-biologically attuned shared positive affect state with the mother and a dyadic amplification of the emotions of joy and excitement. Instead, the infant experiences a shocking mis-attunement when the mother says "No! That's dirty!" while manifesting a facial expression of disgust, horror, anger, or fear. Neuroscientific work suggests that such abrupt mis-attunements can trigger an immediate collapse of arousal, with the infant moving sharply from a heightened, sympathetic-driven state into a more subdued parasympathetic mode. This parental response initiates a sudden halt in the infant's arousal, producing an inhibitory, withdrawal-like state that provides the physiological groundwork for early shame experiences. This downshift is often accompanied by gaze aversion, covering of the eyes or face, and a great deal of internal and/or externally visible distress.

The powerful negative affect of shame is "too potent for older infants to sustain for very long" (Malatesta-Magai, 1991, p. 219), and since the infant cannot yet regulate by herself this shock-induced deflation of narcissistic affect, she is dependent on the mother to repair. If the repair is timely and sensitive (e.g., "Oh honey. I scared you, didn't I? I'm so sorry I yelled at you. I got scared because the litter box is dirty. It's OK. I love you.") the mother's soothing reorganizes the infant's physiological and emotional state, restoring relational harmony and helping the child modulate and recover from the shame response. This effect is neurochemically mediated by a resumption of endorphin production and a reactivation of the dopamine-sensitive limbic circuit (Schore, 1994, p. 248). These neurobiological shifts support the maturation of prefrontal–limbic connections, which gradually enhance the infant's capacity for emotion regulation, including the ability to manage shame without caregiver assistance. Put simply, when caregivers help infants recover from early shame experiences, those interactions support the maturation of prefrontal systems and their connections with emotion-responsive regions—changes that underpin the child's later capacity for regulating feelings. Such experiences also create an internalized object-relations sequence, in which the infant comes to understand that "Not only my wishes, but those of other people are also important."

Normal Shame and Guilt

We retain the capacity to feel shame throughout our lives, usually when we are rejected, excluded, or put down by other people or when we fall short of an important standard of our own. The current understanding of the evolutionary function of shame is that it allows adaptation to cultural/group/familial standards by creating a classically conditioned mechanism for social control (Gilbert & McGuire, 1998). In other words, shame is a necessary social adhesive. Many writers emphasize the difference between shame and guilt, with shame being the feeling "I am bad" and guilt being "I did something bad" (Tagney & Fischer, 1995). But distinguishing shame from guilt is a developmental achievement that is not emotionally available to most children nor to many adults, with the result that they experience shame even if they "did something bad." When we have had many experiences of shame being regulated and repaired by attachment figures, we are able to tolerate shame and experience guilt when appropriate. This is adaptive because the action tendency associated with guilt is the desire to make amends (Tomkins, 1987). Healthy shame and guilt are associated with kindness and generosity, and individuals who show healthy embarrassment and shame are well liked by those who know them (Gilbert & Andrews, 1998).

Pathological Shame

Next I turn to the topic of pathological shame. As an example, I recommend that you watch a video on YouTube that has received attention over the past 15 years. It is called "Single Ladies Devastation" and can be found at the following url:

http://www.youtube.com/watch?v=sb9eL3ejXmE The video shows a three-year-old boy singing a song while on a family trip with his parents and his sisters in the car. The song is by Beyoncé and is called "All the Single Ladies." The boy is full of joy and exuberance at first, dancing to the beat of the song from his car seat. Then his father, who is driving, shames him by telling him, "You can't be a 'single lady!'" (presumably because he is a boy). The boy deflates and immediately begins to cry. The father tries to "take back" what he said ("You *can* be a 'single lady'"), but the boy is not soothed until his mother acknowledges his shame ("Did that hurt your feelings?") and initiates a repair by touching him. Interestingly, the father also appears to go into shame and calls himself a "bad father."

We now understand that shame becomes a negative influence on psychological maturation and development when parents' socializing prohibitions are: (1) especially harsh and intense, (2) extensive, and include punishments for actions and behaviors that are normal and essential to the ongoing development of the child, and (3) not followed by an appropriate repair (George, 2025). Because it is generally understood that shame is "one of the least tolerable affects for humans" (Malatesta-Magai, 1991), unrepaired shame is especially destructive because it becomes associated with a painful self-disorganizing state that cannot be interpersonally or internally regulated, and therefore is consciously avoided, dissociated, or "bypassed" (Lewis, 1971). As Retzinger (1989) noted (as quoted in Schore, 1994): "When shame is not acknowledged, it … creates a form of self-perpetuating entrapment in one's own isolation. If one hides this sense from the other due to shame, it creates further shame, which creates a further sense of isolation" (p. 5).

There is one other path to pathological shame that I have witnessed over the years—significant emotional neglect during childhood. One striking example was when the Adams brought their 16-year-old daughter, Millie, for a Therapeutic Assessment, puzzled and frustrated about her "low self-esteem." Millie was attractive, an excellent student, a good athlete, and the first chair flute in her school orchestra. But she insisted that she was ugly, the other girls in school didn't like her, and kept refusing invitations to sleepovers and other social events. Her parents understandably questioned Millie's thinking and pointed to all the evidence that contradicted her self-views, but this only made Millie feel worse. Their main question for the TA was, "Why does Millie feel so badly about herself in spite of how accomplished and wonderful she is?" The crucial piece of evidence that helped me in my case conceptualization came when I learned that Millie had been adopted at 14 months of age from an orphanage in a disadvantaged country where she had been severely emotionally and physically neglected before being adopted. With the help of an excellent pediatrician, the Adams had addressed Millie's severe malnutrition and delays in development. But no one had counseled them about how to understand and handle the emotional aftereffects of the severe emotional neglect she had experienced. I was able to help them understand that Millie's shame was not their fault and that "cheerleading" her was not helpful. As they showed more compassion, Millie gradually became surer of herself. This is an example of extreme neglect leading to shame, but I have seen many clients over the years whose shame was puzzling and at first glance inexplicable. Through the AAP and other tools like the EMP, we eventually understood that their negative views of themselves were tied to attachment trauma and neglect early in their lives. (See George, 2025, for research on this topic.)

Besides negative self-views, pathological shame is associated with many of the struggles that bring clients to our offices: depression, anxiety, paranoia/distrust, addictions, eating disorders, body dysmorphic disorder, dissociative disorders, PTSD, personality disorders, family violence, and suicide. Helen Block Lewis (1987) called shame "the sleeper in psychopathology," and our assessment tools often bring shame into focus when clients are at first unaware of it. Furthermore, I believe one of the major ways Therapeutic Assessment benefits clients is by helping them develop more self-compassionate narratives about why they struggle. (See Aschieri et al., 2023 for research evidence.) Often people feel a great deal of self-blame about their depression, anxiety, compulsive behaviors, anger outbursts, etc. By helping clients understand that forces beyond their control have contributed to these struggles, we help them take themselves "less personally," and often this leads to less shame and immediate improvement in their symptoms.

Dissociation of Affects

Another result of unacknowledged and unrepaired shame has been described in recent years by a series of authors working within the framework of short-term dynamic psychotherapy. The triangle schema shown in Figure 7.1 was first developed by Ezriel (1952) based on Freud's structural theory and has been adapted and used by Malan (1976, 1979), Davanloo (1978), McCullough Vaillant (1997), Fosha (2000), Frederickson (2013), and others. It depicts the relationship between shame, core affect states, and psychological defenses, and helps us understand the role of shame in various forms of psychopathology. The basic idea is that shame becomes classically conditioned through the types of experiences depicted in the video I referenced—where a core affect state or exploratory behavior is met with condemnation, rejection, anger, fear, or disgust—such that the presence of or even thought of such emotions and behaviors quickly results in shame or anxiety (defined in the diagram as signal affects). Because these painful emotional states are intolerable when not dyadically regulated, the individual then develops a host of psychological coping mechanisms—such as dissociation, acting out, grandiosity, and/or denial (more later about these)—to shut off the experience of and expression of these emotions and impulses (see Figure 7.2). And if the environment continues to support this accommodation

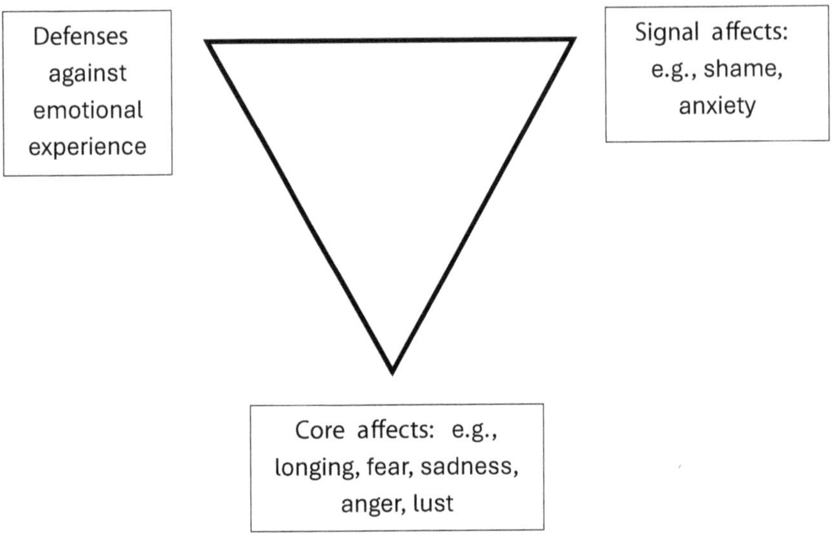

Figure 7.1 The triangle of conflict.

Source: Adapted from Fosha (2000).

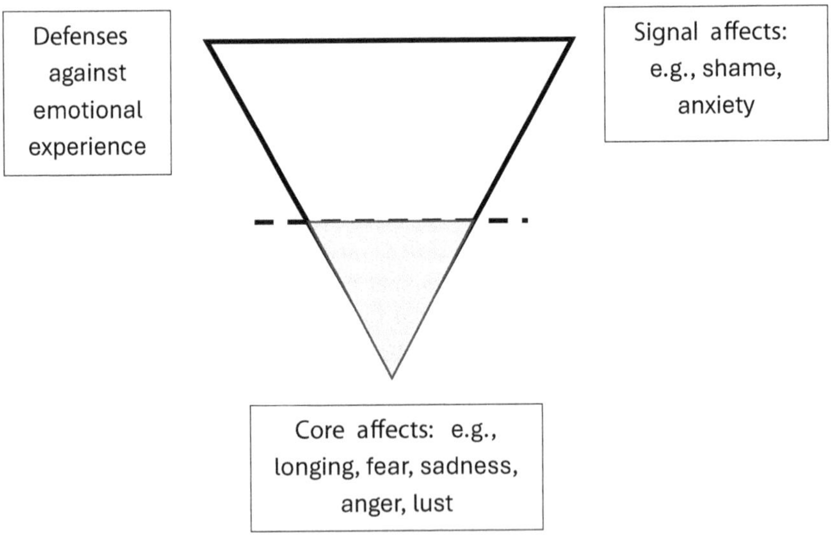

Figure 7.2 The dissociation of core emotions due to shame and defenses.

over time, the individual can end up with adaptive emotional states that are completely inhibited or dissociated,[1] and which continue to affect the person for years. To return to the example of the "Single Ladies Devastation" video, if the parents had not initiated a repair, and if this type of occurrence repeated itself many times, this boy might have become constricted around a number of positive affect states, including expressions of spontaneous joy and vitality. He could also develop an internal self-representation that he was "different than others" and that he could be rejected or shamed if he tried to act as if he belonged.

You can probably think of examples of people with dissociated affect states from your own life or practice, but one person who comes to mind is a man I worked with several years ago who sought a psychological assessment because of his complete inability to accept help from others. Tim, age 43, was a highly successful entrepreneur who had recently experienced the loss of his mother. This event led him to be more self-reflective, and he had noticed how hard it was for him when others expressed sympathy about his recent loss. Tim's main question for the assessment was, "Why am I so unable to ask for and accept help from others? I even have trouble asking help from people I pay to help me!" Tim's MMPI-2 was unremarkable, except for a slight elevation (66T) on Scale 4 that was due mainly to the social and emotional alienation content. I saw his profile as that of a "sturdy survivor" who had long ago developed a self-sufficient, dismissing attachment adaptation (Caldwell, 2001). (I'll write about Tim's Rorschach later.) When I asked Tim to complete the Early Memory Procedure (EMP), he reported the following as his clearest, most negative memory. As you may know, Bruhn (1990) sees such memories as likely metaphors for an important unresolved core issue of the client.

> I was playing with my friend Maureen on the front lawn of our house. It was summer and the door was open and my mother must have been listening from the inside of the house. I asked Maureen, "Can we go over your house and ask your mom to make us those peanut butter and jelly sandwiches like she did yesterday? Those were so good." Suddenly, the screen door slammed open, and my mother came out with a horrible look on her face and the paddle in her hand. She yanked me up by my arm and started to beat me with paddle, yelling "We don't beg in this family. Don't let me EVER let you hear you begging again. It's disgusting. We don't beg." I was completely shocked and confused. I didn't even know what she meant, and I cried and cried. She then told Maureen to go home and dropped me in the front yard crying. I don't remember what happened next, but I think I stayed outside alone for a while and was terrified to go back in the house. I think I was 4 years old.

Clearly, this was an instance of traumatic, toxic, unrepaired shame, and Tim and I eventually came to understand that this incident (and others like it) "taught" him that it was completely unsafe and contemptible to ever ask anyone for anything. This lesson (and other similar ones) generalized in such a way that it got him to "split-off" all longings for dependency and caretaking, with the result that he flinched when people expressed sympathy about his mother's death and felt shame even when paying people to help him with various activities around the house. To meet his goal of becoming more comfortable accepting help, Tim would first need to become aware of his healthy dependency needs and then extinguish the anxiety and shame that would arise if these needs became conscious. Fortunately, assessment tools can be used to help identify clients' potentially dissociated affect states and then to help them become aware of and begin to integrate these emotions.

In my experience, there are three clinical signs of dissociated affect states that appear fairly frequently in Therapeutic Assessment in outpatient settings: (1) Assessment Questions that reflect ways clients find themselves to be a "mystery," such as "Why have I been successful in many areas of my life, but have never had a successful long-term intimate relationship?" or "Why am I normally mild-mannered, but occasionally I get angry and lose it?" or "Why am I so terrified of public speaking when normally I am fairly self-confident?" (2) Discrepancies where difficult affect states appear evident in performance-based tests such as the Rorschach, AAP, EMP, or Wartegg, but these do not show up on self-report tests such as the MMPI-3, PAI, or NEO-PI-R. For example, although Tim—the client I discussed earlier—was not conscious of any urges to be taken care of by others, his Rorschach had two Food responses and three Textures. He was consciously aware of his discomfort receiving help from others but was unaware of how much he desired to be taken care of, or how this split-off longing contributed to his excessive independence. Bornstein (2002) explained this situation using a "process dissociation" framework, and I have written about how to give feedback to clients with this pattern of test results (Finn, 1996). (3) A third marker of dissociated emotions is when clients are not aware of healthy emotions that other people would typically feel. An example might be a female client who is being mistreated terribly by her boyfriend, but who says she feels no anger at him, even though she is aware other people might feel this. In my experience it is almost certain that a client like this grew up in an environment where expressions of anger or positive entitlement were shamed and punished.

Not only are assessment tools useful in showing the dissociation of healthy emotions, but they also provide a way for us to help clients identify and begin to reintegrate these affects. To return to Tim again, he and I discussed his early memories at length, and I asked about his response to the EMP follow-up question for the "begging" memory: "If you could change the memory in any way, what would that be?" Tim had originally written "not have asked for the peanut butter and jelly sandwiches." I said I could understand this response completely but wondered if there were another way to change the memory. I explained that from my point of view Tim seemed to be putting the responsibility for his punishment squarely on himself, but I thought that asking for the sandwiches was completely normal and it was his mother's response that was out of line. Here is an excerpt from the session:

Tim: I see what you mean. What I did wasn't terrible. I guess this was some strange sensitivity of my mother's.

Steve: But I imagine you didn't think that at the time. You believed you had done something shameful. Am I correct?

Tim: That's right. And I guess I overlearned that lesson, which is why I ended up here. Now I'm so afraid of "begging" that I can't even let my employees help me. But what do I do?

Steve: Are you willing to try an experiment?

Tim: Yes.

Steve: Imagine we are dropping you as the adult you are now into the scene with that boy who has just been paddled by his mother. What would you say to him?

Tim: That he didn't do anything wrong.

Steve: Good. Speak right to him if you can. Can you imagine being there with him?

Tim: Yes. (closes his eyes) *"I'm so sorry your mother got angry with you and screamed at you just now. That was shocking and really frightening. And I know she said you were wrong to ask for the sandwiches from Maureen's mother. But it wasn't wrong.* (Tim starts to cry.) *You didn't do anything wrong at all. It was an innocent thing to do. This is your mother's problem."*

At a 6-month follow-up session, Tim told me that he was now at ease asking others for help and even felt a bit surprised that he had difficulty doing so in the past.

Defenses against Shame

Because shame is so painful, so few of us have experienced adequate shame repairs, and therefore have little ability to tolerate shame—many of us have developed coping mechanisms to escape feeling shame. We may lash out at others, get drunk, distract ourselves, or deny we did anything wrong. These natural "escape hatches" can create problems on their own, including more shame, and psychological tests can be used to name and help people understand how many problematic behaviors are related to deep shame. Nathanson (1992) devised a schema to understand shame defenses, which he called the "Compass of Shame." There are four poles to the Compass, and each describes a common defense against shame: Withdrawal (isolating oneself, hiding), Attacking Other (lashing out verbally or physically, "turning the tables"), Avoidance (distraction through thrill seeking, using drugs or alcohol), and Attack Self (self-criticism and self-deprecation). Elison (2006) developed a self-report measure, the *Compass of Shame Scale*, which can be used with clients to measure and discuss their usual ways of handling overwhelming shame. The Thurston Cradock Test of Shame (TCTS) also has a coding system for shame defenses and is also very useful as it can be used as a therapeutic tool with clients, discussing their stories to the TCTS cards, giving labels to self-conscious emotions (embarrassment, shame, humiliation, and mortification), how the characters cope with or defend against shame, and envisioning more adaptive endings. For an example of using the TCTS in an Assessment Intervention Session, see Finn (2019).

Implications for Psychological Assessment

So what are the implications of these understandings of shame for the practice of applied psychological assessment? I want to discuss eight points:

#1 —*Shame is a frequent and perhaps inevitable occurrence during psychological assessment, whether we or our clients are aware of it.*

Psychological assessment is an extremely vulnerable context for almost every client, but especially for those clients with histories of toxic shame. Think about it: the client is asked to provide information to a near stranger, who may be seen as an "all-knowing" expert, whose job is to assess the client, observe the client's performance on a host of puzzling and mysterious tests, and then draw conclusions about the client that will be conveyed to others and that may influence aspects of the client's life in unknown ways. On top of this, the focus of the assessment is often on those areas of life where the client is struggling, feels incompetent, or has been judged wanting by important others and society. And standardized administration procedures for many psychological tests do not allow for much reassurance or interaction as the client's struggles are revealed and exposed. This is a perfect recipe for shame.

#2 —*Shame is tied to many of the problems in living that our clients consult us about.*

Toxic shame appears to predispose people to depression, emotion regulation difficulties, addictions, dissociative disorders, anxiety disorders, personality disorders, and a host of other difficulties. Defenses against shame also create a host of puzzling behaviors that often bring people for assessment. Furthermore, almost all clients have some degree of shame about their struggles, which can create a vicious cycle—where shame leads to pathology that creates shame, which then snowballs or is defended against, and never gets worked through. On top of this, contemporary American culture seems to place a premium on "feeling good," "thinking positively," and "believing in oneself," with the result that many clients develop shame about their shame (about their shame). This is often accompanied by the defense of grandiosity.

#3 —*Our assessment procedures can be helpful in identifying shame and naming it for clients.*

A positive side effect of the shame-arousing aspects of psychological assessment is that if clients have unresolved shame, it most likely will come to the fore, where a sensitive assessor will be able to note it. Very few clients use the word "shame" (although some do), but the astute clinician will notice frequent apologies, self-criticism or deprecation, anxiety, avoidance of specific topics, as well as behavioral cues like blushing, yawning, breaking of eye contact and especially a downward gaze, or covering of the face, eyes, or mouth with the hand. There are now several excellent measures of shame that are useful clinically, such as the TCTS, and our standard psychological tests have scores that are related to shame, such as the Low Self-Esteem Scale of the MMPI-2, the Self-Doubt Scale of the MMPI-3, Self-Criticism codes on the Wartegg, and Vista and Morbid responses on the Rorschach.

I have repeatedly found that simply naming shame for clients can have a powerful therapeutic effect. For example, recently a newly married couple came to me for a brief Therapeutic Assessment because they sometimes ended up in vicious screaming fights during which they said incredibly hurtful things to each other. Both had come from difficult childhoods and had found refuge in each other, and they realized if they couldn't stop the fights, they would damage their relationship. I asked the couple to take the MMPI-3 and both had very high scores on the Self-Doubt scale. Just discussing this one test had a profound effect on the couple. They realized that each had a lot of shame and that when shame got triggered, they would "toss the hot potato of shame" back and forth, using the Attack Other defense to try to regulate themselves. The couple did not have the resources to pursue therapy at that time, but they said that the brief TA had helped them immensely.

#4 —*Performance-based tests can also be very useful in identifying affect states that are dissociated because of early toxic shame experiences, and which the client may need to integrate to reach important goals.*

Examples of this can be found throughout this book, especially with Thomas in Chapter 4 and Ben in Chapter 5. As another example, although Tim—the client I wrote about earlier—was not conscious of any urges to be taken care of by others, he was able to begin to get in touch with these through an Extended Inquiry of his Food and Texture responses to the Rorschach. Eventually he told me, "I think I'm afraid if I open that door [of depending on others] I'll never be able to close it." At that point we were able to discuss how to "open the door" safely.

#5 —*If we are not attentive to shame, psychological assessment can increase clients' shame and traumatize them.*

As I wrote about earlier, shame experiences need not necessarily be toxic; this happens mainly if they are unacknowledged and unrepaired. Unfortunately, this is all too frequent in many settings where clients undergo psychological assessments, and I believe it can affect clients' feelings about assessment and about psychology for years to come. For example, I have seen many children over the years with various types of learning disabilities and cognitive deficits who have come to dread their periodic cognitive evaluations because they experience them as times when their humiliating deficiencies are revealed for all to see. Clients who have undergone personality assessments, especially against their will, can also be traumatized and shamed by psychological assessment, especially when they receive written reports afterwards that describe their difficulties in cold, uncompassionate, pathologizing terms. I would like to make a special challenge to those of you who do forensic assessment to think about ways to conduct your work and maintain your required neutrality without giving clients experiences of toxic shame.

#6 —*Assessor silence in the face of clients' shame will always intensify clients' shame.*

I reiterate, shame itself is inevitable and not necessarily a bad thing. It only becomes toxic when it is not acknowledged or addressed interpersonally. As mentioned earlier, properly supported shame experiences facilitate the development of brain areas associated with emotion regulation. In fact, the opposite is also true: overwhelming, unacknowledged shame is known to create a neurochemical environment in the brain that is destructive to further development of the orbitofrontal cortex and its subcortical connections in the limbic system. To translate, overwhelming experiences of humiliation and shame are toxic to the brain, and they increase one's susceptibility to feeling more shame. Unfortunately, my experience is that many well-meaning clinicians never bring up the shame their clients feel as they undergo psychological assessment or make any attempt to address it. As Nathanson (1992) noted:

> Therapeutic passivity—the decision to remain silent in the face of a humiliated, withdrawn patient—will always magnify shame because it confirms the patient's affect-driven belief that isolation is justified.
>
> (p. 325)

Another error I have seen is for the assessor to make well-intentioned comments that are meant to contradict shame, but that intensify it, e.g., "Everybody has tests they do well on and ones they don't. No reason to worry." "Don't be ashamed—I've heard everything at this point in my career." Or my favorite: "Are you always so hard on yourself?" It's not that these comments can't ever be useful, but timing is essential. It is essential to be able to "sit with" and mirror the client's shame first, before offering information that reframes it, for example:

> I can see why you feel bad after having been shamed by your parents and teachers for years about your learning disability. How awful! But the learning disability is not your fault. It's just the way your brain was made!

Last, recent developments in psychotherapeutic technique have proved that when clients feel shame because a previously dissociated aspect of their personalities is on view, the clinician must be *very* active in the session in helping the client recognize, name, and tolerate the shame that will inevitably result, and it is sometimes essential to first ask the client to look at your face, where she can reality test her assumption that you find her contemptible or disgusting at that moment.

#7 —*Assessors' own shame can lead to "blind spots," "projections," or subtle rejections of clients during the process of psychological assessment.*

As you can imagine, if one of our tasks as clinicians is to help clients overcome shame about parts of themselves they have split off and denied, and to find and reintegrate these aspects of themselves—there is a problem if we ourselves have dissociated and/or are ashamed of the same facets of ourselves. A personal example comes from when I first started working with under-responsible, underachieving young adults whose parents were highly successful overfunctioners. Such parents were often frustrated by their "slacker" children, who never seemed to take adult responsibility for anything, and I often found myself completely on the side of the parents, being tempted to lecture or criticize the kids. It took me a while and some personal growth to realize that these young adults were typically manifesting a split-off part of their parents' personalities and for me to find and appreciate this split-off aspect in myself. I remember a supervisor asking me, "Steve, can't you find a part of yourself that would like someone to peel all your grapes and to never have to work or be responsible?" Frankly, because of my own shame about my dependency needs, it wasn't so easy for me to find this part of myself at the time. Now I still work hard, but I also really like to relax and be pampered, and I can appreciate the balance these underfunctioning children bring to their family systems. And sometimes, if I can get parents to start slacking off a little themselves, these young adults start getting it together.

#8 —*When assessors are skilled at recognizing and managing shame with clients, the healing of shame can be one of the major therapeutic benefits of psychological assessment.*

Last, I want to emphasize how much I have come to believe that assessment can be a powerful tool in helping clients heal from shame. Because our assessment instruments are so good at revealing aspects of clients they hide from themselves and others, and because our tests help us understand clients' dilemmas of change in new ways, we can offer clients more compassionate understandings of their struggles and help them come out of the isolation of shame and reconnect with others.

Some of you have heard me talk about one of my early summary/discussion sessions with a client about her MMPI results. After the feedback, which went very well, this eloquent woman sent me a note I still treasure. It read:

> I totally dreaded coming to see you the other day and envisioned the scene would be like appearing before St. Peter at the pearly gates. I was certain we would review all my faults and shortcomings, and then you would pronounce judgment about whether I was a 'hopeless case' or had a chance of overcoming these faults. In fact, we did talk a lot about my struggles and things I feel totally ashamed about. But you were so compassionate in helping me understand why I do what I do, and that it was connected to things I had no control over, that I now have more compassion for myself and more hope. Thank you from the bottom of my heart.

In closing, I want to acknowledge that it takes considerable expertise and work on ourselves to be able to help clients heal from shame. I hope this chapter helps you understand a bit of what is involved.

Notes

1 In the current literature this is called "structural dissociation" as opposed to "state dissociation," which refers to the altered state people go into when overwhelmed by emotions. See Chapter 13 for a discussion of state dissociation.

References

Aschieri, F., van Emmerik, A. A. P., Wibbelink, C. J. M., & Kamphuis, J. H. (2023). Collaborative assessment methods. In C. E. Hill & J. C. Norcross (Eds.), *Psychotherapy skills and methods that work* (pp. 399–428). Oxford University Press.

Benau, K. (2022). *Shame, pride, and relational trauma: Concepts and psychotherapy*. Routledge.

Bornstein, R. F. (2002). A process-dissociation approach to objective-projective test score interrelationships. *Journal of Personality Assessment, 78*(1), 47–68.

Bruhn, A. R. (1990). *Earliest childhood memories, Vol. 1: Theory and application to clinical practice.* Praeger.
Caldwell, A. B. (2001). What do the MMPI scales fundamentally measure? Some hypotheses. *Journal of Personality Assessment, 76*, 1–17.
Cook, D. R. (1996). *The Internalized Shame Scale (ISS).* North MHS.
O'Leary, J.Cradock (2017). Using the Thurston-Cradock Test of Shame to uncover shame dynamics in therapy and assessment. *The TA Connection, 5*(1), 4–7.
O'Leary, J.Cradock , Kelley, D., & Parrish, C. (2020). From swallowing to savoring emotions: A therapeutic assessment using the Thurston Cradock Test of Shame as an assessment intervention. *Rorschachiana, 41*(2), 181–199.
O'Leary, J.Cradock , Nakamura, N., & Finn, S. E. (2020). Using the Thurston-Cradock Test of Shame as a crucial "empathy magnifier." *Rorschachiana, 41*(2), 144–161.
Davanloo, H. (Ed.). (1978). *Basic principles and techniques in short-term dynamic psychotherapy*. Spectrum.
Elison, J. (2006). Investigating the Compass of Shame: The development of the Compass of Shame Scale. *Social Behavior and Personality, 34*(3), 221–238.
Ezriel, H. (1952). Notes on psychoanalytic group therapy: Interpretation and research. *Psychiatry, 15*, 119–126.
Finn, S. E. (1996). Assessment feedback integrating MMPI-2 and Rorschach findings. *Journal of Personality Assessment, 67*, 543–557.
Finn, S. E. (2019). Therapeutic Assessment of Madeline. In C. Hopwood & M. Waugh (Eds.), *Personality assessment paradigms and methods: A collaborative reassessment of Madeline G* (pp. 13–34). Routledge.
Fosha, D. (2000). *The transforming power of affect: A model for accelerated change.* Basic Books.
Frederickson, J. (2013). *Co-creating change: Effective dynamic therapy techniques.* Seven Leaves Press.
George, C. (2025). Attachment, shame, and trauma. *Brain Science, 15*, 415. https://doi.org/10.3390/brainsci15040415
Gilbert, P., & McGuire, M. T. (1998). Shame, status, and social roles: Psychobiology and evolution. In P. Gilbert & B. Andrews (Eds.), *Shame: Interpersonal behavior, psychopathology, and culture* (pp. 99–125). Oxford University Press.
Harder, D. W., & Zalma, A. (1990). Two promising shame and guilt scales: A construct validity comparison. *Journal of Personality Assessment, 55*, 729–745.
Hoblitzelle, W. (1987). Attempts to measure and differentiate shame and guilt: The relation between shame and depression. In H. B. Lewis (Ed.), *The role of shame in symptom formation* (pp. 207–235). Erlbaum.
Izard, C. E. (1991). *The psychology of emotions*. Plenum.
Johnson, R. C., Danko, D. P., Huang, Y. H., Park, J. Y., Johnson, S. B., & Nagoshi, C. T. (1987). Guilt, shame, and adjustment in three cultures. *Personality and Individual Differences, 8*, 357–364.
Kaufman, G. (2004). *The psychology of shame: Theory and treatment of shame-based syndromes*. Springer.
Lewis, H. B. (1971). *Shame and guilt in neurosis*. International Universities Press.
Lewis, H. B. (1987). *The role of shame in symptom formation.* Erlbaum.

Linehan, M. M. (1993). *Cognitive behavioral therapy of borderline personality disorder*. Guilford Press.
Malan, D. H. (1976). *The frontier of brief psychotherapy*. Plenum Press.
Malan, D. H. (1979). Individual psychotherapy and science of psychodynamics. Butterworth.
Malatesta-Magai, C. (1991). Emotional socialization: Its role in personality and developmental psychopathology. In D. Cicchetti & S. L. Toth (Eds.), *Internalizing and externalizing expressions of dysfunction: Rochester symposium on developmental psychopathology, Vol. 2* (pp. 203–224). Erlbaum.
Vaillant, L. McCullough (1997). *Changing character: Short-term anxiety-regulating psychotherapy for restructuring defenses, affects, and attachment*. Basic Books.
Morrison, A. P. (1996). *The culture of shame*. Random House.
Nathanson, D. L. (1992). *Shame and pride: Affect, sex, and the birth of the self*. Norton.
Retzinger, S. R. (1989). *Marital conflict: The role of emotion*. Unpublished manuscript.
Schore, A. N. (1994). *Affect regulation and the origin of the self*. Erlbaum.
Schore, A. N. (1998). Early shame experiences and infant brain development. In P. Gilbert & B. Andrews (Eds.), *Shame: Interpersonal behavior, psychopathology, and culture* (pp. 57–77). Oxford University Press.
Schore, A. N. (2003a). *Affect dysregulation and disorders of the self*. Norton.
Schore, A. N. (2003b). *Affect regulation and repair of the self*. Norton.
Stern, D. N. (1985). *The interpersonal world of the infant*. Basic Books.
Tangney, J. P., & Fischer, K. W. (1995). *Self-conscious emotions: The psychology of shame, guilt, embarrassment, and pride*. Guilford.
Tangney, J. P., Wagner, P., & Gramzow, R. (1989). *The Test of Self-conscious Affect*. George Mason University.
Thurston, N. S., & O'Leary, J. A.Cradock (2009). *Thurston Cradock Test of Shame*. www.testofshame.com
Tomkins, S. (1987). Shame. In D. L. Nathanson (Ed.), *The many faces of shame* (pp. 133–161). Guilford Press.

Chapter 8

Integrating the Work of Luria and Vygotsky in Modern Personality Assessment

Scaffolding and Collaboration in Therapeutic Assessment*

Alexander Luria is generally viewed as the father of modern neuropsychological assessment (Mikadze, Ardila, & Akhutina, 2018) and his friend and colleague, Lev Vygotsky, is routinely associated with dynamic assessment, a form of interactive cognitive assessment used in education (Haywood, 2012). I will summarize central aspects of their work and then discuss how their theories and practices are useful in modern personality assessment.

Alexander Romanovich Luria (1902–1977)

Luria was a Russian scientist and neuropsychologist whose contributions were so transformative that they reshaped modern understanding of brain–behavior relationships. Drawing on earlier work by figures such as Jackson and Head (see Christensen, Goldberg, & Bougakov, 2009), Luria synthesized and extended existing ideas into a comprehensive theory of *functional brain systems*. In a series of influential books (Luria, 1948, 1962, 1963, 1973, 1974), he argued that brain mechanisms: (1) serve as instruments for carrying out goal-directed activities; (2) develop over time through a person's engagement with the demands and opportunities of their life; and (3) are shaped in important ways by cultural tools, particularly language.

One well-known (though possibly apocryphal) story illustrates this last point. During scientific expeditions to Central Asia in 1931–1932, Luria and his colleagues administered cognitive tasks—including classic visual illusions such as the Ebbinghaus and Müller–Lyer illusions—to rural populations and found that their responses differed markedly from those of subjects in Moscow. According to tradition, Luria once sent a telegram to Vygotsky saying, "The Uzbeks have no illusions!" (Lamdan, 2013). Although interpretations of these findings have been debated, Luria's studies were among the first to provide systematic evidence

* This chapter is based on a webinar I presented for the Therapeutic Assessment Institute in April 2020.

DOI: 10.4324/9781003602231-8

that culture, education, and life experience influence even basic cognitive processes such as perception—implying that psychological tests must always be interpreted within the broader context of a person's lived world (Luria, 1974).

In his clinical work, Luria took an individualized, dynamic, and qualitative approach aimed at understanding a person's difficulties and potential within their particular social milieu (Mikadze, Ardila, & Akhutina, 2018). He frequently repeated tests with slight variations in instructions to observe how problem-solving changed under different conditions, and he insisted that no test score has a single, fixed meaning. A result could only be understood in relation to other data and through dialog with the assessee. Luria also emphasized the practical implications of assessment and believed that evaluation and intervention were inherently connected (Christensen et al., 2009). His work inspired later developments in neuropsychological assessment, including the Luria–Nebraska Neuropsychological Battery (Golden, 2004) and the NEPSY (Korkman, Kirk, & Kemp, 1998), even though these instruments differ in important ways from his strictly qualitative method.

Lev Vygotsky (1896–1934)

Vygotsky, a close colleague of Luria, was a Russian developmental psychologist who had also taught secondary school. As a developmentalist, he viewed test scores as windows into a person's functioning at a given moment rather than as immutable indicators of who they "are." Together with Luria, he helped establish the cultural–historical approach in psychology, a tradition later elaborated into what is now known as Cultural-Historical Activity Theory (Cole, 1996). Their work drew partly on the dialectical ideas of the German philosopher Hegel, a major precursor to phenomenology, emphasizing that a person's abilities and characteristics at any point in time arise from the dynamic interplay of individual development, cultural tools, and lived experience.

One of Vygotsky's major contributions is the concept of the "zone of proximal development (ZPD; Vygotsky, 1986)," which he articulated in the last 10 years of his life. In short, Vygotsky realized that you can't measure a person's learning potential or ability by one or more isolated tests. You have to see how the person functions in a supportive social context, as the environment has a great influence on a person's rate of learning. This understanding has greatly influenced developmental psychology and education and underpins cognitive assessment methods such as dynamic assessment (Haywood, 2012), Lezak's (1983) flexible neuropsychological assessment approach, and the Boston Process Approach (Kaplan, 1988) (Figure 8.1).

A simple example of these dynamic approaches is that of "testing the limits" during cognitive assessment (Axelrod & Schutte, 2011). For example, a child may get a low score on the Block Design subtest of the WISC-V. After the standardized administration, the assessor may redo one or more items of the subtest without imposing a time limit to help figure out if the child's struggles have to

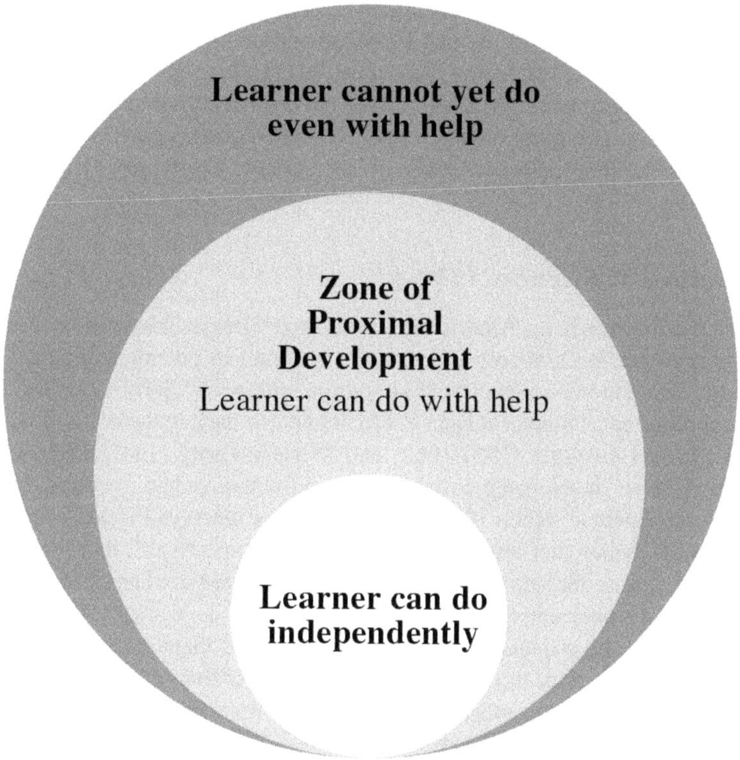

Figure 8.1 The Zone of Proximal Development.

do with deficits in visuospatial abilities or with slower processing. Whatever the result, this added information will be helpful in understanding how to remediate the child's difficulties. Testing of the limits has also been applied in performance-based personality assessment, especially with the Rorschach (Hutt & Shor, 1946) but I have never seen Vygotsky's work cited in this context. In fact, because of its association with cognitive assessment, most psychologists think about the ZPD as only applying to the assessment of abilities; but as I will write about below, I see it as highly relevant to personality assessment. Since I will refer to it later, let me also define one other term.

Scaffolding

In psychology, "scaffolding" is a term developed by Jerome Bruner and his colleagues (Bruner, 1978; Wood, Bruner, & Ross, 1976) based on Vygotsky's work. Scaffolding is the process of supporting learning by providing temporary assistance to individuals so they can achieve goals that are just beyond their reach. The objective is to give just enough help but no more than necessary. This instructional approach leads to the highest rate of growth and learning, and successful scaffolding requires dynamic assessment methods, since the ZPD shifts over time as an individual learns (Haywood, 2012). Once again, I believe assessment psychologists who are familiar with the term scaffolding mainly think of it as relevant to cognitive testing, cognitive remediation, and education, but it has come to hold an important place in Therapeutic Assessment (Kamphuis & Finn, 2019).

Constance T. Fischer (1938–)

Constance Fischer is an American clinical psychologist who was a longtime faculty member in Duquesne University's program in phenomenological psychology. She and her colleagues at Duquesne embraced Giorgi's (1970) vision of psychology as a "human science," which harkens back to the work of Husserl (1913/1962), Heidegger (1927/1962) and Merleau-Ponty (1945/1962). In this context, Fischer developed a collaborative, individualized approach to psychological assessment (Fischer, 1985/1994). The major tenets of Fischer's approach included the belief that knowledge is always "perspectival;" thus, the assessor must always collaborate with the client to make sense of test data (Fischer, 2001). Fischer also emphasized focusing on the "life world" of the person being assessed rather than on test scores, and believed that assessment provided a snapshot of a person moving through time, rather than a description of the fundamental traits of the individual. The goal of assessment in Fischer's mind was to help clients identify "existing patterns" and understand the contexts in which those patterns occur. Then the assessor can help clients recognize that the patterns they are currently living are not the only ones available to them, and that they can begin to author their lives differently (Fischer, 1985/1994). In this sense, psychological assessment could be "therapeutic in its own right" (Fischer, 2001, p. 29). One can see the many similarities of Fischer's view of assessment to those of Luria and Vygotsky, especially the connection between assessment and intervention, but when asked, Fischer said she was not aware of having been directly impacted by their work.[1]

Not only did Fischer's point of view resemble those of Luria and Vygotsky, many of her assessment practices did as well. She was focused on the assessment of process and often modified test instructions—including those from personality tests—in a dynamic way to explore competing hypotheses that came from her or her clients. She also used assessment sessions to help clients explore alternative approaches to persistent problems, emphasizing that these new ways must "branch off from where the client is now"—very similar to Vygotsky's concept of the ZPD. However, Fischer never referred to the ZPD or to scaffolding in her writings and differed from Luria and Vygotsky in the extent to which she collaborated with clients throughout an assessment. For example, Fischer routinely "co-labored" with clients to make sense of test results and routinely asked clients to review and comment on her written assessment reports before she sent them to the referring professional (Fischer, 1985/1994).

Scaffolding in Therapeutic Assessment

Therapeutic Assessment (TA; Finn, 2007) incorporates many of the principles and techniques of Fischer's collaborative, individualized assessment but also explicitly draws on concepts related to the work of Luria and Vygotsky, including the ZPD and scaffolding (Kamphuis & Finn, 2019). For example, the "Assessment Questions" co-developed with clients at the beginning of a TA are seen as guides as to what test results might be "Level 1, Level 2, or Level 3 information," i.e., which information is farther from clients' existing self-views and therefore will require more scaffolding to be assimilated (Fantini et al., 2022). This scaffolding is accomplished through "Extended Inquiries" of standardized psychological tests and "Assessment Intervention Sessions." The latter are very similar to Fischer's (1994) "assessment of process" and have the goal of exploring existing and alternative patterns and helping "Level 3 information" (very discrepant from clients' existing narratives) become "Level 1 or 2 information" (coherent with clients' narratives). Let me now present two TA case examples to better explain my current ideas about scaffolding.

Al

Al was a 30-year-old man referred for a TA by the psychotherapist he had been seeing for 5 years. Al was an extremely talented artist but was not as successful as he might be because of social anxiety and difficulties promoting himself. In fact, Al refused to enter art competitions and had turned down several galleries that had offered to present his work because of anxiety and dread about being expected to attend the opening of the exhibitions. He had a small group of patrons who loved his paintings, and so he made enough money to live on, but his therapist wanted to help Al move past his blocks and become better known. Al was also very interested in the TA and posed the following Assessment Questions: (1) *What is getting in the way of me being more successful in my creative life?* (2) *Why don't numbers make sense to me?* When I asked about the second question, I learned that Al had a history of severe learning problems, especially in math, that were not recognized or remediated in the private elementary and high schools he had attended. He could not read a clock, count money, and did not know whether 10,000 or 100,000 was the bigger number. Clearly, he met the criteria for a diagnosis of dyscalculia, a brain-based disorder that can be addressed through specific instructional methods. But this was not recognized by his school or parents. Instead, Al had been punished for years by his teachers and parents, who believed he simply was "not trying hard enough." He did manage to graduate from high school, and he loved reading. But after attending university for one semester, Al dropped out and devoted himself to his art.

It was clear to me from Al's MMPI-2 that his school experiences (and others I learned about) had taken an enormous toll on his self-image. He scored very high on the Demoralization scale (RCd = 86*T*) and his score on the Low Self-Esteem scale was almost the highest possible (LSE = 91T). Al was very prone to experiencing shame and anxiety, and this was a major factor holding him back from being more successful. Also, the MMPI-2 (PSY-5 AGG = 36*T*) suggested that Al's anger was dissociated (see Chapter 7) and held in check by shame. Although this had been adaptive as a child when he was being humiliated by teachers and his father, it made it impossible for him to promote himself in the competitive art world.

I wanted a chance to work on this shame with Al, and after some thought, I suggested that we do the Wechsler Adult Intelligence Scale, Fourth Edition (WAIS-IV; Wechsler, 2008) together. He agreed, and it was an enlightening and moving experience. As is typical, I administered the Block Design subtest first, but I had to interrupt it when Al started having a panic attack and became very confused and disoriented. I helped him breathe through the anxiety and then inquired what had happened. Al told me he was having a flashback to a scene in high school where his father was yelling at him over his geometry homework and telling him that he was "an idiot" who would "never amount to anything." I said this had been traumatic, which apparently no one had ever said. And Al wept a bit as I named the confusion and shame he must have felt at the time. He then told about numerous other instances of being emotionally abused by his father and teachers at school. When I said I was appalled at how he had been treated for his obvious learning differences, Al asked many questions, including "So this wasn't my fault?" I firmly said no and explained about the kind of help I wished Al had been given. We then connected Al's experiences with school to his social anxiety and fear of having an art show. He quickly saw the relevance to his Assessment Question, "What is getting in the way of me being more successful…?"

In the next session, with Al's consent we returned to the WAIS-IV. He achieved extremely high scores on Similarities (16) and Vocabulary (17) but struggled again terribly on the Arithmetic subtest. He got the first two items correct, which had to do with addition and subtraction, but then failed the next three items, reaching the point where I discontinued the subtest. I then asked Al what he had experienced:

AI: It was maddening!
SF: Tell me more.

AI: *It was the equivalent of the red and white* [the stimuli for Block Design]. *The shapes and the colors.*

SF: Ah.

AI: *With the numbers it is very similar to you know when I take my car in. They ask, "How many miles are on your car?" And all the sudden I look at the numbers and it's you know... cascading. It's like, you know, "He has 75 and sells 8 but he gets rid of 2." All I hear is "Doo doo doo" with the numbers. And all the other information is lost, and it gets piled up into this just emptiness of, "I have no idea." Just like a chasm of nothingness. You know, I can't! It's empty. I couldn't find the answer for the life of me.*

SF: It's so overwhelming.

AI: *Exactly, yeah. It's basically like being thrown into space and saying, "Find hydrogen." Or "Explain why this star is glowing like that" without any kind of pre information. You know I can't explain it.*

SF: Exactly. It feels so beyond you.

AI: Exactly. It's basically galactic. It's decoding a language I don't understand.

We then discussed the shame Al typically felt in these situations and the voice in his mind (internalized from his father) that called him an "idiot." He said that since the previous week's session he had felt more accepting of himself and less frightened, which he attributed to the "safe environment" we had created. I said I was glad of this, then asked if we could experiment more with math problems. Al said he was curious and agreed.

I then chose the first of the Arithmetic items Al had just failed and reread it. I asked Al what he heard.

AI: Um I know that it's a matter of division.

SF: Ok great. That's a good start.

AI: I do know that. But whether it's 4 divided by 20 or 20 divided by 4, I have no idea. The only thing I know is it's division. That's pretty much as far as I can get.

SF: Ok great.

AI: Would each one get 4?

SF: No, but good trying. You know that it's division, but you're not sure which way the division goes.

AI: *Yes. Maybe does it matter which way it goes? If you flip it around, is it the same answer? 20 by 4 is 4 divided by 20? Is that the same answer?*

SF: No. That's multiplication. So, let me think... Let's start with something simpler. So, suppose it was this. There were 20 toys and 2 children, and each got the same number.

AI: *That would be 10.*

SF: Ok, great. And then 10 toys and 2 children.

AI: *Uh, 10 toys. 5.*

SF: Yeah. So that would equal 20 toys and 4 children. I don't know if you could see that.
Al: No

It was clear to me that I had lost him. I thought for a second, remembered that Al was an artist, and intuitively put my notepad on the table between us. I drew 20 small circles in the middle of a page and 2 smiley faces for children on each side.

SF: Ok so 20 toys divided by 2 groups of children...
Al: *Ok, is the 10.*
SF: And then so we could even think of it as, here's toys, 4 children. So, you can even first give each pair of 2 children the same number of toys. So, 20 toys between 2 groups is...10 (pointing). *Then each child in the groups gets the same amount.*
Al: Ok, so it would be 5?
SF: Yes. Yes!
Al: Ok, yeah, that's good. Yeah, yeah. I see that now!
SF: So then let's keep this same schema. So, let's say there are 40 tickets divided equally among 4 children.
Al: *Ok, um. Would it be 10?*
SF: Yeah.
Al: Ok.
SF: Then let's do another one. Ok, so 60 apples divided among 3 children...?
Al: Um. 15?
SF: No. Not quite. Did the drawing help?
Al: Yes!
SF: So, let's draw that one and see if that helps. Do you want to draw or shall I?
Al: You please.

In my mind, this excerpt shows classic scaffolding in the spirit of Luria and Vygotsky and collaboration in the spirit of Fischer. I was identifying Al's *zone of proximal development* and using scaffolding to help Al learn to do simple division. Al was signaling to me about the kind of help he needed, and I believe that communication between our two right hemispheres (Schore, 2012) was helping us work together as a team. I knew that what we were learning would help design a remediation program for Al's dyscalculia if he wanted to pursue it, and in the meantime, we were addressing Al's shame and, it turns out, giving him hope.

In the client feedback form Al filled out after the assessment, he wrote:

> The time we worked on the division problems is a beacon for me when I think back on the assessment. I had never had anyone be so patient with me or try so hard to find the EXACT kind of help I needed to do those problems.

> It was an incredible experience of being seen after so many years of intense loneliness. I left the session feeling better about myself, more real, and more hopeful—not just about me—but about all of humanity.

At the end of the TA, I suggested to Al and his therapist that they work more on his past academic traumas. I also found a cognitive rehabilitation program that could take what we had learned and work with Al on his dyscalculia. At a follow-up session one year later, Al had made great progress and could read a clock, report his odometer reading, make change from money (although slowly), and most importantly, was getting ready for his first art show. I was left in awe at the power of scaffolding and of the importance of being seen.

Hana

Hana, a 30-year-old Japanese woman, was referred by her psychiatrist/therapist for a TA because of a sudden resurgence of obsessive-compulsive symptoms after years of their being absent. Hana had been successfully treated for OCD in her 20s and both she and her therapist were puzzled about her "relapse." Hana's main Assessment Questions were: (1) *Why did my OCD suddenly become worse?* and (2) *How can I become less anxious?* Her OCD manifested in a checking compulsion. She would become anxious when she was leaving the house to go to work, worrying that she had left the stove on, the door unlocked, or the clothes iron plugged in. This led her to go back and check numerous times, sometimes arriving several hours late to her job. When I asked what her worst fear was, Hana said, "That I would make a mistake and be the cause of someone else getting hurt." She said she would find this "intolerable." Interestingly, multiple people in Hana's family across several generations suffered from OCD, leading me to think she had a significant genetic vulnerability to this disorder.

In the initial session, I explored the timing of Hana's OCD symptoms and learned that they coincided with a miscarriage she had after 2 months of pregnancy. At first, Hana did not think the two events were related, but as I asked more, she admitted that she had been very upset by the miscarriage as she and her husband very much wanted to have a child. Also, her husband, parents, and obstetrician had all been very unempathetic to her loss, telling her, "You can get pregnant again," so she felt very alone with her feelings. I was shocked hearing this but contained my reaction as Hana clearly did not want to criticize these people, and she largely spoke about her childhood, her parents, and her husband in very positive terms. But I began to develop a hypothesis that Hana's OCD was related to her unprocessed grief about the miscarriage, which it appeared those around her could not help mentalize.

Because I was curious about Hana's family relationships, I selected the Adult Attachment Projective Picture System (AAP; George & West, 2012) as one of the tests administered. I was struck by her response to the Window drawing, which depicts a small girl standing alone in front of a large picture window. This was Hana's story:

> Uh it looks like she just moved into a new house and is looking at the scenery from her house. She kind of looks sad...probably thinking about the place she lived before. And what happened right before, right? [SF: Yes] I think she was dealing with a different place. She just finished moving. [SF: What happens after?] She will eventually go to a new school and make friends. And I can see her house is very big and she might be the daughter of a rich family. [SF: Anything else?] Nothing more that I can tell.

After I had administered the AAP, I asked Hana if there were any of the drawings she related to. She pointed to Window:

H: Maybe this one, because my parents have a house with land and we are planning to build another house in their yard.
SF: I see. Pretty common in Japan, yes? So that's where your new house will be eventually.
H: Yeah. I thought she just moved in, so I was thinking of me moving into another house and starting a different life.
SF: And I'm trying to remember how you said she was feeling (reading notes) *...You said, "sad, thinking about the place she lived before." Anything feel familiar with that?*
H: I'm excited to move. Just the moving reminded me of me.
SF: OK. (pause) *Did you move at all as a girl?*
H: Not until I was 18. Wait, I forgot.... I stayed with my grandparents for 1 year when I was in elementary school. In the United States, in second grade.
SF: You went in second grade to your grandparents?
H: Uh huh.
SF: So, you were seven or so?
H: Yeah, seven or eight.
SF: What was that like?
H: It was, as you say, "The fish doesn't notice it's wet."
SF: I see.
H: I didn't have a choice. My mother wanted me to learn English. Only my mother came with me.
SF: Your mother came with you, but your father did not.
H: Yes. It wasn't anything like my parents had to move for work. It's just my parents wanted to take me and my sister to the United States for one year.
SF: And it was all you knew, so you accepted it. And didn't feel like you had a choice.
H: Right.
SF: In retrospect, looking back, was it hard?

Hana then proceeded to talk about the difficulties she had faced with the move, saying her mother had "thrown her" into public school with very little English; she had not even known how to write the Roman alphabet. She also said she missed her father a lot and Japanese food. She admitted she had been very sad, then suddenly changed the topic to something positive:

H: It was difficult, but I was the best student. I did well in Math and English.
SF: You learned quickly. You learned English very quickly.
H: Thank you. When the students did good things, my teacher would tell me to put a marble in the jar and count the marbles every week and see who did well or not, and I was always the one who was putting in the marbles.
SF: I get it. So, achievement really helped with the sadness.
H: Yes, every week we had a spelling test. My grandmother and my mom and I worked hard on it. And in the whole year I only made two mistakes.
SF: Oh, my gosh!
H: While other native English speakers spell wrong.
SF: Yes, wow. So not making mistakes was a huge advantage!
H: Uh huh. I wonder, maybe that was sort of part of the OCD?
SF: I wonder. It's sort of like you learned how important it was not to make mistakes, and that not making mistakes and achievement help with hard things.
H: Yes. Now thinking of my experience, I don't know if I would want my child to experience that.
SF: Right. I agree ... So maybe this drawing really is not just about moving—you could relate to this sad little girl too. And maybe something there is tied to your OCD. So, Hana, as we hear more about your childhood, I do hear some stressful things.
H: Now I notice that too while talking.

I was pleased that I was able to use scaffolding to help Hana understand that the sadness she saw in the girl in the AAP drawing related to her too, then connect it to her childhood experiences, and even to her OCD. As with Al, my experience of this sequence was not totally "left-brain." I was listening carefully, remembering Hana's Assessment Questions, paying attention to her facial expressions, following wordless hunches, and responding to her willing collaboration. I am convinced that this type of scaffolding is dependent largely on the right hemisphere (McGilchrist, 2009), and when I look back on it, I always feel a kind of awe when it succeeds in helping a client grasp understandings that previously were out of reach.

After the AAP, Hana and I talked about how her OCD had first appeared when she was in graduate school in the USA—another time period in which she had felt lonely and sad—and that it had recurred right after the miscarriage, when others could not "hold" her sadness. Again, this idea was not an interpretation I presented, but rather the result of Hana and me co-laboring to put the pieces together, with me at times leading the way by half-steps. It also prepared us to later discuss the results of the AAP coding. Hana's attachment status on the AAP was "Insecure-dismissing." When I explained secure and insecure attachment to her, Hana began to talk about ways her parents had "abandoned" her as a child to focus on her older sister who was very problematic. She told me that if she did have a baby, she wanted to do everything she could to be a sensitive caregiver and give the child a secure attachment.

The most moving session in the Therapeutic Assessment was the Assessment Intervention Session. Hana had asked me to think with her about what to do with the fetal remains from her miscarriage, and I proposed we design a ritual she could use to handle them. As I asked questions, Hana suddenly remembered an ancient Japanese rite she had read about of putting cremains in a small paper boat and floating them out to sea. She decided she wanted to do this, and I suggested she include her husband and her parents, which she agreed to. I later met with her and her husband to discuss this idea, which he liked. He had been concerned that Hana had kept the fetal remains and that it kept her focused on the loss of their baby. I saw he was a kind man who had been unsure how to help Hana with her grief and thought it was better not to talk about the miscarriage. But he was very open when I told him she needed help "holding" the sadness together—it was too big for her alone.

Shortly after this session, Hana's obsessions and compulsions suddenly went away. Several years after the TA, I spoke with her therapist and learned that she and her husband had a young son, and that Hana's OCD symptoms had not reoccurred.

Scaffolding from the Point of View of Interpersonal Neurobiology

From these and other experiences, I am convinced that scaffolding is an incredibly powerful technique that gives clients a sense of being mentalized (Allen, Fonagy, & Bateman, 2008), of "feeling felt" (see Chapter 2), and (to use Al's word) of being "real." I believe this is partly due to the healing power of empathy (see Chapter 3) but also to a powerful experience of intersubjectivity related to the inevitable mechanics of scaffolding. You see, when we attempt to find a client's zone of proximal development, we can't do so perfectly. At times we overshoot and offer help that is too difficult or we undershoot and give help that is too easy. Ideally, we realize this based on the client's response and make a correction until we find the next step that is "just right." I believe clients sense the effort that goes into this process and not only feel cared about but also less lonely and more hopeful as a result. To know that we "exist" in the mind of another who wants the best for us and is trying to help us meet our goals is truly transformative, especially for those of us who have experienced existential aloneness before we were old enough to handle it. For all these reasons, I believe training therapists and psychological assessors in the finer points of scaffolding will help their clients grow at the fastest rate possible without being overwhelmed.

Notes

1. Fischer and I wondered if the similarities in their approaches might be due to the Russian psychologists' interest in Hegel (Fischer, 2020). Hegel influenced Husserl and Heidegger, who were fundamental to Fischer's grounding in phenomenological psychology (Fischer, 1994).

References

Allen, J. G., Fonagy, P., & Bateman, A. W. (2008). *Mentalizing in clinical practice.* American Psychiatric Pub.

Axelrod, B., & Schutte, C. (2011). Testing the limits. In J. S. Kreutzer, J. DeLuca, & CaplanB. (Eds.), *Encyclopedia of clinical neuropsychology* (pp. 3438–3439). Springer

Bruner, J. S. (1978). The role of dialogue in language acquisition. In A. Sinclair, R. J. Jarvelle, & W. J. M. Levelt (Eds.), *The child's conception of language* (pp. 241–256). Springer-Verlag.

Christensen, A. L., Goldberg, E., & Bougakov, D. (Eds.). (2009). *Luria's legacy in the 21st century.* Oxford University Press.

Cole, M. (1996). *Cultural psychology: A once and future discipline.* Harvard University Press.

Fantini, F., Aschieri, F., David, R. M., Martin, H., & Finn, S. E. (2022). *Therapeutic Assessment with adults: Using psychological assessment to help clients change.* Routledge.

Finn, S. E. (2007). *In our clients' shoes: Theory and techniques of Therapeutic Assessment.* Routledge.

Fischer, C. T. (1994). *Individualizing psychological assessment.* Routledge. (Original work published 1985.)

Fischer, C. T. (2001). Psychological assessment: From objectification back to the life world. In B. D. Slife, R. N. Williams, & S. H. Barlow (Eds.), *Critical issues in psychotherapy* (pp. 29–67). Sage.

Fischer, C. T. (2020). Personal communication to Stephen Finn.

George,C., & West, M. (2012). *The Adult Attachment Projective Picture System: Attachment theory and assessment in adults.* Guilford.

Giorgi, A. (1970). *Psychology as a human science: A phenomenological approach.* Harper and Row.

Golden, C. J. (2004). *Luria–Nebraska Neuropsychological Battery: Manual.* Western Psychological Services.

Haywood, H. C. (2012). Dynamic assessment: A history of fundamental ideas. *Journal of Cognitive Education in Psychology, 11*(3), 217–229.

Heidegger, M. (1962). *Being and time.* SMC Press. (Original work published 1927).

Husserl, E. (1962). *Ideas: General introduction to pure phenomenology.* Collier. (Originally work published 1913.)

Hutt, M. L., & Shor, J. (1946). Rationale for routine Rorschach "testing-the-limits." *Rorschach Research Exchange, 10*(2), 70–76.
Kamphuis,J. H, & Finn, S. E. (2019). Therapeutic Assessment in personalitydisorders: Toward the restoration of epistemic trust. *Journal of Personality Assessment*, 101(6), 662–674.
Kaplan, E (1988). The process approach to neuropsychological assessment. *Aphasiolology, 2*(3–4), 309–311.
Korkman, M., Kirk, U., & Kemp, S. (1998). *NEPSY: A developmental neuropsychological assessment.* Psychological Corporation.
Lamdan, E. (2013). Who had illusions? Alexander R. Luria's Central Asian experiments on optical illusions. *Dubna Psychological Journal, 3*, 66–76.
Lezak, M. D. (1983). *Neuropsychological assessment* (2nd ed.). Oxford University Press.
Luria, A. R. (1948). *Restoration of function after brain injury.* Macmillan.
Luria, A. R. (1962). *Higher cortical functions in man.* Basic Books.
Luria, A. R. (1963). *Human brain and psychological processes.* Harper & Row.
Luria, A. R. (1973). *The working brain: An introduction to neuropsychology.* Penguin.
Luria, A. R. (1974). *Cognitive development: Its cultural and social foundations.* Harvard University Press.
McGilchrist, I. (2009). *The master and his emissary: The divided brain and the making of the modern world.* Yale University Press.
Merleau-Ponty, M. (1976). Phénoménologie de la perception (1945). *Libraqire Gallimard.*
Mikadze, Y. V., Ardila, A., & Akhutina, T. A. (2018). A. R. Luria's approach to neuropsychological assessment and rehabilitation. *Archives of Clinical Neuropsychology, 34*(6), 795-802. 1–8.
Schore, A. N. (2012). *The science of the art of psychotherapy.* Norton.
Vygotsky, L. S. (1986). *Thought and language.* MIT Press. (Original work published 1934.)
Wechsler, D. (2008). *Wechsler Adult Intelligence Scale-fourth edition.* Pearson.
Wood, D. J., Bruner, J. S., & Ross, G. (1976). The role of tutoring in problem solving. *Journal of Child Psychiatry and Psychology, 17*(2), 89–100.

Chapter 9

Therapeutic Assessment in Personality Disorders

Toward the Restoration of Epistemic Trust*

Jan H. Kamphuis and Stephen E. Finn

Therapeutic Assessment (TA) is a semi-structured method of collaborative psychological assessment, designed to help clients gain new insights and make positive changes in their lives. Throughout TA, the client and assessor work collaboratively. This process starts with the formulation of individualized assessment questions that subsequently orient the testing phase, joint discussion of client test responses and behaviors during the Extended Inquiry of standardized testing, targeted experiential "experiments" in the assessment intervention session, an interactive summary and discussion session, a written synopsis of the process and results provided to the client in accessible language, and finally a follow-up session (see Table 9.1). Collaborative Assessment (CA), TA's "close cousin," uses many of the principles and techniques of TA, but in a less structured way. See Finn, Fischer, and Handler (2012) for distinctions between TA, CA, and similar approaches.

Accumulating empirical evidence suggests that TA and CA can be effective interventions in various settings, and several summaries of the extant research have recently been published (Aschieri, De Saeger, & Durosini, 2015; De Saeger et al., 2014). A meta-analysis on psychological assessment used as an intervention (Poston & Hanson, 2010) showed effect sizes consistent with moderate improvement for process variables (e.g., alliance or satisfaction) and treatment outcome variables (e.g., symptom improvement) combined, and with strong improvement when limited to treatment process variables only. In the following, we present a selective, more fine-grained analysis of the research on the effectiveness of TA. Next, as the main objective of this article, we use the evolutionarily informed theory of epistemic trust (ET) and epistemic hypervigilance (EH) articulated by Sperber et al. (2010) and elaborated by Fonagy and his colleagues (Fonagy & Alison, 2014; Fonagy, Luyten, & Allison, 2015; Fonagy,

* This chapter is based on an article previously published in the *Journal of Personality Assessment*, 2019, 101(6), 662–674. Therapeutic Assessment in Personality Disorders: Toward the Restoration of Epistemic Trust. Article DOI: 10.1080/00223891.2018.1476360 https://www.tandfonline.com/

DOI: 10.4324/9781003602231-9

Luyten, Allison, & Campbell, 2017a, 2017b) as a lens to consider the effectiveness of TA (Finn, 2007).

Typical Steps in a Therapeutic Assessment and Their Relationship to Epistemic Trust/Epistemic Hypervigilance (ET/EH)

Selective Empirical Observations on the Effectiveness of TA

We believe ET theory provides a highly plausible framework for understanding (at least) five intriguing findings that have emerged from extant research on the effectiveness of TA and CA. First, how is it that TA is effective with a wide variety of disorders and client types—without the need to make major modifications in one's procedures? If one combines controlled group designs with repeated-measure single-subject experiments, TA has shown benefits to clients in residential treatment for substance abuse (Blonigen, Timko, Jacob, & Moos, 2015); college students seeking counseling for depression, anxiety, and interpersonal problems (Finn & Tonsager, 1992); couples in which one member suffers from chronic pain (Miller, Cano, & Wurm, 2013); latency age boys with oppositional defiant disorder (Smith, Handler, & Nash, 2010); outpatient clients with borderline personality disorder and suicidal ideation (Morey, Lowmaster, & Hopwood, 2010); multi-problem families with emotionally disturbed children (Tharinger et al., 2009); and clients with complex PTSD (Smith & George, 2012; Tarocchi, Aschieri, Fantini, & Smith, 2013); among others. This breadth of impact suggests that metatheoretical change processes are at work, but what are they?

Second, how is it that such a brief intervention can have clinical impact? Most of the studies already cited and almost all of those cited in the aforementioned meta-analysis involved fewer than five client sessions, yet the average impact of assessment as an intervention was close to that found in meta-analyses of much longer interventions. How is this possible?

Third, how is it that TA can affect clients who are notorious for being resistant to change and who generally need long-term, intensive, relationship-based treatments (i.e., those with personality disorders [PDs])? We conducted a Randomized Controlled Trial (RCT) with 74 clients with complex personality pathology awaiting treatment at a tertiary care facility. This study, comparing the effects of TA to those of a highly credible structured motivation pretreatment intervention—and a qualitative follow-up study—together yielded a pattern of results that led us to step back and reflect (De Saeger, Bartak, Eder, & Kamphuis, 2016; De Saeger et al., 2014). In fact, self-report ratings of demoralization and psychological symptoms did not improve immediately following the five-session TA protocol. However, clients undergoing TA expected more success from their treatment, perceived more progress toward treatment, were more satisfied, and felt more allied to the clinician than did clients in the control condition (with moderate effect sizes ranging from .56–.68). The qualitative analysis of subsequent semi-structured interviews in a subset of clients suggested that (often newly experienced) relational aspects of TA were crucial to its impact, with clients describing feeling empowered, feeling validated, and gaining new personal insights. These client reports were echoed by the great enthusiasm of other therapists and staff in the treatment setting. In other words, TA was deemed very meaningful by both clients and staff, despite it not translating directly to short-term symptomatic improvement. It appears that during TA something of value is taking place in PD clients in a relatively short period of time, and that "something" might be preliminary and perhaps even prerequisite to the type of treatment utility more narrowly defined as symptom improvement (Hayes, Nelson, & Jarrett, 1987).

Fourth, what accounts for TA's positive effects on clients' motivation for treatment and subsequent alliance with treatment professionals? We have already described the results of our own RCT. Various other studies have also documented TA's effect on alliance, engagement, and treatment satisfaction, such as clients being significantly more likely to follow through with recommended psychotherapy following Collaborative/Therapeutic Assessment (CTA) as opposed to traditional assessment (Ackerman, Hilsenroth, Baity, & Blagys, 2000), client-assessor alliance during CTA being a significant predictor of client–therapist alliance in subsequent outpatient therapy (Hilsenroth, Peters, & Ackerman, 2004), client–therapist alliance increasing mid-therapy following a TA with another clinician (Smith, Eichler, Norman, & Smith, 2014), clients in residential treatment having better alliance with staff and better relationships with other residents if they took part in a CTA first (Blonigen et al., 2015), and inpatients with suicidal ideation showing significant increases in working alliance over the course of a structured intervention that began with CA (Ellis, Green, Allen, Jobes, & Nadorff, 2012).

Last, in multiple studies of TA, it has been noted that the greatest positive effects of the intervention were not found immediately after the TA was completed, but at some interval (e.g., 2–8 weeks) afterward (Aldea, Rice, Gormley, & Rojas, 2010; Finn & Tonsager, 1992; Newman & Greenway, 1997; Smith, Handler, & Nash, 2010). What accounts for this "delayed" effect of TA, whereas most psychotherapies show a decline in their positive effects once treatment is completed?

Clearly, empirical research into the specific therapeutic mechanisms of TA is needed to answer these questions, but such investigations are likely to be most useful when guided by clinical theory. We believe the theory of epistemic trust (ET) provides encompassing and plausible answers to the aforementioned questions about the efficacy of TA, and that it might help us understand, in particular, what makes TA effective in clients with PDs.

Epistemic Trust and Personality Disorders

ET, according to Fonagy and his colleagues, is trust in the authenticity and personal relevance of interpersonally transmitted knowledge (Fonagy & Alison,

2014, p. 372). When ET exists in a certain relationship, an individual is able to take in, accept, and learn certain information from another and begin to integrate it into his or her view of self and the world. ET is extremely important to the survival and adaptation of both the individual and the species because each human generation must learn and apply an enormous amount of culturally relevant information to function well, adapt to changing circumstances, and continue to advance our culture. On the other hand, epistemic vigilance about the accuracy and usefulness of information offered by another is also highly adaptive because it protects individuals from accepting and using information that is not accurate. As Sperber et al. (2010) explained from an evolutionary perspective, competitors will try to misinform others to gain an advantage, and it is important for individuals to have healthy skepticism (appropriate epistemic vigilance) to not be misled.

Although both epistemic trust and epistemic vigilance can be adaptive (depending on the interpersonal context), Fonagy and colleagues have written extensively about a situation of pervasive distrust they call *epistemic hypervigilance* (EH), which they believe is particularly prominent in PDs. Individuals with PDs cannot flexibly exercise ET and epistemic vigilance as appropriate, with the result that their views of self and the world are highly resistant to change. EH results in an inability to learn from social experience, broad cognitive inflexibility, and severe problems in interpersonal relationships, all hallmarks of PD. In their recent writings, Fonagy et al. (2017a, 2017b) clarified that even epistemic petrification could be viewed as an adaptive solution to childhood maltreatment, although it is tied to communication failures and social dysfunction later in life. Finally, as we return to later, we believe epistemic *hypovigilance* (or naive trust) is also prevalent in PD, and that many clients vacillate between states of epistemic hypovigilance and hypervigilance.

Epistemic Trust, Attachment, Mentalization, and Ostensive Cuing

How do individuals achieve the flexible integration of ET and epistemic vigilance, which then leads to the greatest level of adaptation and growth? Fonagy and colleagues theorized an important link between ET and attachment, stating, "secure attachment is unlikely to be necessary for generating epistemic trust but it may be sufficient to do so, and, further, it is the most pervasive mechanism in early childhood because it is a highly evolutionarily effective indicator of trustworthiness" (Fonagy & Allison, 2014, p. 374). The underlying reasoning here is that from an evolutionary perspective it is most adaptive to trust and take in information from our secure attachment figures because they are likely to share our genetic heritage, to be invested in our survival, and to refrain from intentionally misleading us. Fonagy and colleagues cited research information (e.g.,

Corriveau et al., 2009) showing that securely attached infants are more flexible in their ability to achieve ET and also to rely on their own appraisals when it would be adaptive. Fonagy et al. (2015) also cited Mikulincer (1997), who suggested that adults with insecure attachment are more likely to reject information that challenges their working models of self and the world in part because their sense of self is vulnerable and they are trying to keep themselves from being emotionally overwhelmed. As a result, insecurely attached adults are more likely to adopt stereotypes and show dogmatic thinking.

Fonagy and colleagues focused on two important processes to explain how secure attachment figures promote appropriate ET in children: mentalization and ostensive cuing. *Mentalization* is an aspect of sensitive caregiving in which a parent actively observes and responds to a child's intentional state (Fonagy, 1998), seeing the child as having his or her own thoughts, desires, wishes, and emotions (i.e., mental states) and responding in ways that match the child's subjective experience of himself or herself. Fonagy and Allison (2014) cited a large body of research showing that parents' ability to mentalize their child "increases the chance of secure attachment, enhances his/her resilience to adversity and promotes cognitive, social-cognitive, and emotion-regulating capacity" (p. 373). Parent mentalization is also important in creating ET, and it "triggers the opening of an evolutionarily protected 'epistemic superhighway' that signals readiness for knowledge acquisition" (Fonagy et al., 2015, p. 584). This is promoted by the *ostensive cues* secure attachment figures frequently give to their infants, for example by making eye contact, taking turns in emotional communication (e.g., peek-a-boo), and calling the infant by name. Both in childhood and in adulthood, ostensive cues create a readiness to take in information that follows, or as stated by Fonagy et al. (2015), "When the listener is paid special attention to and noticed as an agent, he/she adopts an attitude of epistemic trust and is thus ready to receive personally relevant knowledge" (p. 583). Ostensive cuing (which is evidence of mentalization) signals the recipient that he or she is in the presence of a deferential source who has his or her best interests in mind and that the knowledge that follows the ostensive cuing can be treated as relevant to his or her adaptation and survival.

Epistemic Trust and Psychotherapy

In earlier writings, Fonagy and others argued that mentalization is a common factor in all successful psychotherapies and that "the potential effectiveness of all treatments depends not so much on their frame but on their ability to increase a patient's ability to mentalize" (Bateman & Fonagy, 2004, p. 46). Recently, in an attempt to identify what it is about mentalizing that brings about therapeutic change, Fonagy and colleagues focused on ET. Their current point of view is that, "Seeing the world from the patient's standpoint opens the patient's mind by establishing epistemic trust in creating a collaboration. The patient becomes able to trust the social world again as a learning environment" (Fonagy et al., 2015, p. 595) and to change "previously rigidly held beliefs" (p. 597). This is especially true for many personality-disordered clients, who are in a state of what Fonagy and colleagues called epistemic petrification (pervasive EH).

As argued by Fonagy and colleagues (Fonagy & Allison, 2014; Fonagy et al., 2015; Fonagy et al., 2017a, 2017b), when psychotherapy is effective, three cumulative cycles of learning are triggered that (a) help move clients from EH to ET, (b) yield increased mentalization on the part of the client, and (c) ultimately, restore more broadly the ability to learn from the outside social world (i.e., relationships outside the consultation room). Thus, by reestablishing ET, the personality-disordered individual is able to eventually leave the consulting room and engage in ongoing social learning in his or her world of interpersonal relationships, select more positive environments, and create a virtuous cycle in which appropriate ET and epistemic vigilance create more self-confidence and ability to be close to others (Fonagy et al., 2017b). To us this implies that psychological interventions that specifically address ET are highly desirable.

Distinctive Elements of TA That Foster ET

In fact, we believe that in principles and procedures, TA is optimally geared to promote an individual's willingness to (re)consider communication conveying new knowledge from someone else as trustworthy, generalizable, and relevant to the self; that is, to lower EH and promote the restoration of ET. Further, we have come to believe that this process of restoring ET and lowering EH might be the general meta-theoretical ingredient that could help account for the remarkable efficacy of TA across settings and disorders. We now elaborate how different aspects of TA are relevant to ET and EH (see Table 9.1).

The Core Values, Intersubjective Stance, and Major Goals of TA

TA first and foremost shows respect for clients as agentic beings with their own goals, desires, and important perspectives. TA's basic interpersonal position is exemplified in the following orienting statement:

> I see myself as a consultant to you to help you better understand what your situation is now. Therefore, I'd like us to figure out what questions you'd like to have answered from the assessment. Then we'll use testing to help answer your questions. Today, I'll also be asking you about yourself so I can understand your assessment questions, and I'll answer any questions

Table 9.1 Typical steps in a Therapeutic Assessment and their relationship to epistemic trust/hypervigilance (ET/EH)

Step	*Goals/procedures*	*Relevance to ET/EH*
1. Initial Session(s)	1. Assessor listens/mirrors/ supports client, attempts to avoid eliciting shame, or helps manage shame if it arises 2. Assessor and client co-construct Assessment Questions (AQs) 3. Assessor asks about past assessment experiences and addresses any reservations/ hurts 4. Assessor invites questions about TA procedures and about himself or herself	1. By listening and responding in an attuned manner, assessor gives evidence of mentalizing the client and promotes ET 2. AQs elicit curiosity and motivation from client and help build ET 3. Listening to and addressing past hurts lowers EH 4. Normalizing clients' curiosity promotes ET; appropriate transparency lowers EH and builds ET
2. Testing Session(s)	1. Assessor selects tests based on client's AQs and explains to client how each test is relevant to client's concerns 2. Assessor uses Extended Inquiries to scaffold new information from testing that is relevant to client's AQs 3. By using multiple tests across different sessions, assessor slowly builds on previous understandings and gradually introduces Level 2 and 3 information (i.e., information that is incongruous with client's existing working model); assessor and client begin to co-construct a new narrative the is more coherent, accurate, compassionate, and useful	1. Clients see their own goals are taken seriously, which promotes ET; tests are viewed as authoritative sources of information, which facilitates ET; assessors acknowledge that clients' input is necessary to understand test results, which lowers EH 2 + 3. AQs serve as a form of ostensive cuing that elicits ET and facilitates clients taking in new information; attuned scaffolding helps prevent clients from being overwhelmed and allows them to incorporate new information at the fastest rate possible; clients and assessors develop new language to describe clients' experiences and dilemmas

(*Continued*)

Table 9.1 (Continued)

Step	*Goals/procedures*	*Relevance to ET/EH*
3. Assessment Intervention Session(s)	1. Using test materials, assessor devises "controlled experiments" that help client "discover" Level 2 and 3 information that might otherwise be rejected 2. Assessor tells client that goal of the session is to help address specific AQs 3. As the "experiment" proceeds, assessor enlists client as co-observer and scaffolds new understandings 4. Assessor offers emotional support and helps manage client's shame and anxiety as new information is taken in 5. When new solutions are tried and judged to be successful, clients are urged to "try it at home" and to report back at the next session	1. Case conceptualization underlying choice of procedures requires sophisticated mentalizing of clients by assessor and sets the stage for ET 2. AQs are used as ostensive cues to facilitate ET in the face of potentially overwhelming information 3. New narratives arise from the collaboration of clients and assessors, which lowers EH and promotes ET 4. By assessors sharing responsibility for regulating for clients' affect, EH is lowered and ET grows 5. Exporting solutions to real life helps clients transfer learning and new ways of being to their social world
4. Summary/ Discussion Sessions	1. Assessor structures discussion of assessment results using client's AQs 2. Assessor references client's experiences and shared understandings from earlier assessment sessions 3. Assessor shows test profiles and references test scores and findings from nomothetic research 4. Client is framed as "expert on him- or herself" and is invited to confirm, modify, or reject test findings 5. Client is asked to give examples of how assessment findings show up in outside life 6. Assessor offers emotional support and helps manage shame and anxiety 7. Instead of making recommendations, assessor offers "possible next steps" and asks client for input and modifications 8. Client is reminded of written feedback, upcoming follow-up session, and possibility of future contacts	1. AQs serve as ostensive cues that help open the "information superhighway" and facilitate clients' assimilating and accommodating new information 2. EH is lowered by referring to clients' own insights and experiences 3. Tests are seen as authoritative sources, which facilitates ET 4. Clients are seen as final arbiters, which lowers EH 5. Making connections to outside world promotes virtuous cycle 3 (transfer outside the assessment relationship) 6. Assessor helps regulate client's affective reactions, which lowers EH 7. By recognizing client's power to act on new understandings arising from assessment, EH is lowered 8. Clients feel assessor is continuing to hold them in mind, which lowers EH and promotes ET

(*Continued*)

Table 9.1 (Continued)

Step	*Goals/procedures*	*Relevance to ET/EH*
5. Written summary provided to client	1. Assessor structures written summary of assessment results using client's AQs 2. Assessor writes summary in plain, jargon-free language adapted to client's intellectual, educational, and developmental level 3. Assessor refers to important experiences/understandings from assessment sessions and uses shared language developed by assessor and client 4. Assessor summarizes nomothetic information discussed during the summary/discussion session 5. Assessor refers to confirming examples provided by client, as well as modifications and disagreements 6. Assessor writes summary in professional but also personal and warm tone (as culturally appropriate) 7. Assessor invites client to comment or ask questions about the written summary and to provide written feedback to the assessor 8. Assessor reminds client of Follow-Up Session	1. AQs serve as ostensive cues that facilitate ET 2. Language and content of letter gives clients the experience of being mentalized by assessors and helps ET 3. Collaborative communication and invoking shared memories facilitates ET 4. Scientifically grounded tests are seen as authoritative sources and this facilitates ET 5. Referencing clients' input gives evidence that they were heard and that their opinions are held in mind, which facilitates ET 6. The combination of professional and personal tone helps clients feel respected and valued, which facilitates ET; clients can refer back to written summary to remember assessor and assessment findings 7. Assessors' interest in and openness to clients' opinions and feedback helps them feel respected and valued and increases ET 8. The possibility of further contact with the assessor helps clients feel valued and increases ET
6. Follow-Up Session(s)	1. Assessor shows interest in client and mirrors any positive strivings 2. Assessor asks client if there are questions about or reactions to the TA 3. Assessor asks for feedback from client about the TA 4. Assessor formally says goodbye	1. Clients' feeling remembered and seen facilitates ET 2. Clients and assessors continue to collaboratively work on new narrative; some clients mention information previously rejected now seems accurate and useful; the fruits of increased ET are often visible 3. Assessors' openness to clients' opinions and feedback helps them feel respected and valued and increases ET 4. A formal, structured termination helps manage emotional impact of assessment relationship, lowers EH, and facilitates ET

> you have about me, the testing, or the feedback session that we'll have at the end of the assessment. Okay?
>
> (Finn, 1996a, p. 7)

What will be evident from this statement is that in TA the client is heavily involved in the problem definition, and there is less of a power imbalance than is generally the case in regular assessment (or psychotherapy). In fact, the model treats "clients as integral participants in a collaborative process, whose goal is to observe, understand, and rethink their problems in living" (Finn & Tonsager, 2002, p. 12). The philosophical stance is clearly humanistic, recognizing the innate healing potential of clients and emphasizing the practice of transparency and authenticity. Also, this stance illustrates the core values of TA, which have been articulated as "collaboration, respect, humility, compassion, openness, and curiosity" (Finn, 2009). TA's viewpoint is also intersubjective, with assessors being trained that "all knowledge is perspectival" and that they, too, must be curious and open to learning about themselves and their tests during their interactions with clients. These core principles of TA promote mentalization on the part of both assessors and clients, and as such create an optimal environment for the reestablishment of ET.

TA's overarching goal is to understand clients' core narratives and then help "each client to get the feeling of being an 'author' of his or her new story, a story which is more compassionate, useful, emotionally viable, and coherent than the previous one" (Aschieri, Finn, & Bevilacqua, 2010, p. 257). Essential to this endeavor is building a secure alliance. In addition to the emphasis on more broadly used techniques such as emotional attunement, collaborative communication, and repair of disruptions, TA includes a number of specific elements that promote the reduction of EH and the cultivation of ET. In what follows, we review those elements.

Enlisting Clients' Curiosity by Co-Constructing Assessment Questions

We believe there is a central part of every TA that helps build alliance early in the intervention; every TA begins with one or more sessions in which assessors and clients work to co-construct Assessment Questions (AQs) that form the basis of the collaborative exploratory process (Finn, 2007). Early on, the clinician asks the client something like this: "So what things would you like to learn about yourself from the assessment?" "Are there some things you have been wondering about yourself that you'd like to understand better?" "What questions do you have about yourself that we can try to answer together?" Clients' AQs are collected in their own words, signaling that the clinician takes their personal agendas seriously. This is an essential point: By not telling the client what is important and what needs changing, but instead, by centering the assessment on their personal concerns and agendas, TA builds in a motivation for clients to engage themselves in the process of assessment in an open and honest fashion. It often is, as one client noted, "the first time [the client] was actually involved in defining the nature of the problem."

To illustrate how AQs function, we refer to Finn's (2012) report on the TA of "Ben," a 27-year-old man with prominent borderline features who was in group and individual psychotherapy focused on managing his dangerous sexual behaviors. (See Chapter 5.) Ben and Finn developed the following questions for his assessment: "Why do I keep sexually acting out in dangerous ways, even though I know that it's really stupid?" "What am I going to have to do to stop acting out?" "Why do I hate myself?" As Finn (2007) explained, such AQs serve multiple purposes:

1. They give information about the client's current internal working models1. For example, Ben revealed his extremely negative self-image and his confusion and judgment about his sexual behaviors. This is useful knowledge for a clinician who wishes to affect Ben's views of himself and others.
2. AQs also enlist clients' curiosity about themselves as the TA intervention begins, which helps to lower EH and foster mentalization. In this way, Ben's questions can be seen as "open doors" he was pointing Finn toward, as if to say, "Approach me in this way and I will let you in."
3. By accepting the clients' questions as defining the boundaries of the assessment, the clinician also fosters the client's trust, as if to say, "I understand that this is where you are open to input. I will respect your limits and not directly challenge other aspects of your working model."

We now believe the co-construction of AQs serves as a form of *ostensive cuing*, which helps establish a safe relationship with the client and moves the clinician into the role of a deferential source of information. This happens for several reasons. First, by referencing clients' questions throughout the assessment, TA clinicians establish the relevance of the information they are about to convey. As Sperber et al. (2010) explained, relevance is highly significant to epistemic vigilance because it is inefficient to put energy into comprehending information that is not personally relevant. By tying new information to the client's AQs, the assessor effectively communicates, "You might want to listen closely now, as what I'm about to say is pertinent to your personal goals." Also, by focusing on the client's AQs, the clinician demonstrates his or her goal of helping the client in the way he or she is willing and ready to receive. As summarized by Hilsenroth and Cromer (2007), research supports this assertion in showing that "collaboratively developing individual treatment goals and tasks" greatly helps clinicians foster a positive alliance with clients. This type of strong alliance is essential for circumventing EH in clients (e.g., those with PDs) who tend to be distrustful of treaters' desire to "fix" aspects of them they are not ready to change.[1]

Attentiveness to Self-Verification and Disintegration

TA theory gives central importance to two constructs that are highly related to ET: self-verification and disintegration. *Self-verification* (Swann, 1997) is the natural human tendency to take in information that confirms our internal working models and to screen out information that would disconfirm them. Although normal, self-verification is an especially strong motive for individuals with fragile senses of self, as they are prone to emotional overwhelm and *disintegration*[2] (Kohut, 1984) when confronted with information that contradicts their working model. As mentioned earlier, this stance typifies the personality-disordered individuals Fonagy and colleagues described as showing epistemic petrification (pervasive EH). Although such individuals are highly challenging for clinicians to work with, TA assessors try to maintain empathy for these clients, remembering Kohut's (1984) insight that disintegration experiences are unbearable affective-cognitive states and that fragile clients understandably will do anything they can to avoid them.

TA assessors are trained to use a particular strategy to affect the internal working models and personal narratives of individuals showing EH or petrification. As already mentioned, this strategy involves (a) reducing the clients' anxiety by recognizing their power as collaborators, enlisting their curiosity about themselves, and building a secure alliance; (b) presenting the client with a number of experiences (typically using psychological tests) that create opportunities for "bottom-up" learning (described later), and (c) slowly working both to confirm aspects of clients' working models (self-verification) and then gradually expanding those working models, all the while providing emotional support. In TA, this approach is called moving from *Level 1 information* (that matches clients' working models) to *Level 2 information* (that does not fundamentally contradict, but expands clients' working models) to *Level 3 information* (that challenges clients' internal working models; Finn, 1996a, 2007). ET is fostered not only by the TA clinician coming to be a privileged source through ostensive cuing, and by the clinician's using the AQs to signal the personal relevance of the information that will be offered, but also because the clinician sensitively conveys information that is similar enough to the client's evolving views that it does not engender epistemic distrust.

In fact, this strategy is fully consonant with the theory of epistemic vigilance by Sperber et al. (2010). They distinguished between vigilance toward the source of new information and vigilance toward its content. As mentioned earlier, relevance is one content criterion we all use to regulate epistemic vigilance, but research shows that other content characteristics are also important, such as whether the new information is coherent, logical, and whether it fits with existing "background beliefs." If new information is too divergent from existing beliefs, we are likely to reject it, even if it comes from a deferential source (Sperber et al., 2010).

Attentiveness to Shame

A related aspect of TA that we believe helps restore ET in clients with PDs is its focus on shame. In an interesting theoretical contribution, Schoenleber and Berenbaum (2011) articulated how shame regulation might be central to the development and maintenance of each of the PDs listed in the *Diagnostic and Statistical Manual of Mental Disorders* (4th ed. [DSM–IV]; American Psychiatric Association, 2000). Shame regulation could be primarily preventive, attempting to preclude shame experiences (e.g., in obsessive–compulsive PD, where a person might adopt extreme standards to avoid the shame of exposure of imperfections), or escape-oriented in the face of immediate or imminent shame (e.g., in avoidant PD, where a person might excessively withdraw from interpersonal situations that could yield social evaluation); or aggressive to self or others, to regulate present or past shame experiences (e.g., in borderline PD, where deliberate self-harm is exercised to cope with unbearable shame, at the same time often creating a source of shame). Irrespective of its specific form, shame works as a major "rigidifier" of the client's experiential and behavioral repertoire. It signals the aspects of self that cannot be addressed, are "off limits," and hence impermeable for updating on the basis of new evidence.

TA theory recognizes that shame is one of "the least tolerable affects for humans" (Malatesta-Magai, 1991) and TA clinicians are trained to address it in multiple ways (Aschieri, 2016; Finn, 2007). First as mentioned earlier, a central tenet of TA is to provide an atmosphere where clients are treated as competent collaborators, experience a lack of judgment from the clinician, and become curious about themselves. This basic therapeutic stance is identical to that recommended by experts for intervening with shame (e.g., Gilbert, 2011). Also, by allowing clients to delineate their own AQs, TA allows them to avoid topics (at least initially) that would be too shame producing to explore (i.e., shame prevention, as explained by Schoenleber & Berenbaum, 2011). Valid psychological tests can enhance a clinician's empathy for where shame "landmines" lie, while also providing opportunities for discussing sensitive topics the client might have planned to avoid. If TA clinicians inadvertently elicit shame from their clients, they are trained to make repairs in a way that can actually strengthen the therapeutic alliance (cf. Safran & Muran, 2003). Finally, the overarching goal of TA, of helping clients construct more compassionate narratives about their problems in living, directly addresses shame (i.e., shame repair; Schoenleber

& Berenbaum, 2011). When reframed in these terms, shameful "dysfunctional behaviors" that might not be discussed can be transformed into contextualized "problems in living" that can be either addressed or are in need of acceptance.

We strongly believe that shame vulnerability is a major factor that contributes to EH in PD and other clients. In fact, many of the most difficult and alienating aspects of PD (e.g., grandiosity, blaming others, impulsive behaviors) can be conceptualized as defenses against shame (Schoenleber & Berenbaum, 2011; see Chapter 7). None of us is likely to reduce our epistemic vigilance until we are assured that a communicator will not give us information that would be incredibly painful to hear. By helping clients to avoid and regulate shame, TA clinicians both cultivate ET in their relationships with those clients and also help move them into a position of lower EH in general.

Use of Assessment Instruments

Mapping the Structure and Content of Clients' Internal Working Models

Many a novice psychotherapist is cautioned against making "premature interpretations." If one wishes to avoid triggering epistemic distrust by presenting Level 3 information to clients, TA might have a distinct advantage. By using standardized psychological tests as a central part of their intervention, TA clinicians have a direct and formalized way of gaining information about the structure and content of clients' working models and about aspects of clients' difficulties that they might not yet be ready to acknowledge.

For example, in the case example mentioned earlier of Ben (Finn, 2012), the young man Finn helped get curious about his dangerous sexual behavior, Finn asked him early in the TA to complete the Minnesota Multiphasic Personality Inventory–2 (MMPI–2; Butcher et al., 2001), a self-report measure of personality and psychopathology that generally provides the clinician with a mix of Level 1 and Level 2 information. The resulting profile was highly consistent with Ben's self-presentation in revealing a difficult-to-interrupt pattern of risky and impulsive behavior. However, the MMPI–2 also suggested that the major driving force behind this behavior was that it helped Ben temporarily escape intense shame and other negative affect states of which he was somewhat aware (as shown by his AQ of "Why do I hate myself?"), but the depth and importance of which he failed to comprehend (as shown by his AQ of "Why do I keep sexually acting out in dangerous ways, even though I know that it's really stupid?"). In addition, as is typical in TA, Finn used several empirically grounded performance-based personality instruments with Ben. Such tests can help reveal aspects of internal working models of which clients are not fully aware (i.e., Level 2 and Level 3 information; Finn, 1996b, 2012). From the Rorschach (Exner, 2003) and Early Memory Procedure (Bruhn, 1990), Finn learned that Ben was prone to falling into intensely painful affective states. These affects appeared to have their origin in severe attachment trauma during childhood related to Ben's mother being hospitalized repeatedly for depression, Ben's feeling responsible for her depression, and Ben and his brother being left to manage their fear and loneliness largely on their own. All of this was Level 3 information, as Ben's working model explicitly involved his having had "good parents" who loved him and had provided him with a "good childhood," and it was clear that he held onto this point of view very strongly.

Our point here is that by using assessment instruments, TA clinicians gain a detailed map of clients' working models, and this allows them to navigate—within a relatively short period of time—the potential "minefield" of therapeutic interactions with personality-disordered and other clients, by understanding what types of interpretations or interactions are likely to enhance ET or reify EH. Finn knew that to help Ben, he could not directly challenge Ben's positive view of his childhood and instead needed a way to help him become aware of his shame and the role it played in his sexual acting out.

Tests Provide Opportunities for Top-Down and Bottom-Up Learning

When used in a collaborative manner, psychological tests also enhance ET by providing opportunities for both top-down as well as bottom-up learning. These two terms refer to complementary methods of knowledge acquisition and transmission (Sun & Zhang, 2004). Top-down learning moves from explicit to implicit knowledge; for example, a clinician says to a client, "I think you are feeling shame right now because your eyes are downcast, your face is red, and you look like you want to disappear," and the client accepts the term "shame" as a descriptor for this kind of experience. Bottom-up learning involves going from implicit perceptions to explicit conclusions; for example, the clinician asks the client, "Can you describe what you're experiencing right now?" and the client replies, "I can't look at you, my face is hot, and I want to run away or disappear." The clinician might ask, "Do you have a word for this experience?" and then work with the client's response, perhaps even asking, "Does the word 'ashamed' fit for what you are experiencing?" Although results vary by context and the nature of the knowledge being transmitted, it is generally found that some combination of top-down and bottom-up learning leads to the most efficient and effective learning (Sun & Zhang, 2004). Fonagy and Alison (2014) seemed to acknowledge this in their statement, "It is important that in this process both patient and therapist come to see each other more clearly as intentional agents. It is not sufficient for the therapist to present their 'mentalizing wisdom' to the patient if they are not themselves clearly seen as an agentive actor" (p. 377).

We have found that for clients with EH, such as those with personality pathology, an effective strategy is to prioritize bottom-up learning, especially early in a TA, and for the clinician to intentionally avoid positioning himself or herself too much as an "expert." Then, in the middle stages of the TA, psychological tests are selected that create situations relevant to clients' problem behaviors and AQs, and the clinician and client work together to draw conclusions. Two core TA techniques are particularly useful here, extended inquiries and assessment intervention sessions (AISs).

In *extended inquiries*, TA clinicians engage clients in discussing their experiences and responses to a psychological test, with the hope of achieving new understandings (an example will follow later). As documented in many published TA case examples, such tactics can lead even clients with EH to incorporate new views of themselves they might otherwise have found to be threatening or overwhelming (e.g., Finn, 2015; Kamphuis & De Saeger, 2012; Kamphuis, De Saeger, & Mihura, 2018). Because the new information that emerges is based on the client's own test responses and behaviors, EH is relaxed.

In the *AIS*, TA clinicians use their test-heightened empathy to arrange potential bottom-up learning experiences for clients concerning Level 3 information (which is incompatible with the current working model), often again using psychological tests or test stimuli. For example, Finn hoped to help Ben understand the relationship between his negative feeling states and his compulsive use of sex as a tension-reducing behavior. Finn also wanted a way to begin to shift Ben's view of himself as having had a "good childhood" because this narrative led Ben to blame himself for the difficulties he had as an adult. So, in a TA session, Finn first asked Ben to rate—on a scale from 1 to 10—"how sexually compulsive" he felt at that time. Ben rated himself at 1. Finn then showed Ben a series of Thematic Apperception Test (TAT) cards and asked him to tell stories that fit the cards. The first three cards were chosen to be emotionally neutral, so when Finn asked Ben to rate his sexual compulsivity, Ben's ratings were low. Finn then showed Ben three highly dysphoric cards, and to two of them, Ben told stories about female figures who were depressed (possibly unconsciously referencing his mother). The third card, TAT 13B, depicts a young boy sitting in a doorway looking dejected, and Ben told this story:

> He's left alone again. There's no one there for the boy. His parents are gone, his brothers and sisters are off somewhere, and he has no friends. He's tired of all this and is sitting there waiting for his ... someone to come home. [SF: What is he thinking and feeling?] Awful. Alone. I mean I guess it's better off to be dead...(Ben started to cry) since nobody cares and notices.

When Finn asked Ben a few moments later to rate his level of sexual compulsivity, Ben took stock, seemed surprised, and exclaimed that it was at a 10. With Finn's guidance, Ben then was able to agree that the "sexual acting out is a way to cope with these awful feelings." Ben also began to spontaneously revise his working model of his childhood, saying about his last TAT story that, "I guess that was me… that was me when I was growing up. But I don't like to admit that." He and Finn were then able to construct a new narrative, in which Ben's parents were "good people" who "loved him" but who had been overwhelmed with Ben's mother's illness and so left Ben alone frequently with painful feelings that were too much for him. Ben's epistemic vigilance seemed to be relaxed because this new narrative made sense of his own experience in the AIS and he therefore seemed able to incorporate it into his working model.

Tests as "Authoritative" Outside Sources, as well as Opportunities for Play

As Sperber et al. (2010) explained, one other source characteristic that affects ET is *reputation*, with the implication that all exchanges of information exist in both a personal and a social context: "No act of communication among humans, even if it is only of local relevance to the interlocutors at the time, is ever totally disconnected from the flow of information in the whole social group. Human communication always carries cultural features" (p. 379). This means that inevitably, the extent to which a client believes what a particular clinician says is affected by what the client has heard about that clinician from other clients and staff, what other trusted sources (e.g., peers and family members) believe about the clinician, and by the general reputation in the client's social group of psychologists, psychotherapists, psychiatrists, or other mental health professionals. The client's personal experience of the source will still be important for believability, but these contextual variables are nevertheless influential, probably especially early in a communication exchange when a client is deciding whether to even listen to the source.

In TA we are aware that psychological tests are seen as an authoritative source by many clients. This does not mean that PD clients in a state of epistemic petrification will easily revise their working models on the basis of nomothetic test results. Still, we have noticed that even the most skeptical clients will listen more intently when we share information relevant to their AQs from standardized tests and when we back it up talking about research, percentile ranks, and so on. Our sense is that this openness is at least partly related to a cultural reputation of tests being more "objective" or "neutral" than personal (even expert) opinion.

Conversely, the test plane can also make trying on new personally relevant information less consequential. The same dynamic might be conceptualized from a psychoanalytic perspective. Tests, especially in the context of the AIS, can serve as "potential space," Winnicott's (1971) term for a sense of an inviting and safe interpersonal field in which one can be spontaneously playful while connected to others. In other words, test stimuli can serve as transitional objects to (more safely) play with, try on, and to infuse with personal meaning, before actually internalizing the emerging insights. In AIS, we deliberately use this "transitional space" (Winnicot, 1971) provided by the consulting room or test environment as a safe haven, and encourage clients to embark on a self-relevant, collaborative mentalizing experiment.

Scaffolding and Targeting the Zone of Proximal Development

Those readers with a background in education might see an overlap between TA's schema of levels of information and the concepts of the zone of proximal development and scaffolding; we believe both are relevant to ET and EH. The *zone of proximal development* (ZPD) is a concept introduced by Vygotsky but developed more fully by others after his death (cf. Zaretskii, 2009). Vygotsky recognized that knowledge acquisition always occurs in a social, interpersonal, and cultural context, and that beyond just assessing what an individual can do alone, it is also useful to know what he or she can do with help, and what is out of reach even with assistance. The ZPD—where supported learning takes place—is the "golden target" in teaching that leads to the most rapid acquisition of knowledge by the learner. *Scaffolding*, a concept developed by Bruner and others (Bruner, 1978; Wood, Bruner, & Ross, 1976) based on Vygotsky's work, is the process of providing temporary active assistance to help individuals achieve goals that are just beyond their ability. If one can give just enough help, but no more than necessary, a learner will show the fastest rate of knowledge acquisition.

Although Vygotsky applied the ZPD primarily to cognitive skills, and Bruner originally elucidated scaffolding with regard to language learning, both concepts can be broadly applied, are relevant to epistemic trust, and are highly applicable to helping clients update their working models during psychotherapy. In TA, clinicians are trained to deliberately "half-step" (i.e., scaffold) clients toward Level 3 information that is emerging from a psychological assessment, using tests as communication tools, maps of the clients' working models, and as opportunities for bottom-up learning.

For example, Finn (2007) reported on an extended inquiry of the Rorschach with a middle-aged man, Jeff, done as part of a couples' TA. Jeff and his wife, Ann, had sought help because of marital problems related to Ann's depression. Jeff found himself increasingly enraged about Ann's struggles, and one of his main individual AQs was, "How can I deal with the feelings I get when Ann tells me she has slept all day?" Statistical results from Jeff's psychological testing suggested that he had a dismissing attachment status and tended to avoid negative affects and focus on achievement. Also, Jeff's Rorschach scores suggested an underlying depression that he kept at bay through a variety of characterological coping mechanisms (minimization, intellectualization, withdrawal, and manic avoidance). When taken together, this information led Finn to hypothesize that Jeff could not be appropriately empathic to Ann's depression because he was defended against his own; in fact, from a systemic point of view, the couple appeared to be engaged in mutual projective identification where Ann "held" the depression for both, and Jeff "held" the capacity to keep going and disconnect from emotion. Finn's dilemma was how to explore this hypothesis with Jeff and eventually, with the couple. The following is an excerpt from the extended inquiry of Jeff's Rorschach. Finn had just finished the standardized administration of the test. Notice the "half-steps" Finn used to help Jeff revise his working model that Ann was depressed, but he was not.

SF: What was that test like for you?

J: OK ... I'm curious how you make anything out of it.

SF: Of course! I'll be scoring your responses and then we'll discuss your scores and see if they give us any information about your AQs. But for now, I'm curious—did you notice anything in particular about your test responses?

J: Not really. Did you?

SF: Perhaps, but I'm not sure. Can I read you back some of your responses and get your thoughts?

J: *Sure.*

SF: Here are some I noticed: "A bat with holes in its wings" (Card I); "A smashed bug" (Card II); "A ripped tuxedo" (Card III), "An upside-down bat, hanging by its feet in the dark in a cave" (Card IV). (Pause) Any impressions from those?

J: They all seem gloomy and a bit upsetting.

SF: I thought so, too. Do you think they tell us anything about your situation?

J: *Well, if I let myself, I could feel really depressed about the situation at home.*

SF: I can imagine. That makes sense. And what do you think if I tell you that each of these responses would get a score for depression in the research-based scoring system for the Rorschach?

J: I'm not really surprised. There's a lot of depression, but I don't let myself feel it.

SF: How do you do that?

J: *Well in my German family, people don't get depressed. You just put one foot in front of the other and go to work every day.*

SF: Oh, maybe that explains the order of your responses on that last card.

J: *How so?*

SF: Well, your first response, the bat hanging upside down in the dark, gets a score for depression.

J: I can sorta see that. That might be me when I just can't take it anymore. I go in my man cave downstairs, drink beer, and watch football.

SF: That fits! And do you remember your next response?

J: (Pause) *The "Keep on Trucking Guy"?* (a reference to the famous Robert Crumb poster)

SF: Yes. (Pauses and looks at Jeff.)
J: That's what I do! When I'm depressed, I just keep on trucking. And I don't understand why Ann can't do that, too.

This led Finn and Jeff to discuss how different people have different coping mechanisms, and that Ann might not be able to push her feelings to the side the way Jeff did. Jeff said he understood this and that he had always appreciated Ann's emotional sensitivity in contrast to his family's denial of emotions. Finn asked if Jeff had ever told Ann that he, too, struggled with feelings of depression, and Jeff said he hadn't because he didn't want to "burden" her. Finn wrote, "It's difficult to describe the wonder and relief that showed on Jeff's face at that point, as he recognized his own depression, found a framework for his frustration with Ann, saw that he was being unfair to himself by not talking to Ann about his depression, and realized that his own mind had given the key for understanding all this through what he saw on the Rorschach" (Finn, 2007, p. 154). Jeff's choice to eventually discuss his depressive feelings with Ann in a subsequent couples' session was a significant step in the couple's achieving a better relationship.

To return to ET, we propose that when clinicians successfully engage in the kind of scaffolding illustrated earlier, it has the potential to reduce EH and restore ET. Successful scaffolding requires empathy, sensitive and timely attunement, collaborative communication, and repair of disruptions—the hallmarks of secure attachment—and it is a demonstration of the clinician's ability to mentalize the client. Although we have described scaffolding up to this point as being led by the clinician, it clearly is an intersubjective process to which both assessor and client contribute. Finn imagined something about Jeff's inner world that he was able to communicate in a way Jeff could grasp, and Jeff helped elaborate Finn's notion so that it was more useful and complete.

How TA Addresses Blind Trust

As Sperber et al. (2010) stated, "Vigilance … is not the opposite of trust; it is the opposite of blind trust" (p. 363). This assertion spurred us to bring up another difficulty we have noticed frequently in our PD clients: blind trust or epistemic hypovigilance. Some clients seem to be much too open to taking in information from others, with sometimes disastrous consequences, yet do not appear to learn from such experiences to develop appropriate ET and epistemic vigilance. Not uncommonly, some clients swing between epistemic hypovigilance, which tends to lead to relational traumas, and then inevitably switch to a stance of EH. Clients with dependent or borderline features come to mind, but we have seen a similar pattern with PD clients with prominent narcissistic, antisocial, avoidant, or even paranoid features. Our hypothesis is that such clients learned early in life to discount important internal cues that regulate ET and vigilance, in part because their primary caregivers were not reliable and trustworthy. Although adaptive when basic survival was at stake, this is highly problematic in adulthood. Such clients appear to quickly sort people into "friends" and "foes" based on superficial or inconsequential information, and then rigidly maintain such categorizations even when there is ample evidence that they should be modified.

TA has several ways that it addresses epistemic "blind trust" and hence also EH. First, again, the basic collaborative frame of TA puts the client in the driver's seat and helps build self-efficacy, confidence, and "taking one's own authority." For example, not uncommonly, clients come for an initial TA session bringing AQs that have been suggested to them by another person (e.g., referring therapist, parent, spouse) and that they might not fully understand. Unless such AQs address the clients' own areas of concern, this behavior can be evidence of epistemic hypovigilance in action. In such situations, TA clinicians are encouraged to help clients explore their own agendas, which might or might not be related to the concerns others have. Almost always, the AQs suggested by others are abandoned or are greatly modified by the end of the initial session.

In general, during testing sessions, ongoing invitations to clients to describe their experiences, observe their own behavior, check tentative hypotheses against their own lives, and correct or disagree with the assessor serve to help clients pay attention to the cues that guide appropriate ET and epistemic vigilance.

Ensuring Transfer to the Outside World

Fonagy and his colleagues believe that promoting transfer to the outside world (i.e., change beyond the consulting room) is a cornerstone of effective psychotherapy. In other words, it is crucial that any intervention systematically promotes the third "virtuous cycle" (Fonagy et al., 2017b). We hold that this emphasis is even more crucial in clients with EH, such as those with PD. Generally, PD clients do not show up at the clinic doorstep complaining about their personality pathology. Instead, they contemplate treatment because their interpersonal style has adverse effects on life outcomes (e.g., job functioning, intimate relationships; see also Emmelkamp & Kamphuis, 2007).

We believe TA processes mentioned earlier (e.g., integration of bottom-up and top-down learning, scaffolding, enlisting clients' curiosity) all promote assimilation and accommodation of new information, and as such, promote transfer of learning. Importantly, TA's use of collaboration to build clients' self-efficacy also helps them gain confidence in themselves and take risks after they finish the assessment. In addition, several other procedures integral to TA seem highly relevant to the third virtuous cycle mentioned by Fonagy and colleagues (Fonagy et al., 2017b). First, and perhaps foremost, inviting and co-constructing AQs in the clients' own words about what it is they want to learn about themselves from the assessment will very likely yield questions that are ecologically valid to (PD) clients. Generally, PD clients will formulate questions that center on recurring problems in their social and relationship functioning (e.g., "Why don't I work harder?" or, "Why do I cheat on my partner even though I really love him?" or, "How come I am not happy with myself, despite all my accomplishments?"). Consistently exploring these questions as the central frame for the assessment helps keep focus on what it is that matters to the client "outside." Moreover, the semi-structured AIS and summary and discussion session specifically include steps to check for ecological validity. In the AIS, for example, after inducing a central personality dynamic deemed central to the case conceptualization, the clinician asks the client to (a) name the behavior, and then (b) check it for fit with the problem behaviors outside (Finn, 2007). When new solutions are tried during the session and found to be successful, clients are encouraged to "Try it at home!" and then come back and report what they learned. Likewise, in the summary and discussion session, after each piece of personally relevant feedback, clients are not only asked to check it for accuracy, but also to see if they can provide an example of how the element just discussed shows up in their lives (similar to the interactive style of test interpretation described by Claiborn & Hanson, 1999, in the context of career counseling, and fully consistent with two very early advocates of client participation in test interpretation; Dressel & Matteson, 1950). Also, many clients have told us that the personalized written feedback in TA has been essential in their continuing to remember and try out learnings achieved during the assessment. Finally, in Follow-Up Sessions clients and assessors discuss how insights and suggestions derived from the assessment have helped them or not in their real-life contexts. Such procedural elements systematically foster transfer from the sessions to clients' wider social world.

Conclusions

Theorizing by Fonagy and colleagues (Fonagy & Alison, 2014; Fonagy et al., 2015; Fonagy et al., 2017a, 2017b), as well as writings of Sperber et al. (2010), offer a new, evolutionarily informed theoretical account of the nature of psychopathology and the workings of effective psychotherapy. The central thought guiding the model is that effective interventions specialize in generating epistemic trust in individuals who struggle to relax their epistemic vigilance in more ordinary social situations, and that the restoration of ET is perhaps the most important outcome of psychotherapy. The main objective of this article was to use this model as a lens to consider the effectiveness of TA (Finn, 2007).

Our review of philosophical and procedural characteristics of TA aims to elucidate how TA might bring about restoration of epistemic trust, the prerequisite for clients with personality pathology to consider relating differently to themselves, others, and the world at large. We hold that as a package TA might be particularly effective in dislodging and motivating PD and other clients to try on new thoughts, feelings, and (interpersonal) behaviors in subsequent therapy, and ultimately, in everyday life. Moreover, we believe ET theory is uniquely suited to provide an encompassing explanation for the previously described set of five intriguing findings in the TA/CA literature on its effectiveness.

First, how is it that TA appears to benefit many different types of clients with different problems in living? Although we have given special attention to PD clients in this article, addressing EH and restoring ET is likely to be crucial to helping many clients; therefore, if TA is particularly effective in promoting ET it should show wide utility. Second, how is it that such a brief intervention can be impactful? By enlisting clients as collaborators, arousing their curiosity and lowering EH, and using personally relevant AQs as ostensive cues, TA assessors become deferential sources who are able to use the "epistemic superhighway" and information from psychological tests to help clients update their working models in a relatively short period of time, and immediately begin trying out new understandings in assessment sessions and in real life. Other forms of therapeutic intervention might need more time both to establish a positive alliance and then to collect and put together an effective case conceptualization that can be used to guide treatment. Third, TA as a brief intervention can exert powerful positive effects on patients with PD because of its sensitive attunement to their (initially) low levels of ET, and through its variety and sequencing of techniques fostering ET. These benefits to treatment readiness could pave the way for ultimate outcomes further on, be it in subsequent treatment or not. Fourth, TA's particular emphasis on building alliance early in the intervention and maintaining it throughout the intervention by shame regulation and avoiding disintegration experiences is likely to account for its positive effects on clients' motivation and alliance with subsequent treatment professionals. It appears that many clients leave a TA more or less concluding, "[Some] mental health professionals will respect my competence, hold me in mind, not shame me, judge me, or overwhelm me, and provide emotional support and useful ideas about how to think and act differently in ways that are important to me." With such an updated working model, clients are more likely to accept referrals for additional treatment and enter those situations with an open attitude. Fifth and finally, ET theory seems uniquely positioned to explain why many of the positive effects of TA continue to grow after clients leave an assessment. If TA truly leads to a lowering of EH and an increase in ET, and to learnings that aid clients in their natural social environments, they should continue to have more success in social interactions and in understanding and addressing any difficulties that arise.

Implications for Assessment

To the extent that a goal of assessment is to positively affect clients, many techniques of TA could be particularly effective, including (a) gathering clients' questions about themselves and their problems at the beginning of an assessment, (b) involving clients as collaborators throughout an assessment, (c) using scaffolding and top-down and bottom-up methods in presenting assessment results with clients, (d) using tests as authoritative sources, or conversely as opportunities for play, and (e) applying the TA concept of levels of information to organize how assessment materials are discussed with clients. All of these features of TA appear to give clients an intense and possibly life-changing experience of being mentalized (seen and held in mind) by the assessor, which greatly affects ET and the ability of clients to return to their worlds with a new capacity for social interaction, ongoing interpersonal learning, and increased flexibility.

Implications for Psychotherapy

Therapists are often given general advice to "avoid premature interpretations" and "build alliance" with clients, without being taught how to implement these ideas. We believe that explicitly teaching concepts of scaffolding and top-down versus bottom-up learning to new psychotherapists could greatly help them operationalize what it means to "hold clients in mind." Also, although many psychotherapists are not trained to use tests, collaborating with other colleagues who do, and who work collaboratively with clients, can provide essential information about places where clients are vulnerable to disintegration experiences and to therapeutic disruptions. There are many points where a CA or TA might be useful in treatment with PD clients, but two that seem particularly obvious are (a) at the beginning of treatment where there is evidence that TA fosters alliance in subsequent psychotherapy (Ackerman et al., 2000), or (b) mid-treatment, especially when clients and assessors might feel stuck (Smith et al., 2014). A final area that could be strengthened in psychotherapy training is better awareness of shame: how to recognize it, how to understand it, and how to intervene when it arises. TA's learnings about shame can be extended to psychotherapy as well as psychological assessment.

Implications for Research

We echo the call of the original authors of ET theory for integral testing of the assumptions undergirding the model in clinical contexts and especially as regards PD (Fonagy et al., 2017b). A key challenge will be to derive testable hypotheses, as ET is an encompassing developmental and interpersonal theory based on concepts that are not easy to operationalize. As a research priority, we advocate that a (state) measure of level of ET versus EH be developed, although we presume that a straightforward self-report might not lend itself well to this task. In fact, we surmise that ET theorizing could more readily serve as a heuristic and clinical roadmap than as a framework for experimental testing of its core constructs. Moreover, we conjecture that hypothesis testing might be better done indirectly; that is, by comparing the effectiveness of (novel) interventions and strategies that are oriented to or based on this model, versus those that are not (explicitly). In so doing, research designs are recommended that are described in the classic article by Hayes et al. (1987), particularly the manipulated (use of) assessment designs. (One approximation is the study by De Saeger et al., 2014.) For example, one might test the incremental validity of assessment models that pay explicit attention to the cyclical nature of ET (i.e., clients dropping back to lower levels of ET because of negative outside experiences, or therapists' misattunement) versus those that do not.

As an example of a novel ET-based intervention, we offer our work (in progress)[3] that we have internally coined "TA-extended." It concerns an assessment-driven intervention for clients with PD who are deemed not (yet) suitable for regular evidence-based treatment programs (often clients with a PD not otherwise specified diagnosis, or with narcissistic features). TA-extended is kicked off by a full TA as described in this article (cf. virtuous cycle 1, holding the client in mind); followed up by a 3-month, 5-hr-per-week program combining verbal and nonverbal therapies systematically seeking enhancement of mentalization around the core themes developed in the TA (cf. virtuous cycle 2; increased mentalization). This is followed by a 3-month self-guided period (i.e., no or minimal treatment) in which clients are expected to independently apply the new learnings in their social surroundings (cf. virtuous cycle 3; social transfer); and concludes with two booster sessions reviewing progress and remaining work (which might or might not lead to referral for additional treatment; integration). As one can see, this intervention closely follows the progression of the three virtuous cycles as proposed by Fonagy (Fonagy et al., 2017a, 2017b). We are currently working on a preliminary report describing this intervention in more detail, along with preliminary data and a case analysis.

Notes

1 "Internal working model" is a term first developed by Craik (1943) and later used by Bowlby (1969/1982) to describe the implicit "map" a person has about how the world functions, and especially what to expect in close, protective relationships.
2 By disintegration I mean an experience of great emotional distress, disorientation, and fear that can result when an individual is unable to refute evidence that some tightly held core belief about the self is wrong.
3 This research was yielding promising results but was interrupted during the pandemic due to funding issues and was never completed.

References

Ackerman, S. J., Hilsenroth, M. J., Baity, M. R., & Blagys, M. D. (2000). Interaction of therapeutic process and alliance during psychological assessment. *Journal of Personality Assessment*, *75*, 82–109.

Aldea, M. A., Rice, K. G., Gormley, B., & Rojas, A. (2010). Testing perfectionists about their perfectionism: Effects of providing feedback on emotional reactivity and psychological symptoms. *Behavior Research and Therapy*, *48*, 1194–1203.

American Psychiatric Association (APA). (2000). *Diagnostic and statistical manual of mental disorders* (4th ed., Text Revision). Author.

Aschieri, F. (2016). Shame as a cultural artifact: A call for reflexivity and self-awareness in personality assessment. *Journal of Personality Assessment*, *98*(6), 567–575. https://doi.org/10.1080/00223891.2016.1146289

Aschieri, F., de Saeger, H., & Durosini, I. (2015). L'evaluation therapeutique et collaborative: preuves empiriques [Therapeutic/Collaborative Assessment: Empirical studies]. *Pratiques Psychologiques*, *21*, 307–317.

Aschieri, F., Finn,-S. E., & Bevilacqua, P. (2010). *Therapeutic Assessment and epistemological triangulation. In V. Cigoli & M.Gennari (Eds.), Close relationships and community psychology: Aninternational perspective* (pp.249–264). Franco Angeli.

Bateman, A. W., & Fonagy, P. (2004). Mentalization-based treatment of BPD. *Journal of Personality Disorders*, *18*, 36–51.

Blonigen, D. M., Timko, C., Jacob, T., & Moos, R. H. (2015). Patient-centered feedback on the results of personality testing increases early engagement in residential substance use disorder treatment: A pilot randomized control trial. *Addiction Science and Clinical Practice*, *10*(9). https://doi.org/10.1186/s13722-015-0030-9

Bowlby, J. (1969/1982). *Attachment, vol. 1.* (2nd ed.). Basic Books.

Bruhn, A. R. (1990). *Earliest childhood memories, Vol. 1: Theory and application to clinical practice*. Praeger.

Bruner, J. S. (1978). The role of dialogue in language acquisition. In A. Sinclair, R. J. Jarvelle, & W. J. M. Levelt (Eds.), *The child's conception of language* (pp. 241–256). Springer-Verlag.

Butcher, J. N., Graham, J. R., Ben-Portah, Y. S., Tellegen, A., Dahlstrom, W. G., & Kaemmer, B. (2001). *MMPI-2: Manual for administration, scoring, and interpretation, revised edition.* University of Minnesota Press.

Claiborn, C. D., & Hanson, W. E. (1999). Test interpretation: A social influence perspective. In J. W. Lichtenbeg & R. K. Goodyear (Eds.), *Scientist-practitioner perspectives on test interpretation* (pp. 1–14). Allyn & Bacon.

Corriveau, K. H., Harris, P. L., Meins, E., Fernyhough, C., Arnott, B., Elliott, L., … de Rosnay, M. (2009). Young children's trust in their mother's claims: Longitudinal links with attachment security in infancy. *Child Development*, *80*, 750–761. https://doi.org/10.1111/j.1467- 8624.2009.01295.x

Craig, K. J. W. (1943). *The nature of explanation*. Cambridge: Cambridge University Press.

De Saeger, H., Bartak, A., Eder, E. E., & Kamphuis, J. H. (2016). Memorable experiences in Therapeutic Assessment: Inviting the patient's perspective following a pretreatment randomized controlled trial. *Journal of Personality Assessment, 98*, 472–479. https://doi.org/ 10.1080/00223891.2015.1136314

De Saeger, H., Kamphuis, J. H., Finn, S. E., Verheul, R., Smith, J. D., van Busschbach, J. J. V., Feenstra, D., & Horn, E. (2014). Therapeutic Assessment promotes treatment readiness but does not affect symptom change in patients with personality disorders: Findings from a randomized clinical trial. *Psychological Assessment, 26*(2), 474–483.

Dressel, P. L., & Matteson, R. W. (1950). The effect of client participation in test interpretation. *Educational and Psychological Measurement, 10*, 693–706.

Ellis, T. E., Green, K. L., Allen, J. G., Jobes, D. A., & Nadorff, M. R. (2012). Collaborative assessment and the management of suicidality in an inpatient setting: Results of a pilot study. *Psychotherapy, 49*, 72–80.

Emmelkamp, P. M. G., & Kamphuis, J. H. (2007). *Personality disorders*. Psychology Press.

Exner, J. E., Jr. (2003). *The Rorschach: A comprehensive system* (4th Ed.). Wiley.

Finn, S. E., Fischer, C. T., & Handler, L. (Eds.) (2012). *Collaborative/Therapeutic Assessment: A casebook and guide*. Wiley.

Finn, S. E. (1996a). *A manual for using the MMPI-2 as a therapeutic intervention*. University of Minnesota Press.

Finn, S. E. (1996b). Assessment feedback integrating MMPI-2 and Rorschach findings. *Journal of Personality Assessment, 67*, 543–557.

Finn, S. E. (2007). *In our clients' shoes: Theory and techniques of Therapeutic Assessment*. Erlbaum.

Finn, S. E. (2009). *Core values in Therapeutic Assessment*. Retrieved from http://www.therapeuticassessment.com

Finn, S. E. (2012). Implications of recent research in neurobiology for psychological assessment. *Journal of Personality Assessment, 94*, 440–449.

Finn, S. E. (2015). Therapeutic Assessment with couples. *Pratiques Psychologues, 21*, 345–373.

Finn, S. E., & Tonsager, M. E. (1992). Therapeutic effects of providing MMPI-2 feedback to college students awaiting therapy. *Psychological Assessment, 4*, 278–287.

Finn, S. E., & Tonsager, M. E. (2002). How Therapeutic Assessment became humanistic. *The Humanistic Psychologist, 30*, 10–22.

Fonagy, P. (1998). An attachment theory approach to treatment of the difficult patient. *Bulletin of the Menninger Clinic, 62*, 147–169.

Fonagy, P., & Allison, E. (2014). The role of mentalizing and epistemic trust in the psychotherapeutic relationship. *Psychotherapy, 51*, 372–380.

Fonagy, P., Luyten, P., & Allison, E. (2015). Epistemic petrification and the restoration of epistemic trust: A new conceptualization of borderline personality disorder and its psychosocial treatment. *Journal of Personality Disorders, 29*, 575–609.

Fonagy, P., Luyten, P., Allison, E., & Campbell, C. (2017a). What we have changed our minds about: Part 1. Borderline personality as a limitation of resilience. *Borderline Personality and Emotional Dysregulation, 4*(11). https://doi.org/10.1186/s40479-017-0061-9

Fonagy, P., Luyten, P., Allison, E., & Campbell, C. (2017b). What we have changed our minds about: Part 2. Borderline personality, epistemic trust, and the developmental significance of social communication. *Borderline Personality and Emotional Dysregulation*, *4*(9). https://doi.org/10.1186/s40479-017-0062-8

Gilbert, P. (2011). Shame in psychotherapy and the role of Compassion Focused Therapy. In R. L., Dearing & J. P., Tagney (Eds.), *Shame in the therapy hour* (pp. 325–354). American Psychological Association.

Hayes, S. C., Nelson, R. O., & Jarrett, R. B. (1987). The treatment utility of assessment: A functional approach to evaluating assessment quality. *American Psychologist*, *42*, 963–974.

Hilsenroth, M. J., & Cromer, T. D. (2007). Clinician interventions related to alliance during the initial interview and psychological assessment. *Psychotherapy: Theory, Research, and Practice*, *44*(2), 205–218.

Hilsenroth, M. J., Peters, E. J., & Ackerman, S. J. (2004). The development of therapeutic alliance during psychology assessment: Patient and therapist perspectives across treatment. *Journal of Personality Assessment*, *83*, 331.

Kamphuis, J. H., & De Saeger, H. (2012). Using Therapeutic Assessment to explore emotional constriction: A creative professional in crisis. In S. E. Finn, C. T. Fischer, & L. Handler (Eds.), *Collaborative/Therapeutic Assessment: A casebook and guide* (pp. 133–155). Wiley.

Kamphuis, J. H., De Saeger, H., & Mihura, J. (2018). The broken zombie: Using R-PAS in the assessment of a bullied adolescent with borderline personality features. In J. Mihura & G. Meyer (Eds.), *Using the Rorschach Performance Assessment System* (pp. 65–83). Guilford Press.

Kohut, H. (1984). *How does analysis cure?* University of Chicago Press.

Malatesta-Magai, C. (1991). Emotional socialization: Its role in personality and developmental psychopathology. In D. Cicchetti & S. L. Toth (Eds.), *Internalizing and externalizing expressions of dysfunction: Rochester symposium on developmental psychopathology* (Vol. *2*, pp. 203–224). Erlbaum.

Mikulincer, M. (1997). Adult attachment style and information processing: Individual differences in curiosity and cognitive closure. *Journal of Personality and Social Psychology*, *72*, 1217–1230.

Miller, L. R., Cano, A., & Wurm, L. H. (2013). A motivational therapeutic assessment improves pain, mood, and relationship satisfaction in couples with chronic pain. *The Journal of Pain*, *14*(5), 525–537.

Morey, L. C., Lowmaster, S. E., & Hopwood, C. J. (2010). A pilot study of Manual-assisted Cognitive Therapy with a Therapeutic Assessment augmentation for Borderline Personality Disorder. *Psychiatry Research*, *171*, 531–535. https://doi.org/10.1016/j.psychres.2010.04.055

Newman, M. L., & Greenway, P. (1997). Therapeutic effects of providing MMPI-2 feedback to clients at a university counseling service: A collaborative approach. *Psychological Assessment*, *9*, 122–131.

Poston, J. M., & Hanson, W. M. (2010). Meta-analysis of psychological assessment as a therapeutic intervention. *Psychological Assessment*, *22*, 203–212. https://doi.org/10.1037/A001s679

Safran, J. D., & Muran, J. C. (2003). *Negotiating the therapeutic alliance: A relational treatment guide*. Guilford Press.

Schoenleber, M., & Berenbaum, H. (2011). Shame regulation in personality pathology. *Journal of Abnormal Psychology, 121*, 433–446.
Smith, J. D., Eichler, W. C., Norman, K. R., & Smith, S. R. (2014). The effectiveness of Collaborative/Therapeutic Assessment for psychotherapy consultation: A pragmatic replicated single case study. *Journal of Personality Assessment, 97*(3), 261–270.
Smith, J. D., & George, C. (2012). Therapeutic assessment case study: Treatment of a woman diagnosed with metastatic cancer and attachment trauma. *Journal of Personality Assessment, 94*, 331–344.
Smith, J. D., Handler, L., & Nash, M. R. (2010). Therapeutic assessment for preadolescent boys with oppositional defiant disorder: A replicated single-case time-series design. *Psychological Assessment, 22*, 593–602.
Sperber, D., Cl'ement, F., Heitz, C., Mascaro, O., Mercier, H., Origgi, G., & Wilson, D. (2010). Epistemic vigilance. *Mind & Language, 25*(4), 359–393.
Sun, R., & Zhang, X. (2004). Top-down versus bottom-up learning in cognitive skill acquisition. *Cognitive Science Research, 5*, 63–89.
Swann, W. B., Jr. (1997). The trouble with change: Self-verification and allegiance to the self. *Psychological Science, 8*, 177–180.
Tarocchi, A., Aschieri, F., Fantini, F., & Smith, J. D. (2013). Therapeutic Assessment of complex trauma: A single–case time-series study. *Clinical Case Studies, 12*(3), 228–245.
Tharinger, D. J., Finn, S. E., Gentry, L., Hamilton, A., Fowler, J., Matson, M., Krumholz, L., & Walkowiak, J. (2009). Therapeutic assessment with children: A pilot study of treatment acceptability and outcome. *Journal of Personality Assessment, 91*, 238–244.
Winnicott, D. W. (1971). *Playing and reality*. Routledge.
Wood, D. J., Bruner, J. S., & Ross, G. (1976). The role of tutoring in problem solving. *Journal of Child Psychiatry and Psychology, 17*(2), 89–100.
Zaretiski, W. K. (2009). The zone of proximal development: What Vygotsky did not have time to write. *Journal of Russian and East European Psychology, 47*, 70–93.

Chapter 10

Learning to Navigate Karpman's Triangle

The Healing Potential of Assessing Traumatized Clients*

My work assessing and treating traumatized clients over the course of my career has been one of the most personally growth-producing experiences I have had. In this chapter, I will describe some of what I learned through this work and how these lessons impacted my development as a clinician and as a human being.

A Fairly Common Story among Mental Health Professionals

Let me start by telling my version of a story I have found to be all too common among psychotherapists working with traumatized clients. Perhaps some of you will personally relate to parts of this story. "Jane" was a 28-year-old woman referred for a psychological assessment by her psychiatrist, Dr. Nuñez, who was concerned about Jane's unremitting depression and her increasing inability to function. I was a young clinician, just starting to develop my ideas about the therapeutic potential of psychological assessment, and I was eager to impress Dr. Nuñez and help Jane. Dr. Nuñez also mentioned that she hoped I might see Jane in therapy after the assessment, as she herself only did medication management, not psychotherapy.

Jane was an attractive blonde woman who looked younger than 28, and she had a winsome smile and a shy, vulnerable air about her. I immediately felt protective of her and was happy when the assessment got off to a good start and appeared to be going well. Over the course of our work together, Jane and I came to understand that she not only was depressed but also had been terribly traumatized as a child by a critical and demanding mother, an alcoholic and rageful father, and a series of stepfathers, all of whom had sexually abused Jane

* This chapter is based on a paper presented at the annual meeting of the Society for Personality Assessment, March 21, 2014, Arlington, VA, as part of a symposium "Countertransference and Trauma: Therapeutic Uses of Self in Collaborative/Therapeutic Assessment," Diane H. Engelman, Chair.

DOI: 10.4324/9781003602231-10

and sworn her to silence. Starved for attention and longing to be loved, Jane had kept the secret of her sexual abuse not only from her mother but also from her husband, whom she married when she was 19. The marriage ended after four years in part because of Jane's increasing difficulties having sex. After Jane's husband had left five years previously, she had become increasingly depressed and unable to work.

Dr. Nuñez knew virtually nothing about Jane's early trauma history, and both she and Jane were grateful for the assessment. Jane told me several times that she had never felt so understood as she had by me, and she steadily improved during the assessment and was able to go back to work part-time. As a result of Jane's progress, I eagerly agreed to Dr. Nuñez's request that I see Jane in psychotherapy after the assessment, and Jane was very happy about this arrangement too.

To make a long story short, I saw Jane for several years in psychotherapy, and after about 6 months, things started to happen between us that confused me and that I didn't know how to handle. Early in the treatment, Jane confessed to me that she was afraid that I would eventually "toss her away" as her father and husband had. Touched, I reassured her there was *nothing* she could do that would make me call an end to our treatment. I soon came to rue those words.

As I see it now, Jane proceeded to put me through a series of unconscious tests to see if I meant what I said. She quickly became very depressed again and stopped working. This meant Jane had little money to pay for therapy, for although Jane's mother was wealthy, she and Jane were estranged. I quickly cut Jane's therapy fee by two-thirds, telling myself that it is our duty as psychologists to treat those without economic resources. I did not even blink when Jane asked if she could see me more than once a week, which meant that I was giving up two full-fee slots a week, an economic stretch for me at the time.

Jane also began to fill more of my time in between sessions, calling frequently in tears, desperate and suicidal, and asking for my help. I always called back as soon as I could, even if the call was late at night or during the weekend. Inevitably, my partner Jim came to know Jane's name and managed to roll his eyes only once or twice when my home office phone rang in the evenings. I myself was unaware of any resentment about Jane's calls and was conscious only of sympathy and anxiety for her. When Jim and I took a 2-week vacation over the summer, Jane panicked, and I sent her a postcard every day to let her know I was thinking of her. (This was before the era of cell phones.)

Despite my attentiveness and reassurance (or, I now see, perhaps because of it) Jane continued to become more depressed and seemed to turn into what I have come to call a "trauma magnet." She was involved in a car accident—that ostensibly was not her fault—but which totaled her car and involved a driver with no insurance. For months she had to rely on public transportation until a friend gave her an old car. Also, Jane's apartment was burglarized and her computer was stolen, which made it more difficult for her to apply for jobs. And one day she tripped going up some stairs and broke her leg badly. She was on crutches for weeks.

It was around this time that I began to be aware of feelings of helplessness and frustration with Jane. There were several times toward the end of therapy sessions when she became so despondent and tearful that I was unable to get her out of my office. I kept other clients waiting 15–20 minutes because of this, and afterwards I felt trapped and resentful. I had been getting consultation for months about my work with Jane, and at my consultant's urging I told Jane one day that we had to end sessions on time, and if she needed time to collect herself, she would have to sit in her car. Jane calmly agreed. She then went home and immediately overdosed on her antidepressant medication. Luckily one of her friends found Jane and called an ambulance, and when the hospital contacted Dr. Nuñez, she insisted that Jane be hospitalized psychiatrically. Jane's mother agreed to foot the bill for inpatient treatment, but only if Jane would go to an excellent hospital in the northeastern United States, near where her mother lived. I saw Jane once before she left, and we had several phone conversations when she reached the hospital. In retrospect, when we talked, we basically apologized to each other. I don't know who felt more ashamed, Jane or me. But our therapeutic relationship was over, and I must admit that I was partly relieved about this. It had become clear that I was not helping Jane and that I was in over my head as a therapist, even with backup consultation. I have spent years thinking about what happened in my relationship with Jane, and I will share some thoughts now and discuss their relevance to the assessment and treatment of traumatized clients.

An Organizing Rubric: Karpman's Triangle

I have written before (Cf. Finn, 2004), about a schema I have found quite powerful in organizing my thoughts about traumatized clients, i.e., Karpman's (1968) "Drama" or "Trauma" Triangle. (See Figure 10.1.) As I understand it, this diagram is a map of the internal object relations of many traumatized clients. That is, their unconscious internal representations (or stories) about the world are that there are three different types of people: (1) perpetrators (i.e., abusers), (2) victims, and (3) rescuers. In their relationships with others, traumatized clients tend to enact one of these roles (for reasons I will explain), and people in close relationships with them often feel a great deal of "role suction" (my word for the internal pressure one feels during projective identification[1]) to enact a complementary role. At the end points of the triangle, one finds "pure" versions of the roles: persecutors are selfish, sadistic, angry, and ruthless; victims are hurt, helpless, and despondent; and rescuers are selfless, overly generous caretakers. One also finds blends of the roles, such as "victim-rescuers"—who will give anyone the shirt off their backs to the point that they end up damaging themselves—or "victim-persecutors," who are so focused on their own pain and so self-involved that they become furious if others do not give them the care to which they feel

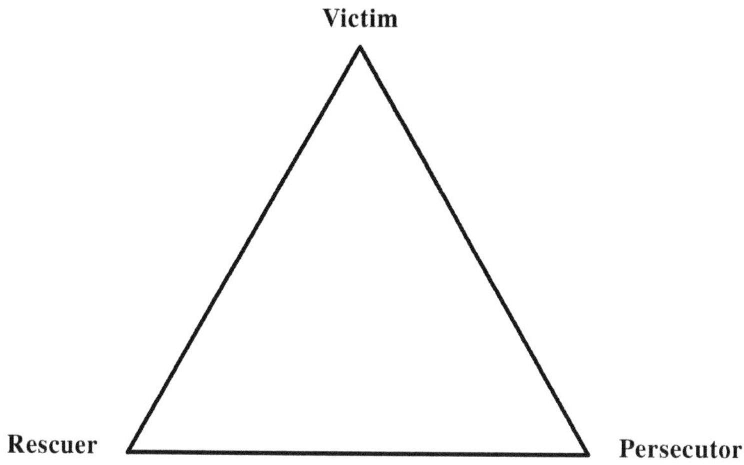

Figure 10.1 Karpman's (1968) Drama Triangle.

entitled. Importantly, as Karpman (1968) explained, the same person may also end up "switching" roles rapidly, one minute being helpless and depressed, and the next being angry and cruel. (See Figure 10.2.) As you might guess from these kinds of sudden shifts, the roles in Karpman's triangle are dependent on the coping mechanism of dissociation, which many traumatized clients learned to use to survive intolerable circumstances.

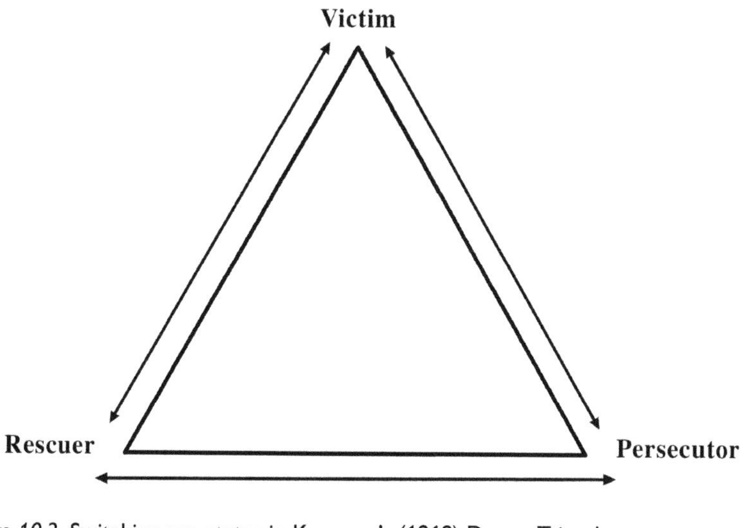

Figure 10.2 Switching ego states in Karpman's (1968) Drama Triangle.

To further illuminate this point, let's talk about the healthy aspects of Karpman's triangle. The ends of the triangle represent exaggerated versions of affects and ego states that are normal and adaptive (found nearer to the center of the triange). The healthy aspect of the victim is the ability to express sadness, tolerate grief, and ask for and accept help. The healthy aspect of the persecutor is the ability to express anger, do what it takes to protect oneself, and be assertive. The healthy aspects of the rescuer are empathy for others and a desire to help those in need. (See Figure 10.3.)

A person living from the "center" of the triangle has flexibly integrated all three of these states and can express them in a balanced way as the context requires. From my point of view, that kind of balance is what we want to foster in ourselves and in our clients (see Figure 10.4).

The challenge is that through traumatic learning, some of these adaptive ego states become split-off and dissociated and are no longer available to a person when the context requires.[2] For example, Jane's testing showed that she was completely unable to express appropriate anger because she had grown up in an environment where to do so would have been extremely dangerous. If she had shown anger, her rageful and abusive father would have beaten her more, and her mother would have cut her off from the little bit of caretaking she provided. Now as an adult, Jane was so determined to be different from her abusers that she couldn't even tell a friend she was angry when the friend stood her up for a movie. This showed up, for example, in the PSY-5 protocol of Jane's MMPI-2. (See Figure 10.5.) She had the lowest possible score on Aggressiveness. This is a sign of highly dissociated anger.

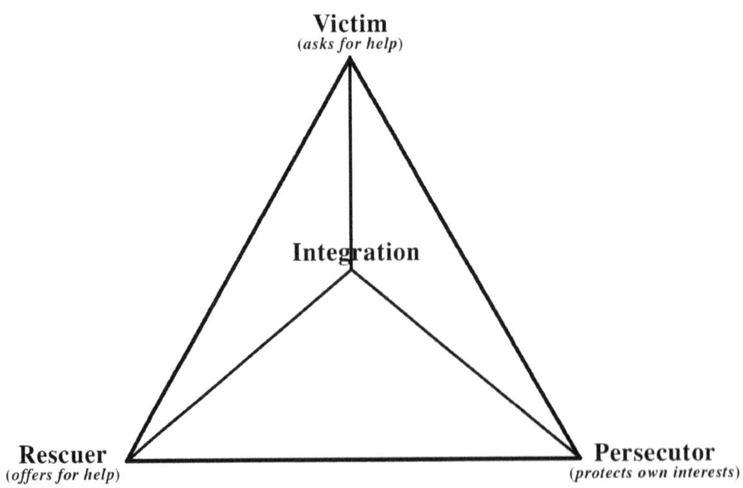

Figure 10.3 Healthy aspects of Karpman's (1968) Drama Triangle.

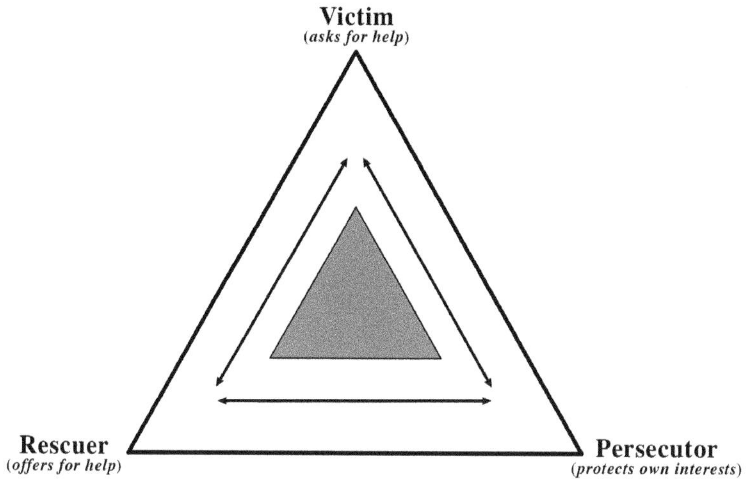

Figure 10.4 The healthy resolution of Karpman's Triangle: Integration of ego states.

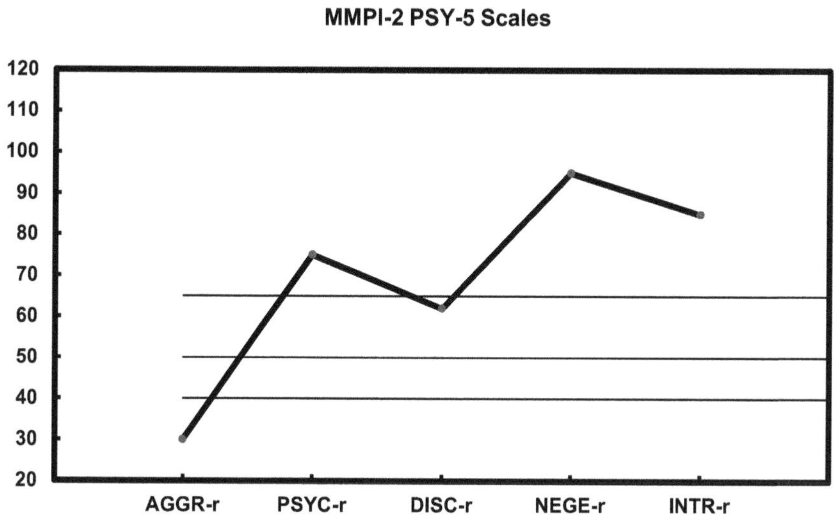

Figure 10.5 Jane's MMPI-2 PSY-5 Protocol.

To further complicate things, very rarely Jane went into a flying rage (remember the rapid shifts I talked about earlier), but afterwards she always felt horrified with herself and deeply ashamed. This underlying anger was evident in her Rorschach protocol, in which Jane had eight Aggressive Content (AgC) responses. The Rorschach also showed that Jane's empathy was blocked at times

(Pure H = 1; Fr + rf = 2; Isolate/R = .26) because: (1) she was so overwhelmed (D = -4) that she couldn't tolerate experiencing others' pain, and (2) once more, caretaking impulses had been inhibited when she was growing up. On the Early Memory Procedure (Bruhn, 1990) one of the incidents Jane wrote about was of trying to comfort her mother at age seven when her mother was crying after a fight with Jane's father. Jane's mother had rebuffed her harshly (probably due to her own shame), saying, "Will you just leave me alone? You're always in the way, you brat!" Jane said the strongest feelings associated with the memory were "despair" and "self-hate" for "being a burden." As you can see from the diagram (Figure 10.6), because both anger and empathy were split off, Jane was set up to "live" at the far end of the "Victim" corner in Karpman's triangle.

This kind of person can be difficult for many of us to be around, unless we're fortunate enough to have come from families where all three healthy ego states were accepted and supported. For you see, when a person who lives in one corner of the triangle invites us to play a reciprocal role (the aforementioned "role suction" or projective identification), we are psychobiologically prone to engage in this form of unconscious enactment (Schore, 2012). What is needed to "pass the test" is to respond from the "middle" of the triangle. When Jane confessed that she was terrified she could push me to the point of abandoning her, an integrated response might have been, "Well, there surely are things you could do that would make it impossible for us to continue our work together. Let's talk about those and how we can prevent that from happening." When Jane lost her job and could no longer pay my full fee, I might have said, "I can give you 10 therapy sessions at a reduced rate, but my own finances do not allow me to

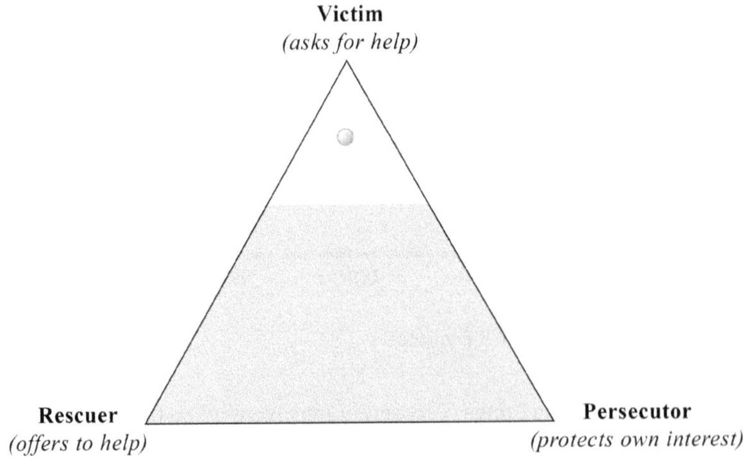

Figure 10.6 The Victim Role adaptation.

do more than that. Shall we discuss how you can get work so you can pay my full fee after that, or if you prefer, we can discuss where you can get treatment you can afford to pay for long-term?" And the first time Jane had trouble leaving my office when our session time was over, I might have brought this up at the next meeting and asked her to strategize with me about how to prevent that in the future. Possibilities might have been that we: (1) start to wrap up much earlier in the session, (2) schedule longer sessions (for which Jane would pay an additional fee), and/or (3) suspend any emotionally arousing therapy work until Jane had more emotion regulation skills in place.

Now one major problem was, at this time of my life, I also had my own dissociated affect states. I grew up in a family where my father was abusive, my mother was a consummate victim, and I was trained as my mother's emotional caregiver. I had been "giving therapy" to my mother for years before I ever went to graduate school, and the whole family had benefited from this. In short, I was highly rewarded for being a "victim-rescuer." In fact, this kind of background is so common among psychotherapists that it creates a set of characteristics I have termed "therapist disease."

(See Figure 10.7). Therapists with this adaptation are self-sacrificing, have a host of needy clients who require their time, and build their self-esteem on being "helpful" to others. In my experience, if these therapists don't become more integrated themselves, they eventually burn out or develop stress-related medical illnesses. I remember one therapist who consulted me years ago about how to handle a very disturbed client who had moved into the space under the front porch of the therapist's office and would not leave. The therapist wanted

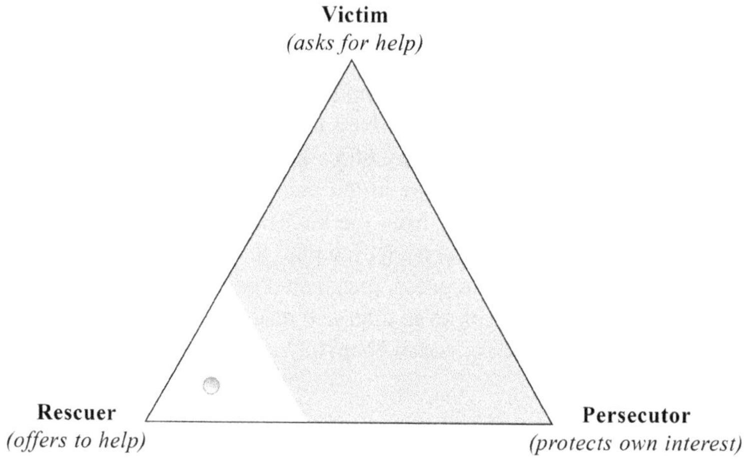

Figure 10.7 "Therapist Disease": The Rescuer Role adaptation.

my opinion about what to do, but she flinched when I asked if she had considered calling the police. She could not imagine doing that because she was sure it would "damage" her relationship with the client. And we psychological assessors are not immune to "therapist disease." For example, I know many of us are willing to do complicated assessments and write long, time-consuming reports for very little pay, in part because we so much want to be helpful to our clients and referral sources. And most of us are much more comfortable giving emotional support to others than we are asking for it ourselves. Sound familiar, anyone?

I will write more about psychological assessment below, but before I leave the topic of Karpman's Triangle, I want to clarify one more thing about the projective identification "tests" traumatized clients present to us. Traditional psychodynamic theory sees these as instances of "repetition compulsion" and warns of enacting dangerous countertransference, which is to be avoided at all costs. Modern interpersonal psychoanalytic theory (e.g., intersubjectivity theory) sees minor versions of such enactments as inevitable and as golden opportunities for clients and therapists to collaborate in each other's healing (Davies, 2004; Bromberg, 2012; Schore, 2012) by discussing and coming to understand what occurred. In the years since I treated Jane, I have worked a great deal on "buying back" my own split-off anger and dependency needs, with the result that I am more able to "come from the center of the triangle" when working with traumatized clients and others in my life. The results, both personally and professionally, have been gratifying.

I also strongly believe what Control Mastery Theory (Weiss, 1993) says, that is, traumatized clients *want* and even *long* for us to "pass" their tests, so that we can model for them a new way of living in which they aren't destined to be victims, persecutors, or rescuers. Many of you have read my account (Finn, 2005) of the client I assessed who tended to live in the "persecutor" area of the triangle and had dissociated any feelings of weakness and concern for others. I was asked to evaluate her after she pulled a knife on a man who had refused to have sex with her at a party. When the client arrived for her feedback session at the end of the assessment, she walked into my office holding a bottle of beer. I calmly said, "You can put that in the fridge in the kitchen and pick it up on the way out." When the client came back from the kitchen and sat down in my office, she sighed and said, "Mommy won't let me play in the middle of the highway. That feels good." As you might guess, the client's parents had made no attempt to contain her as an adolescent, even after she made it clear that she was using drugs and engaging in reckless sexual behavior.

Implications for Psychological Assessment

So let me conclude by saying more about the implications of Karpman's Triangle for psychological assessment and offering advice that may be helpful in minimizing the kinds of painful lessons I went through:

1) Pay attention to your feelings about the clients you are working with. These are important assessment results themselves that can greatly help you navigate Karpman's Triangle.
2) If you have a tendency toward being a rescuer, victim, or persecutor in your personal or professional life, watch out for these roles in particular when you work with traumatized clients. And while many of us in this field derive a great deal of satisfaction from being "helpful" to our clients and colleagues, make sure you have other major sources of self-esteem than just that one.
3) Learn to recognize signs of dissociated affect states and of dissociation in general in psychological testing. Many of the papers by Judith Armstrong on this topic are rich and informative (e.g., Armstrong, 1994, 2002). I have also written about how the combination of self-report and performance-based personality tests can be particularly useful in identifying split-off affect states (Finn, 1996, 2011).
4) If you catch yourself in an enactment of Karpman's triangle with a traumatized client, don't despair. See this as an opportunity for personal healing and for your client to also understand important patterns in their lives. As soon as you can, get back to the "center of the triangle," and if you can't get there on your own, get consultation and/or seek help in your own therapy.
5) Be particularly aware when you start making allowances or adjustments in your normal professional boundaries with traumatized clients, e.g., cutting your fee, giving extra time in sessions, not charging for missed sessions, taking phone calls in between sessions, etc. These may be appropriate, but they may also be signs that you are in a rescuer role.
6) And above all, do not lose your common sense. Some of you have heard me talk about what I call the "10 grandmothers' test." This is a thought experiment I developed where I imagine asking ten sensible grandmothers what they would recommend doing in a particular clinical situation. For example, I can imagine asking my Grandma Jessie what to do about a client who had moved in under the porch of her therapist's office and wouldn't leave. "Why honey," she would say, "isn't it obvious? If she won't leave, then the person has to call the police. That situation isn't good for anyone!"

Notes

1 Projective identification has classically been defined as a defensive process in which two individuals collaborate to "hold" and enact complementary emotions and characteristics that are difficult to hold within one person at the same time. Modern views of projective identification are that it is an unconscious form of "right-brain to right-brain" communication in which "events occurring within the dyad are experienced by both parties as being the consequence of behavior in the other" (Schore, 2012, p. 169).

2 This phenomenon is called "structural dissociation" in contrast to "state dissociation," which refers to the state of parasympathetic arousal associated with the freeze response.

References

Armstrong, J. G. (1994). Reflections on multiple personality disorder as a developmentally complex adaptation. *Psychoanalytic Study of the Child, 49,* 349–364.

Armstrong, J. (2002). Deciphering the broken narrative of trauma: Signs of traumatic dissociation on the Rorschach. *Rorschachiana, XXV,* 11–27.

Bromberg, P. M. (2012). *The shadow of the tsunami and the growth of the relational mind.* Routledge.

Bruhn, A. R. (1990). *Earliest childhood memories: Vol. 1. Theory and application to clinical practice.* Praeger.

Davies, J. M. (2004). Whose bad objects are we anyway? Repetition and our elusive love affair with evil. *Psychoanalytic Dialogues, 14,* 711–732.

Finn, S. E. (1996). Assessment feedback integrating MMPI-2 and Rorschach findings. *Journal of Personality Assessment, 67,* 543–557.

Finn, S. E. (2004, March). *"But I was only trying to help!": Therapeutic Assessment and Karpman's triangle.* Paper presented at the Society for Personality Assessment annual meeting, Miami, FL, as part of a symposium, "What Can We Learn from Failed Assessments?" S. E. Finn, Chair. Reprinted in Finn, S. E. (2007). *In our clients' shoes: Theory and techniques of Therapeutic Assessment* (pp. 179–192). Erlbaum.

Finn, S. E. (2005). How psychological assessment taught me compassion and firmness. *Journal of Personality Assessment, 84,* 27–30.

Finn, S. E. (2011). Journeys through the valley of death: Multimethod psychological assessment and personality transformation in long-term psychotherapy. *Journal of Personality Assessment, 93,* 123–141.

Karpman, S. B. (1968). Fairy tales and script drama analysis. *Transactional Analysis Bulletin, 7,* 39–43.

Schore, A. N. (2012). *The science of the art of psychotherapy.* Norton.

Weiss, J. (1993). *How psychotherapy works.* Guilford.

Chapter 11

Use of the Adult Attachment Projective Picture System in the Middle of a Long-Term Psychotherapy*

Can clinicians use assessment tools in the middle of long-term psychotherapy to help clients deepen their work and progress in their healing? I have long been interested in this question, particularly in reference to the Rorschach (Meyer et al., 2011) and the Minnesota Multiphasic Personality Inventory–2 (MMPI–2; Butcher, Dahlstrom, Graham, Tellegen, & Kaemmer, 1989; Finn, 1994, 1996b, 2007). In this article, I present a case in which I employed a relatively new test, the Adult Attachment Projective Picture System (AAP; George & West, 2012), to impact a psychotherapy that was in serious difficulty.

My Background with the AAP

I first became aware of the AAP in 2003 through a presentation given by Carol George, one of the test's developers, at the annual meeting of the Society for Personality Assessment. I had been reading about attachment theory for years and had considered pursuing training in the administration and interpretation of the Adult Attachment Interview (AAI; George, Kaplan, & Main, 1984/1985/1996), but I never did because of the time required to administer, transcribe, and code an AAI. I could not see a way that such a time-consuming procedure would ever be viable in my clinical practice. I was immediately struck by the potential clinical utility of the AAP, and I invited Dr. George to Austin to give a presentation to my colleagues at the Center for Therapeutic Assessment. Shortly after that, a group of us decided to pursue formal training in the AAP, and Dr. George began coming monthly to Austin to work with us. This was an extremely rich training experience, and later I write more about its impact on my clinical work.

Although I eventually decided not to pursue certification as a reliable coder of the AAP (I pay others to code the protocols that I administer), I frequently

* This chapter is based on an article previously published in the *Journal of Personality Assessment*, 2011, 93(5), 427-433. Use of the Adult Attachment Projective Picture System (AAP) in the Middle of a Long-Term Psychotherapy. Article DOI: 10.1080/00223891.2011.595744 https://www.tandfonline.com/

DOI: 10.4324/9781003602231-11

use the AAP in my practice of Therapeutic Assessment and have also used it with clients in psychotherapy. The case I present here concerns the impact of the AAP on a long-term psychotherapy client, and I chose it because it illustrates the potential therapeutic utility of the AAP. At the end of this article I make more comments about the general utility of the AAP in clinical practice.

Case Presentation

"Mike" was an attractive man in his late 40s who I met 4 years before the events I describe, when he and his wife, Sally, were referred to our clinic by friends for a couples' assessment. I was unable to do the assessment myself, so I referred the couple to two colleagues, while agreeing to consult. Sally complained that Mike was condescending and did not really care about her; he saw her as unreliable, childlike, and incredibly selfish. Shortly after that assessment, Mike and Sally separated, with plans to divorce. Mike then called and asked if I would see him for individual therapy, and I agreed. I had been working with Mike in individual therapy for about 2 years before I had the idea of asking him to do the AAP with me.

Early Therapy Sessions

As you might imagine, the early part of Mike's therapy concerned his separation from Sally and the prospect of their divorce. At the time, they had been married for 12 years and had three small children to whom Mike was devoted. He anguished over the thought of hurting his children, and we spent many hours discussing whether it was better for him to stay with Sally—in a marriage that he found increasingly toxic—until his children were older, or whether he should leave then. I was struck by how intense his guilt feelings were and by how overly responsible he felt for Sally and his children.

I commented on this and learned that Mike had been in a caretaker role in various relationships since he was a child. His father was sickly and his mother quite depressed, needy, and egocentric. Mike had taken care of his younger siblings, done most of the chores around the house, and been a star athlete and pupil to boot. The only things that seemed to get him attention and approval from his parents were his academic and athletic achievements, and Mike soared to the top of his chosen sport, earning national titles and at one point almost making it onto the U.S. Olympic team. Although his many activities kept him busy, Mike also remembered many lonely times as a child. He told of one poignant episode when he was eight, had nothing to do, and felt tremendously alone and sad. He went outside and started raking leaves until he felt better. During this period of psychotherapy, Mike came weekly to our sessions, cried a few times, and seemed to become less anxious and guilty.

As we talked about his history as a caretaker, it eventually became clear to Mike that he wanted to end his marriage, and he and Sally finalized their divorce about 6 months after I started seeing him, a year into their separation. I think Mike's decision was aided by the fact that he was starting to get a lot of attention from women he met, for he was an exceptionally attractive and financially successful man. He began dating, still saw his kids almost every day, and succeeded in setting better limits with his parents, who continually asked for his help and attention. It was at this point that Mike's therapy took an unusual course that lasted for over a year.

Second Phase of Therapy

It took some months for me to recognize the pattern that characterized the second phase of Mike's treatment. He would come weekly for a series of 6 to 10 sessions, then disappear for a month or more. Eventually, Mike would call and ask to discuss some crisis, usually concerning Sally or one of the women he was dating. Sometimes, Mike would tell me that he was taking a break from therapy, and that his life was going extremely well and he had nothing to talk about. Other times, he would call and cancel his scheduled appointment, telling me that he would be out of town for work and would call me when he got back. Sometimes he did, in fact, call; other times he would wait until he felt some urgency.

I was not put off by these comings and goings, but I was curious about them. After the second or third repetition, I began to ask Mike to talk about what he was experiencing when he felt like leaving therapy, something he found quite difficult. The most I could get him to say was that he was used to handling things on his own, preferred that way of doing things, and did not want to waste his or my time if he could manage by himself. Although his pattern of coming and going in therapy continued, he did start to get wise to himself and would laugh when he would tell me once again that he thought he was "all cured." Also, after several rounds of this cycle—at my suggestion—Mike came a couple of weeks longer than he otherwise might have, to see what it was like to be in therapy when he did not have an urgent agenda. I remembered how trapped he had felt as a child by his parents' needs, and I never attempted to constrain him when he wanted to go.

During this period, I also kept in mind various aspects of Mike's test results from when he and Sally did the couples assessment, and this helped me be patient with him. (See Figure 11.1 for Mike's MMPI–2 and Table 11.1 for the lower portion of his Structural Summary.) He was one of those clients I have written about elsewhere (Finn, 1996a, 2011b) who had a pretty clean MMPI–2 profile and a much more distressed Rorschach. There was a slight elevation on Scale 6 (Paranoia) of the MMPI–2, which we interpreted at the time of the assessment as due to Mike's feeling persecuted by Sally. Because of the discrepancy between his MMPI–2 and Rorschach, I knew that Mike ran the risk of opening "Pandora's box" and accessing a lot of underlying depression and shame if he really settled into a long-term uncovering psychotherapy. I also remembered that he had an Isolation Index of .25, no cooperative movements (COP), and only 2 Pure H responses in his 32-response Rorschach protocol. Clearly, as he

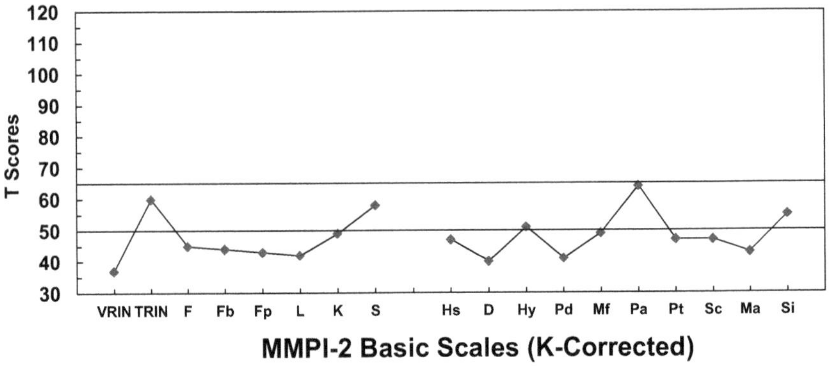

Figure 11.1 Mike's MMPI–2 profile done during the couples' assessment.

Notes: VRIN = Variable Response Inconsistency scale; TRIN = True-Response Inconsistency scale; F = Infrequency; Fb = Back F; Fp = Infrequency Psychopathology; L = Lie; K = Defensiveness; S = Superlative Self-Presentation; Hs = Scale 1, Hypochondriasis; D = Scale 2, Depression; Hy = Scale 3, Hysteria; Pd = Scale 4, Psychopathic Deviate; Mf = Scale 5, Masculinity-Femininity; Pa = Scale 6, Paranoia; Pt = Scale 7, Psychasthenia; Sc = Scale 8, Schizophrenia; Ma = Scale 9, Hypomania; Si = Scale 0, Social Introversion. Minnesota Multiphasic Personality Inventory-2 (MMPI-2) Profile for Basic Scales.

had told me, he was a "solo flier" from way back, who had learned to navigate treacherous territory without others' assistance. It seemed a lot to expect that he would start depending on me.

As this second year of treatment continued, however, Mike began to feel more and more upset with himself. Much of his distress centered on his dating relationships with women. Not unexpectedly, Mike showed the same kinds of conflicts in that arena as he did in his therapy relationship with me. He would meet a new woman, get intensely involved in the relationship, then start to get cold feet after about four to six weeks. He would notice things about the woman he did not like, worry that he was "settling," then eventually break off the relationship, usually to the woman's great surprise, leaving her angry and hurt. This pattern repeated itself again and again, until Mike realized there was something going on in him that made it impossible for him to commit to anyone. We began talking about what might be happening, and how to learn more about his internal dilemma. I had recently completed the basic AAP training, and I suggested to Mike that we do the AAP to see if it would shed any light on his concerns. He was enthusiastic and also agreed to repeat the MMPI–2 and Rorschach.

Table 11.1 The lower portion of Mike's Rorschach CS Structural Summary done during the couples' assessment

Ratios, Percentages, and Derivations

R	= 32	L	= 1.00			FC:CF+C	= 3:0	COP = 0		AG = 1	
						Pure C	= 0	GHR:PHR	= 2:4		
EB	= 4:15	EA	= 5.5	EBPer	= N/A	SmC':WSmC	= 0:1.5	a:p	= 5:4		
eb	= 5:3	es	= 8	D	= 0	Afr	= 0.75	Food	= 0		
		Adj es	= 6	Adj D	= 0	S	= 3	SumT	= 2		
						Blends/R	= 4:32	Human Cont	= 6		
FM	= 2	SumC'	= 0	SumT	= 2	CP	= 0	PureH	= 2		
m	= 3	SumV'	= 1	SumY	= 0			PER	= 0		
								Isol Indx	= 0.25		
a:p	= 5:4	Sum6	= 7	XA%	= 0.63	Zf	= 14	3r+(2)/R	= .36		
Ma:Mp	= 5:1	Lv2	= 0	WDA%	= 0.75	W:D:Da	= 12:14:6	Fr+rF	= 0		
2AB+Art+Ay	= 7	WSum6	= 16	X-%	= 0.37	W:M	= 12:4	SumV	= 0		
MOR	= 1	M-	= 0	S-	= 0	Zd	=+ 7.5	FD	= 0		
		Mnone	= 0	P	= 5	PSV	= 0	An+Xy	= 3		
				X+%	= 0.52	DQ+	= 5	MOR	= 1		
				Xu%	= 0.11	DQv	= 0	H:(H)+Hd+Hd	= 2:4		
PTI = 0		DEPI = 5		CDI = 4		S-CON = 3		HVI = No		OBS = No	

Mid-Therapy Assessment

I asked my colleague who had tested Mike 2 years earlier to administer the Rorschach and AAP, and Mike and I came up with the following assessment questions for the testing:

- *Why don't I let people get really close to me, and/or myself get really close to them?*
- *What keeps me from diving into a relationship, or just saying no, instead of dancing around and sending mixed signals?*
- *Why don't I feel I deserve what I accomplish?*

Before turning to the AAP results, let me briefly discuss Mike's MMPI–2 and Rorschach results.

MMPI–2 (see Figure 11.2). This profile was similar to the one Mike produced in the initial couples' assessment. As you can see, there were no indications of significant psychological distress or psychopathology, and I felt the profile accurately depicted the way Mike presented himself to others, as a man who was psychologically healthy and "had it all together." I noted from Mike's scores on Scale 2 and Scale 7 that he rated himself as less depressed and anxious than the average man in the MMPI–2 normative sample.

Rorschach. Mike's repeat Rorschach Structural Summary was also not that dissimilar from his previous one. As shown in Table 11.2, the protocol suggested that Mike dampened his emotions (FC:CF+C = 2/0; Lambda = 1.23; SumC'/WSumc = 2/1), and relied on intellectualization (2AB + Art + Ay = 5) and other defenses to protect him from underlying feelings of depression, low self-esteem, and shame (DEPI = 6, Vista = 1, 3r+(2)/R = .32). His Affective Ratio (Afr = .81) suggested that he shut down his feelings because he had a tendency to get caught up in his emotions and to have trouble backing away from them. I was pleased to see that there was somewhat more human content in the protocol [Pure H = 3; H + Hd + (H) + (Hd) = 10]—compared to the previous testing [Pure H = 2; H + Hd + (H) + (Hd) = 6]. Also, the Isolation Index (.03) was now in the normal range—whereas the previous year it had been .28—and Mike had one cooperative movement (COP) score, whereas there had been none in the previous protocol. Last, the GHR/PHR ratio was now in the positive direction, indicating that Mike had a more positive view of human interactions. In fact, the Rorschach suggested that Mike had changed over the 2-year interval I had seen him, was more aware of people now and of their potential to be helpful to him and was more likely to turn to them for assistance than he had been earlier.

As mentioned earlier, I have written (Finn, 1996a, 2011b) about the pattern of test results reflected in Mike's assessment, where clients show little distress or disturbance on their MMPI–2 profile (without evidence of intentional defensiveness) and significant distress and disturbance on their Rorschach. At our

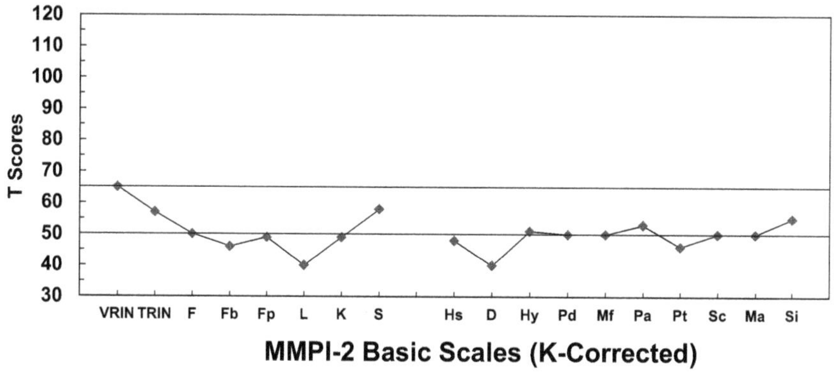

Figure 11.2 Mike's MMPI–2 profile from the mid-therapy assessment.

clinic, many of the clients with this pattern are independent, high-functioning people, who are very successful in business; well-liked by coworkers, neighbors, and friends; and easy to treat in the initial phases of psychotherapy. But these individuals are often unsuccessful in intimate relationships and can become highly disorganized in the middle of long-term psychotherapy if they start to become emotionally dependent on their therapists. Their good MMPI–2 profiles reflect their good character defenses and coping mechanisms; their disturbed Rorschachs reveal a level of "underlying disturbance" that they keep in check with these defenses. I felt I understood Mike's dilemma of change from his Rorschach and MMPI–2 and could answer his assessment questions. Thus, I was curious about what additional light would be shed by the AAP.

AAP. Dr. George coded and classified Mike's AAP protocol. Table 11.3 shows the Coding Summary sheet for Mike's stories. Mike's attachment status was classified as dismissing from the AAP because of his prominent use of the defense of deactivation.[1] All seven of Mike's stories contained Ds (deactivation) markers. However, as can also be seen, all of his stories also showed evidence of cognitive disconnection[2] (coded E in the table).

Here is the transcript of Mike's story to the AAP card labeled Departure, which shows a man and woman standing together with suitcases:

> Um, it looks to me like a couple, perhaps traveling together, um with their hands um in their pockets. They're giving me the idea that they're either in an argument or under stress of some kind, um maybe trying to come up with a plan of some kind about what to do next. Maybe they missed their plane or one of their bags didn't get on the plane and they're waiting, trying to figure out what to do next, wondering if they should get a taxi somewhere. I don't

Table 11.2 The lower portion of Mike's Rorschach CS Structural Summary done mid-therapy

Ratios, Percentages, and Derivations

R	= 29	L	= 1.23			FC:CF+C	= 2:0	COP = 1	AG = 2
						Pure C	= 0	GHR:PHR	= 6:5
EB	= 6:1.0	EA	= 7.0	EBPer	= N/A	SmC':WSmC	= 2:1.0	a:p	= 8:2
eb	= 4: 4	es	= 8	D	= 0	Afr	= 0.81	Food	= 0
		Adj es	= 8	Adj D	= 0	S	= 3	SumT	= 1
						Blends/R	= 2:29	Human Cont	= 10
FM	= 3	SumC'	= 2	SumT	= 1	CP	= 0	PureH	= 3
m	= 1	SumV	= 1	SumY	= 0			PER	= 3
								Isol Indx	= 0.03
a:p	= 8:2	Sum6	= 4	XA%	= 0.66	Zf	= 10	3r+(2)/R	= .32
Ma:Mp	= 5:1	Lv2	= 0	WDA%	= 0.74	W:D:Dd	= 4:19:6	Fr+rF	= 0
2AB+Art+Ay	= 5	WSum6	= 8	X-%	= 0.34	W:M	= 4:6	SumV	= 0
MOR	= 1	M	= 0	S-	= 0	Zd	= +7.5	FD	= 0
		Mnone	= 0	P	= 7	PSV	= 0	An+Xy	= 3
				X+%	= 0.52	DQ+	= 7	MOR	= 1
				Xu%	= 0.14	DQv	= 0	H:(H)+Hd+(Hd)	= 3:7
PTI= 0	DEPI = 6			CDI = 1		S-CON = 2		HVI = No	OBS = No

> sense they're in a fight; generally you would see one of their hands being out showing expression if they were in an argument or something. Both act like they're in some kind of a pickle and trying to figure out what the next move is going to be. (**SF: What might happen next?)** Well, um, something tells me they're going to come up with a plan of action, and eventually pull their hands out of pockets, pick up their bags, and go somewhere but they're not to that point yet of knowing what to do. **(SF: What are they thinking or feeling?**) I don't know ... sadness maybe is a word for it. It looks like both are unhappy and um sort of resigned to the fact that something has gone wrong or is going wrong or something not so pleasant is happening to them and they're just trying to figure out what next the move is. **(SF: Anything else**?) No.

You can see in this story Mike's tendency to approach relational events intellectually, by trying to "figure out what to do next." The couple is functionally involved in trying to solve the problem they face, but there is little sense of their being connected emotionally. You can also see the uncertainty Mike shows over how to handle emotional scenes.

Here is Mike's story to one of the alone cards, called Bench, which shows a person sitting on a bench with their head bowed and knees up.

> Um, looks like a young lady sitting on a bench, uh, it looks like she's trying to deal with a problem or is sad and um not sure how to handle it maybe trying to hide her grief that she's feeling from other people that might be nearby so they can't see her crying. Her head down kind of implies she's alone with her thoughts and trying to figure out how to handle her situation. Um, it looks like it must be in public place of some kind, I wouldn't expect to see a bench like that in someone's house, so maybe she's in a park or on a bench on the street somewhere. It looks like she's barefooted but can't really tell about what her clothing is, but it definitely looks like features or body shape of a woman, maybe in mid-teens to mid-20s and she just appears sad and lonely. **[SF: What led up to it?]** Um I sense that she had been walking, having a lot of thoughts in her head, confused, and just couldn't take it anymore and finally just had to sit down and cry it out. **[SF: What might happen next?]** Well, I think in a while the grief will pass to some extent and she will put her feet down on the ground, sit there a few minutes, figure out what to do next, and eventually get up and walk away. **[SF: Anything else?]** No.

In this story it is easy for us to see Mike's consternation about how to handle grief and sadness, and his belief that he has to hide such feelings from others. Notice that no one comes to help the character with her feelings; she handles

Table 11.3 Coding Summary Sheet for Mike's Adult Attachment Projective Picture System responses

Dyadic	*Personal Exp*	*Synch*	*Ds*	*E*	*Seg*	*Alone*	*Agency*	*Personal Exp*	*Connected*	*Ds*	*E*	*Seg*
Deprt (3)	0	1 Couple Functional	Ds	E		Window (2)	"2" Girl contemplates	0	1	Ds	E	
Bed (5)	0	1 M/son Delay Functional quality	Ds	E		Bench (4)	"2"→ get up Lady Problem solving "thinking"	0	3	Ds	E	
Ambul (6)	0	1 Fractured functional comfort by a stranger Woman/boy/ several ideas as to who is in ambulance	Ds	E	R	Cemtry (7)	"2" Man Reflect, remembers	0	*not coded* *father → parent or grandparent*	Ds	E	
						Corner (8)	1 Kid Rej	0	*not coded*	Ds	E	R

Classification: Dismissing, with a lot of underlying cognitive disconnection.

them on her own and eventually just "puts her feet down on the ground" and walks away. For me, the loneliness in this story mirrored the loneliness and isolation in both Mike's childhood and his adult life.

Summary/Discussion Session. With previous clients, I had taken the case summary that Dr. George had written and then used it to talk to the clients about their AAP results. This time I wanted to do something different, and at my request Dr. George wrote a "client report" for me to use with Mike. He and I had already spent a session talking about his MMPI–2 and Rorschach scores when I handed him this report and asked him to read it. (See Table 11.4 for excerpts.)

Mike read Dr. George's report silently, then put it down and exclaimed, "This is amazing! It nails me!" We then went through the report slowly and talked about it and its relevance to Mike's main Assessment Question of why he couldn't let himself get close to others. We agreed he would take the report home and read it and come back later in the week. I got the following email the next morning:

> Steve,
>
> Had a pretty tough sleep last night. Been thinking about all of the strategies that I have used for so long to control my feelings and it all feels like it has been kind of a big sham. I am feeling better now but am realizing that I am not quite sure who I am any more if I am not the image that I created for myself … I even questioned last night as I tossed and turned whether I really might suffer from depression. As I reflect on my childhood and my life, I think I have had these feelings of suffering and inadequacy my whole life. Should I consider medicine? I went for a bike ride and of course feel much better. I am unsure of how to cope. I don't want to run away from these feelings and want to experience them. Any thoughts?
>
> See … I can reach out for help. Mike

I wrote back to Mike immediately and reassured him that his coping mechanisms were not a big sham, but represented his best effort over time to handle a difficult and complex situation. I praised him for reaching out for support and told him it was okay to take "breaks" from the feelings, and to call me if he wanted to talk before our next session.

Post-Assessment Phase of Psychotherapy

For a year after the AAP assessment, Mike worked steadily in therapy with me—with no breaks! The reassessment, and specifically the AAP report and our ensuing discussions, were a catalyst that helped him access the grief and painful affect he had been avoiding. During this period, Mike felt a lot, including—as I think was unavoidable—some pretty significant depression. He did

Table 11.4 Excerpts from AAP Report written for Mike by Dr. Carol George

What Your AAP Results Mean: The Dismissing Attachment Adaptation
The Adult Attachment Projective (AAP) assesses an individual's fundamental experience and expectations for him- or herself in caring and protecting relationships. Research has shown that what we expect to happen in such relationships is established first in early childhood through experiences with parents. It's as if such relationships help us construct an internal "map" or "picture" of how caring relationships are likely to go....A good metaphor to use for early attachment is that of a protective "dance." In the early years, child and parent are dance partners on life's stage, a stage that confronts every child with challenges, stress, illness, and danger. The young child's role in the dance partnership is to let the parent know clearly and directly that he or she desires or needs care. The parent's role in the dance partnership is to respond promptly and appropriately, thinking carefully about what the child and situation require in order to help the child manage his or her distress...
In many instances, the attachment dance happens easily in a way that appears to be "programmed" by our biology, and an individual is left with what is called a "secure" state of mind regarding attachment ... In other instances, however, the early attachment dance does not happen easily or smoothly. This produces individuals whose attachment state of mind is what we call "insecure"...
Mike, the AAP indicates that your attachment status is what psychologists call "insecure-dismissing." People with this attachment classification generally had early caregivers who were—for various reasons—unresponsive or not well attuned to their children's needs for care and protection. The expectation dismissing individuals developed was, "When I am scared or in need of comfort or protection, it's best if I take care of my needs on my own. I'll reserve asking my parents for help to those times when I feel really distressed. " As a result, such children learned to "armor their hearts" against longing, and deal with emotional upset all by themselves through various practical and functional behaviors...
As adults, the internal "map" of dismissing individuals automatically leads them to select relationships, activities, and life paths that prioritize work, achievement, and intellect over intimacy. Relationships with friends, parents, spouse, and children *are* important to them, but family and friends may complain that they don't *feel* that important to dismissing individuals. This is because dismissing individuals value their individual strengths and abilities to solve problems—qualities that are not balanced with emotional connections in relationships...
There is a paradox about the emotional life of many dismissing individuals. On the whole, they seem to be strong, confident, capable people who have very little emotional distress. "Negative" emotions, such as sadness, distress, loneliness, anger, and even fear, are considered private and sometimes seen as unimportant, unnecessary, or interfering with the problem-solving process. As a result, many dismissing individuals push such feelings aside and are no longer aware of them fully...Avoiding negative emotions also creates a dilemma about becoming more connected emotionally to themselves and other people: If they do so, dismissing individuals may first have to deal with underlying feelings of insecurity, rejection, unworthiness, sadness, and anxiety.

start taking an antidepressant and joined a psychotherapy group for added support. He started to rely on me regularly for emotional support, and this gradually generalized to his turning to friends. He even took a break from dating during this period while we worked on the issues detailed in the AAP write-up. In some of our sessions, we went through Mike's AAP stories in detail, so he could see his own defensive operations at work. This period of therapy was also incredibly productive in terms of Mike's remembering more about his childhood. I remember one session in particular where we sat with a scrapbook of pictures from Mike's early years, and he sobbed as he recalled how alone and lost he had felt during those years. He even asked for a hug at the end of the session, which I gave willingly.

My therapeutic goals during this period of our work were (a) to help Mike access split-off anger and grief that he had had to put aside while growing up to survive, (b) to support Mike as he got in touch with these emotions, so that he would not be overwhelmed and retraumatized by them, (c) to teach Mike that turning to me and other people for emotional support helped him and that it addressed his dilemma of being a solo flier versus being emotionally overwhelmed, (d) to help Mike construct a coherent narrative of how his early upbringing related to his difficulties in adult intimate relationships, and (e) to help reduce Mike's shame. My sense was that we made good progress on all these goals.

Unfortunately, this "working through" phase of Mike's psychotherapy was cut short, in my opinion, by my telling Mike that I would be ending my long-term psychotherapy practice the following year (10 months later). (I continue to do assessments and brief psychotherapy.) Because of Mike's background, I wanted to give us ample time to say good-bye, and I fully expected that we would continue our work for the next 10 months. However, several weeks later, Mike called and left a phone message saying that he "was doing extremely well" and would be taking a break from individual therapy while continuing with group therapy. I called and urged him to come in and talk about his decision, but Mike did not call back. I also contacted Mike's group therapist, who promised to follow up with Mike; I heard back that Mike denied that his decision had anything to do with my closing my therapy practice. Mike apparently insisted that he just did not need the individual therapy at that time. I felt sad, frustrated, and guilty, but I also trusted that the work Mike and I had done would have a positive impact.

Follow-Up

To my surprise and delight, Mike emailed me 11 months later, 2 weeks after the day I officially closed my therapy practice and asked to meet for a "check-up" session. I agreed, and when we met, he joyously told me about a new development in his life. He had been dating a woman steadily for 9 months, and they were starting to talk about getting married. Mike was happy to report that he felt no panic about the commitment, and he was clear in attributing this to our work together and thanked me profusely. I asked Mike what he felt had made the most difference, and he said he was still amazed by the accuracy of the AAP report and how "many tears" he had "locked away" without knowing. He said he had a much larger support network, and that he was setting good limits with his parents and with his ex-wife. I gently brought up his precipitous departure from the individual therapy, and he somewhat abashedly admitted that he had "had all he could take." He denied any anger about my closing my practice, and I let the topic go, satisfied that Mike and I had done what we could do given the circumstances, and that our work was enough to impact a major stuck point in his life.

Of course, I was aware that Mike had started dating his new woman friend shortly after he quit therapy with me. Did this mean that the new relationship was questionable? I did not think so. I reasoned that I had served as an auxiliary attachment figure for Mike during the latter phase of our therapy, and that he had learned that it felt good to lean on someone emotionally. When I announced that I would be leaving, Mike became aware of the pitfalls of using a therapist as an auxiliary attachment figure. (For example, the relationship is a business relationship and therefore can be terminated by the therapist.) Mike's finding a new attachment figure—in an adult romantic partner—was a healthier, more natural choice. I believed the work we had done made it possible for him to attach to his girlfriend, and that in fact, he no longer needed me or another therapist as he had previously. Six months after my meeting with Mike, I heard from a colleague (who saw a friend of Mike's in psychotherapy) that he was engaged to the woman he had been dating. I was delighted with this news, and of course, hope the best for Mike and his new wife. I am hoping that he might come to see me again in the future, and that if so, I might convince him that we should redo the AAP, so we could see how his attachment system is healing.[3]

Summary and Conclusions

In summary, the AAP was incredibly useful to me and my client, Mike, in many ways. First, the AAP—and the theory it is based on—gave me a coherent and parsimonious way to understand his relational challenges. Although some of the information derived from the AAP was contained in the MMPI–2 and Rorschach, the AAP spelled out the likely origin and nature of Mike's difficulties in detail, in a way that other tests could not. The AAP write-up seemed to lessen his shame; it resonated with him deeply, and it helped him see through his defenses. Of course, the slow and careful work I had done with Mike previously set the stage for his being able to use the AAP results, but Dr. George's write-up spoke to him forcefully and was the opportunity for an "optimal disintegration experience" (Dabrowski, 1967) that led him to his next piece of work in therapy.

Second, the AAP cards were "experience-near" for Mike, and he and I did very meaningful work as we discussed his stories and what they revealed about how he handled relationships. As I have done with other clients, in several therapy sessions, Mike and I "tried out" alternative stories to some of the cards, for example, with the girl in the bench card reaching out to others for help. In this way, Mike was able to feel his way into his own dilemma of change, to track the internal shifts he was experiencing, and to notice where he was still blocked. We both found these sessions extremely moving, and Mike repeatedly said that they were valuable. Of course, similar work can be done using the Thematic Apperception Test (Murray, 1943) or other picture story cards with clients, and I have previously published cases in which I did so (Finn, 2007). I find, however, that the AAP cards are extremely useful in stimulating discussions of attachment issues, because the cards were specifically designed to stimulate the attachment system (George & West, 2001).

Third, the AAP feedback helped direct Mike to material he had resisted bringing into therapy—the shortcomings of his early years. When I had gently approached this material earlier, Mike had always assured me that he had no resentment toward his parents and knew they had done the best they could. The even-handed neutrality of the AAP client report reassured Mike in a way that I had not been able to, that we could discuss ways his parents had failed him, while also not judging them. Dr. George's report was also perfect for a man who used intellectualization as a major coping mechanism, in that it rationally and coherently explained the connection between his childhood experiences and his current life struggles; it was also based on solid research.

Based on this case and other experiences with clients, I heartily recommend the AAP as a clinically rich assessment tool that has much to offer in a multimodal personality assessment battery. My colleagues and I now routinely include the AAP in adult assessments that concern relational issues and find it extremely valuable in framing clients' dilemmas around close relationships in ways they can understand. Because of its empirical grounding and its connection to the vast research on attachment, the AAP offers insights and information beyond what can be derived from other tests. The AAP is also useful in predicting the way clients will relate to psychotherapists, and I have been able to help other therapists with dismissing clients be patient with those clients' needs to "come and go" in therapy, as Mike did with me. The AAP is also accessible to clients, and the cards are quite emotionally arousing for many clients. In Therapeutic Assessment this provides many opportunities to dialogue with clients about their stories and their emotional experiences of the cards, which can lead to powerful assessment interventions.

Last, I would add that even if one chooses never to administer the AAP to clients, I believe that training in the instrument affords a wonderful way to learn deeply about attachment theory, which is useful in understanding many of our clients' dilemmas. I have found that my AAP training made me more empathic to clients. And there is growing agreement in our field that early attachment experiences are related to many of the difficulties experienced by our clients, and that when these difficulties are understood, they can be effectively addressed in psychotherapy (Fosha, 2000; Schore, 2003; Siegel, 1999; Stern, 2004). Many of us believe that the current integration of attachment theory, developmental neurobiology, and psychotherapy represents the cutting edge of clinical practice (Finn, 2011a). The AAP provides a wonderful entrée into this body of knowledge.

Notes

1 "Deactivation" is a psychological defense first named by Bowlby (1980) in which an individual shifts attention away from attachment events, figures, or emotions to avoid distressing affects.
2 Bowlby (1980) saw "cognitive disconnection" as a defensive process in which distressing emotions are disconnected from their true source, much as in displacement or splitting.
3 Mike did come to see me several years later and was happily married, but I did not ask him to repeat the AAP. However, I have written elsewhere Finn (2023) about the utility of repeatedly administering the AAP in long-term psychotherapy.

References

Bowlby, J. (1980). *Attachment and loss: Vol. 3. Loss: Sadness and depression.* Basic Books.
Butcher, J. N., Dahlstrom, W. G., Graham, J. R., Tellegen, A., & Kaemmer, B. (1989). *MMPI–2: Minnesota Multiphasic Personality Inventory–2: Manual for administration and scoring.* University of Minnesota Press.
Dabrowski, K. (1967). *Personality shaping through positive disintegration.* Little, Brown.
Finn, S. E. (1994, April). *Testing one's own clients mid-therapy with the Rorschach.* Paper presented at the Society for Personality Assessment annual meeting, Chicago, IL. Reprinted as Chapter 5 in Finn, S. E. (2007), *In our clients' shoes: Theory and techniques of Therapeutic Assessment* (pp. 45-53). Erlbaum.
Finn, S. E. (1996a). Assessment feedback integrating MMPI–2 and Rorschach findings. *Journal of Personality Assessment, 67*, 543–557.
Finn, S. E. (1996b). *A manual for using the MMPI–2 as a therapeutic intervention.* University of Minnesota Press.
Finn, S. E. (2007). *In our clients' shoes: Theory and techniques of Therapeutic Assessment.* Erlbaum.
Finn, S. E. (2011a, March). *Implications of recent research in neurobiology for psychological assessment.* Address given to the annual meeting of the Society for Personality Assessment, Boston, MA.

Finn, S. E. (2011b). Journeys through the valley of death: Multimethod psychological assessment and personality transformation in long-term psychotherapy. *Journal of Personality Assessment, 93*, 123–141.

Finn, S. E. (2023). From unresolved to earned secure attachment: The AAP as a powerful clinical tool in psychotherapy. In C. George, J. Wargo Aikens, & M. Lehmann (Eds.), *Clinical application of the Adult Attachment Projective Picture System* (pp. 97–109). Routledge.

Fosha, D. (2000). *The transforming power of affect: A model for accelerated change.* Basic Books.

George, C., Kaplan, N., & Main, M. (1984/1985/1996). *The Adult Attachment Interview.* University of California.

George, C., & West, M. (2001). The development and preliminary validation of a new measure of adult attachment: The Adult Attachment Projective. *Attachment and Human Development, 3*, 30–61.

George,C., & West, M. (2012). *The Adult Attachment Projective Picture System: Attachment theory and assessment in adults*. Guilford.

Meyer, G. J., Viglione, D. J., Mihura, J. L., Erard, R. E., & Erdberg, P. (2011). *The Rorschach Performance Assessment System (R-PAS)*. R-PAS.

Murray, H. A. (1943). *Thematic Apperception Test manual*. Harvard University Press.

Schore, A. N. (2003). *Affect regulation and the repair of the self.* Erlbaum.

Siegel, D. (1999). *The developing mind: Toward a neurobiology of human experience.* Guilford.

Stern, D. N. (2004). *The present moment in psychotherapy and everyday life*. Norton.

Chapter 12

Undoing Preoccupied Attachment Defenses Revealed through the Adult Attachment Projective Picture System

The Grief Underlying Cognitive Disconnection*

Susan was a 52-year-old woman I saw over 10 years ago with her husband Bob as part of a couples' Therapeutic Assessment. The two had been married for over 30 years and had three grown daughters. Both agreed that the marriage had never been easy but said that they had been struggling more during the last four years after their last daughter left home. Bob was a successful businessman who spent long hours at work. Susan had tolerated this while the children were at home, but after her youngest daughter went to college, she found herself increasingly lonely and angry at Bob over his unavailability. He had made some efforts to work less but said frankly that he preferred being at his office—where he was successful, admired, and liked—to being at home with an angry and complaining wife. He said that Susan should pursue her own interests, and that she was unfairly relying on him for her happiness. She agreed that she needed to develop individual friends and hobbies, and that this had been hard. But she also wanted to travel and do fun things with Bob and knew that it was no longer financially necessary for him to work so much.

As illustrated in the flowchart in Figure 12.1, after an initial session with the couple, we separate them and do complete individual assessments with each. During these sessions, we use various performance-based personality tests, including the Rorschach (Meyer, Viglione, Mihura, Erard, & Erdberg, 2011), the Wartegg Drawing Completion Test (Crisi & Palm, 2018), the Early Memory Procedure (Bruhn, 1990), and the Adult Attachment Projective Picture System (AAP; George & West, 2012). As explained in Chapter 11, the AAP is a valid projective test of adult attachment status, and we have found it very useful in our couples' Therapeutic Assessments because of how individual attachment status affects intimate relationships. For example, as you may have already guessed, Bob's attachment classification from the AAP was "Dismissing" (sometimes

* This chapter is adapted from a paper presented at the XXI International Congress of Rorschach and Projective Methods, July 17, 2014, Istanbul, Turkey as part of a symposium, "Using Projective Tests to Help Clients Access Split-off Emotions," Stephen E. Finn, Chair.

DOI: 10.4324/9781003602231-12

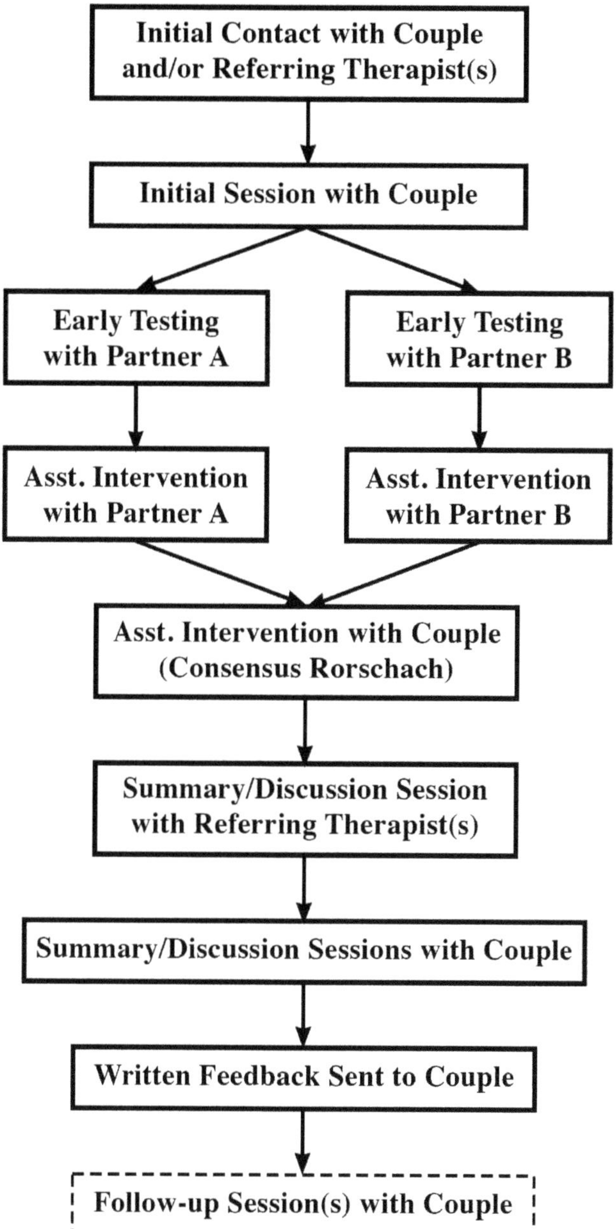

Figure 12.1 Flowchart of Therapeutic Assessment with couples.

called Avoidant) and Susan's was "Preoccupied" (sometimes called Anxious/ Ambivalent). Bob showed a typical dismissing approach to attachment distress: he avoided emotional situations and threw himself into work, in part to soothe himself. Susan showed a typical preoccupied pattern: she worried, got angry, and obsessed about past hurts, without ever reaching resolution. The combination of these two styles formed a perfect systemic storm, where Susan was an angry pursuer and Bob was a resentful avoider. Neither knew how to interrupt this dance, and it was clearly damaging the relationship as it went on. Of note, both people had even spent time working previously in individual therapy, and each seemed to have some appreciation of where their attachment schemas came from. Susan's mother had died when she was 4, and she got very little support around this event. Her father then quickly married another woman who was the quintessential "wicked stepmother"—treating Susan harshly and showing obvious preference for her own biological daughters. Susan knew all these events and could connect them intellectually to her feelings of abandonment. Likewise, Bob understood that his family "didn't do feelings" and that he had grown up largely fending for himself. Early on, he discovered that hard work and achievement made him feel good about himself, and he became a star athlete, straight-A student, and very successful businessman. He knew that he avoided feelings and that he had no idea how to address Susan's distress. But for both people, these cognitive understandings did not help them have better interactions or have more empathy for the other person.

The incident I relate occurred during the Extended Inquiry of Susan's AAP, after I had just completed the standardized administration. Here is her story to one of the AAP stimuli (called "Bench"--depicting an individual curled up on a bench alone) with the AAP coding marked to the side:

Bench	
Now this girl, um I think to me I think it looks like a girl probably	Disconnect
kind of young she looks young to me um and she looks like she is	Agency:
either tired…or um…*thinking* about something, maybe worried.	internalized
Um…I feel like she's kind of been there I don't think she just got	secure base
there I think she's been there sitting there um but I think that	Disconnect
she's probably um either *thinking* hard about something or worried	Agency:
about something or tired. *(SF: What might have led up to it?)* She	internalized
could, she could have had a she could have been like either had	secure base
a fight with somebody or she could have um, she could have just	
been working and really tired just kind of taking a break kind of	Disconnect
resting or she could have had something um happen. I do think	
it's somebody young because I don't think it's easy to get in that	Disconnect
position (laughs). So I do think it's just something kind of like that.	
Kind of like she looks like, like something is maybe bothering her.	
But you know it could be like even, it could be even like a young	
kid like there just playing -and-seek. It could be something even	Disconnect
like that where you put your head down to play hide and seek. *(SF:*	
What might happen next?) I think that she at some point will, will	
lift up her head unfold her arms and get off that bench and go, go	
do something else. *(SF: Anything else?) No.*	Agency: action

The "Disconnect" marker to the side is for an AAP code called "Cognitive Disconnection" that is typical of people with preoccupied attachment status (Bowlby, 1973). It is coded when people tell multiple storylines to a single picture without ever settling on a single story, are uncertain about their stories, or have themes of worry or anger in their stories (George & West, 2012). In attachment theory, this is seen as a coping mechanism that keeps the person from facing the emotionally distressing impact of the scene depicted. All of Susan's stories were full of uncertainty and cognitive disconnection, and I was pretty sure that if she did not use this way of distracting herself, she would connect on a deeper level with the scenes, and with many painful feelings she had pushed out of awareness in order to survive her difficult childhood.

After the AAP, the following discussion occurred:

SF: How was that for you?
S: OK...It was hard though to decide on the stories, because each scene could represent so many things.
SF: I noticed that. It seemed that often it was hard to decide on a single story.
S: Yes, the pictures are so ambiguous.
SF: They are. But may I ask...do you generally have trouble making up your mind when things are ambiguous?
S: Oh yes, it's really hard for me to make decisions, and it often takes me a long time. Bob gets really frustrated because he can make decisions in seconds. I don't think his decisions are always the best ones, but he doesn't fret the way I do.
SF: And does that fretting hold you back?
S: I guess it does. That's one reason I haven't figured out what to do with my time now that my daughter has left. There are so many possibilities, I just don't know what to pursue.
SF: And I think that happened in the stories too. Let me read a few and see what you think. [Reads several stories.]
S: Yes, I had trouble making up my mind.
SF: I see that. And while it didn't really matter, it did interfere with the flow of your stories.
S: Yes. And it makes me look unsure of myself.
SF: I think that's right.

I then asked Susan to do an experiment with me. I handed her back each of the cards and asked her to tell definitive stories with single plot lines. This wasn't easy for her to do, and I had to coach her at several points when she started waffling. On her own initiative, she also decided to stop saying "Maybe..." or "Probably..." as she told the stories. This is what happened when we got to the Bench card, the fourth in the set:

S: I think that…there I go again [catching herself being uncertain] *…this girl has just had something happen to her, and she is sitting on a bench alone sobbing and wishing she could escape her life.*

SF: What happened before?

S: An adult who was supposed to be kind to her was vicious instead.

SF: Go ahead and say who it was…it's your story.

S: Her stepmother was incredibly mean to her in front of a group of guests, saying that she wasn't smart or pretty and was never going to amount to anything.

SF: What is she thinking or feeling?

S: (Starts to cry.) *She feels humiliated, alone…desperate. She can't believe that her father left her alone with this terrible woman, and that he won't protect her at all. Her stepmother complains to him about her and he believes her, without ever asking her what is going on.*

SF: And what happens afterwards?

S: She manages to make it through until she can leave home, but she feels terrified and alone for years afterwards. (Sobbing hard.)

I waited for Susan to compose herself and when she did, she verified that the new story was a reflection of what she had experienced growing up. I said how sorry I was that this had happened to her, and I mirrored how strong she was to have made it through. With very little help from me, Susan was then able to see how these events were influencing her reactions to Bob and how overdetermined her feelings of abandonment were. She got to a calmer place and left my office.

After this event happened, Susan immediately started being calmer and more insightful in meetings with Bob and less angry with him during the day. With help, she still expressed her desire to travel and do fun things with him, but the tone of angry resentment was no longer there, and he began to respond positively. Of course, Bob had his own parallel work to do during the assessment, which I won't get into here. But I can attest that at the end of the assessment, the couple was in a much better place.

References

Bowlby, J. (1973). *Attachment and loss, vol. 2*. Basic Books.

Bruhn, A. R. (1990). *Earliest childhood memories: Vol. 1. Theory and application to clinical practice*. Praeger.

Crisi, A., & Palm. J. (2018). *The Crisi Wartegg System: Manual for administration, coding, and interpretation*. Routledge.

George, C., & West, M. (2012). *The Adult Attachment Projective Picture System*. Guilford.

Meyer, G. J., Viglione, D. J., Mihura, J. L., Erard, R. E., & Erdberg, P. (2011). *The Rorschach Performance Assessment System (R-PAS)*. R-PAS.

Chapter 13

"If Only I Had Looked!"

How Polyvagal Theory Helped a Client Rewrite Her Core Narrative*

Polyvagal Theory and Its Implications

In 1995 Stephen Porges, a prominent psychiatrist and psychophysiologist, published an influential paper on what has come to be called "Polyvagal Theory." Porges's theory was original in proposing a new understanding of the autonomic nervous system (ANS) from a simple fight/flight/freeze model to an evolutionarily evolved system with three aspects: the Social Engagement System (governed by the myelinated ventral branch of the vagal nerve), the Mobilization System (related to the sympathetic nervous system), and the Immobilization System (regulated by the unmyelinated dorsal vagal complex). Porges claimed that the Immobilization System was the oldest, evolving around 500 million years ago; the Mobilization System developed next, around 400 million years ago; and the Social Engagement System was the most recently evolved, from around 200 million years ago (Porges, 1995). I first read about Polyvagal Theory in the early 2000s and was intrigued by its clinical implications[1]

The "Neuroception" of Danger

Porges introduced the idea that the nervous system constantly scans for danger without our being aware of it. This is why we react to sudden loud noises or to other people's facial reactions without thinking. This fit with my observations that clients—especially those with histories of trauma—were unconsciously poised to see if it was safe to be with me. I began to pay even more attention to creating a secure relational environment.

* This chapter is adapted from a presentation I gave at the annual meeting of the Society for Personality Assessment, March 17, 2012, as part of a symposium, "Now It All Makes Sense: Using the Adult Attachment Projective Picture System as a Therapeutic Tool for Clients with Attachment Trauma," Carol George (Chair).

DOI: 10.4324/9781003602231-13

Social Connection as a Core Survival Mechanism

Polyvagal Theory emphasizes that social connection is essential for human survival and health and that "co-regulation" (the mutual calming of two nervous systems) is the main way we create a sense of safety. This idea helped me think deeply about how to help clients feel secure in my presence through a gentle word or smile and helped explain how clients feeling seen during psychological assessment could have such a therapeutic impact.

Dissociation as a Survival Mechanism

Although foreshadowed by Janet (1889), Ferenczi (1932/1988), and others, Porges emphasized that certain complex trauma responses such as dissociation or numbness were adaptive survival mechanisms and not psychological failures. He also explained that dissociation occurred when caring others are not available to help regulate overwhelming emotions. This emphasis helped me assess and treat clients with histories of trauma, as shown in the case example I present below.

Bottom-Up Healing

Porges's work had a huge influence on psychotherapy, emphasizing the importance of paying attention to body states and dissociation, and the need to use "bottom-up" methods rather than purely cognitive ones. This made me even more convinced about the therapeutic potential of such methods in psychological assessment.

Let me now introduce a Therapeutic Assessment that demonstrates the utility of Polyvagal Theory.

Mary

Mary was a 51-year-old woman who volunteered to take part in a Therapeutic Assessment as part of a live TA training I did. Although Mary had worked in psychotherapy at various points in her life—including a six-year treatment with a Jungian analyst—she was still greatly troubled by various aspects of her life, which were reflected in her main questions for the assessment:

Why Am I so Disconnected from My Feelings?

Mary described almost never knowing what she felt, and as a result, having great difficulty making decisions about things. Mary's current therapist complained that Mary never connected with her emotions during their sessions, and that instead she "told stories" that went on and on. I experienced this myself during our assessment sessions and initially found it quite difficult to interrupt Mary as she defensively avoided feelings.

Why Couldn't I Leave My Abusive Boyfriend?

Mary had only recently separated from a boyfriend she had been with for three years, who was possessive and emotionally and physically abusive to her. At the time of the assessment, she was still longing to be with him. This relationship fit a pattern in that both of Mary's previous long-term male partners had abused her physically and emotionally, and she had left those relationships with a great deal of difficulty.

Why Do I Have Uncontrolled Angry Outbursts and How Can I Prevent Them?

At various points in the past year, when being berated by her boyfriend, Mary had become uncharacteristically and violently angry, turning over tables and breaking objects, and afterwards had only a dim memory of her actions. Previously in her life, she had almost never expressed anger directly. In fact, she and the boyfriend had separated only after he made a complaint to the police that she had attempted to murder him during one of these episodes. He had cornered her in her kitchen and had his hands around her neck, and she had reached back, broken a wine glass, and cut him slightly on his arm.

Why Do I Feel Guilty Even When I Don't Have Reason To?

Mary constantly blamed herself for many things, including having cut her boyfriend during their last fight. Part of her knew she was justified, but she still felt guilty about it, in part because the police took her boyfriend's side and issued a restraining order against her. While Mary talked about all this, I sensed shame as well as guilt. I also hypothesized that anger was a split-off affect state for Mary. (See Chapter 7.)

Early in the TA I asked Mary to complete the MMPI-2 and the Early Memory Procedure (EMP). Figure 13.1 shows her basic MMPI-2 profile.

To me, this profile was further evidence that Mary's anger was not well integrated. People with the 3–4 code type are known to split off anger because they don't want to be seen as "mean" or aggressive, but they then lose control of their anger and explode or act out when it becomes too much for them. (Mary's therapist was also concerned about her excessive alcohol use.) The 4–7 code type embedded in the profile suggested that shame was a major underlying dynamic, and that when Mary "acted out," she likely felt unwarranted intense shame. In addition, Mary's extremely low score on Scale 5 (Mf) suggested that she had learned not to express anger directly and had difficulty protecting herself, especially with men. As I discussed the MMPI-2 with Mary, I learned that Mary had been left alone a lot in childhood and had early on adopted a caregiver role relative to her younger siblings. She remembered regularly cooking dinner for the

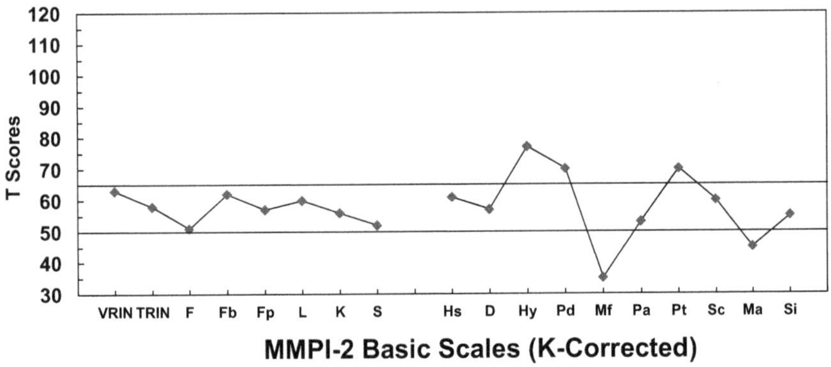

Figure 13.1 Mary's MMPI–2 profile. VRIN = Variable Response Inconsistency scale; TRIN = True-Response Inconsistency scale; F = Infrequency; Fb = Back F; Fp = Infrequency Psychopathology; L = Lie; K = Defensiveness; S = Superlative Self-Presentation; Hs = Scale 1, Hypochondriasis; D = Scale 2, Depression; Hy = Scale 3, Hysteria; Pd = Scale 4, Psychopathic Deviate; Mf = Scale 5, Masculinity-Femininity; Pa = Scale 6, Paranoia; Pt = Scale 7, Psychasthenia; Sc = Scale 8, Schizophrenia; Ma = Scale 9, Hypomania; Si = Scale 0, Social Introversion. Minnesota Multiphasic Personality Inventory-2 (MMPI-2) Profile for Basic Scales. Copyright © 2001 the Regents of the University of Minnesota. All rights reserved. Used by permission of the University of Minnesota Press. "MMPI-2" and "Minnesota Multiphasic Personality Inventory-2" are trademarks owned by the University of Minnesota Press.

family starting at around age 10. Her father was a cold, brusque man—a baker in their small town—who had never hugged her or said the words "I love you" to her before he died. Her mother was warmer, but she was a compulsive caregiver who spent her energy on an array of needy families in their town and gave very little nurturance to her own children.

An important piece of information emerged when I asked Mary to complete the Early Memory Procedure (Bruhn, 1990). Her most negative clear memory—which is believed to capture an underlying emotional schema related to the client's main problem—was of a trauma that was clearly unresolved. When she was 16, Mary was walking home from the house of her boyfriend one night, and a man dragged her off the street into an alley, pinned her to a wall, and raped her. This was a terrifying and life-altering experience for her. During the rape, Mary dissociated, talked to the man while keeping her head turned away, and thus she didn't see his face. The man also told Mary that if she went to the police that he would hunt her and her family down and kill them. She arrived home distressed and disheveled and told her parents what had happened. To their credit, they insisted on her going to the police, but there, things went badly. All but one of the police who interviewed Mary refused to believe that she didn't know who her assailant was and accused her of protecting someone. They aggressively questioned Mary for hours about this, with her repeatedly saying, "I didn't look." Then they dragged male friends of her boyfriend into the police station and interrogated them, although Mary had never suggested they were at fault. This made those friends, their girlfriends, and her boyfriend angry, and they shunned Mary. In short order, all the inhabitants of her small town walked by her on the street as if she didn't exist. They stopped buying at her father's bakery, and the family had no recourse but to send Mary away from home when she was just 18. She went to live with an aunt in a large city and attended university, where she did well in school but developed a drinking problem.

Mary also got little or no emotional support from others about the rape. When she told her father that she was afraid of the rapist returning to kill her, his response was, "Yes, well, they do say that the criminal often returns to the scene of the crime." Years later, when she told her female analyst about the incident, the woman reportedly said, "Well, if you're going to act like a lamb, you have to expect to be led to slaughter!" When I appeared shocked at the analyst's comment, Mary quickly explained that she herself was at fault because she had brought up the rape right at the end of a session, and the analyst hadn't really had time to think about what to say. But when I asked what was said the next time it was talked about, Mary said the incident was never discussed again in four years of subsequent therapy.

As we discussed this event, it was clear to me that Mary was still traumatized by the rape and that it was affecting her a great deal. I was also convinced that her shame about "not looking" was related to her series of abusive relationships, and that perhaps she was unconsciously trying to replay her trauma with a different, more adaptive outcome. I gingerly tried to suggest something along these lines, but Mary could not see a connection. I wanted to help Mary see herself in a more compassionate light, but I wasn't sure how I was going to accomplish this. Pondering this, in the next session I gave Mary the Adult Attachment Projective Picture System (AAP; George & West, 2012).

AAP Administration and Extended Inquiry

Mary struggled throughout the test, but on the very last card, which depicts a young boy in a corner with his head turned away and his hands up, she had even more difficulty than on the previous cards. In a fascinating fMRI study, Carol George and her colleagues have demonstrated that when women with histories of attachment trauma are shown this picture, their right amygdalas become highly activated (Buchheim, Erk, George et al., 2005). As I sat with Mary, I was sure that this card had reactivated her rape trauma. Her face grew pale, she began speaking very rapidly, and her speech became incoherent. This is the exact transcript of her response:

> "Hmmm....hmmm... 'How does this look?' Right. (Laugh.) Ah, yeah, in this photo it's a case of 'How does this look?' He's ah the little boy is doing a mime. He's got hands up like this. (Gestures hands up.) He's looking down like this. 'How do I look like this? If I do it like this is this better? If I do it like this is this better? OK?' And he goes like this. 'And don't laugh at me!' (Laugh.) So, he's ah...in this one he's practicing a scene for a school play. And he's wanted this part in the school play. He really wanted it. He asked his teacher to give him a special part. And now he's really trying to he's really trying to enter into it, he's trying to do it well. And he's got people there watching. 'If I do it this way is this better? If I do it this way, is this better?' And they go, 'No.' And he thinks, 'Ah, gosh, this isn't what I was expecting.' But anyway, he's trying, he's trying his best. And...it's pantomime, actually. He's doing pantomime. It's the school play. And so.... hmmm (Long pause.) I'm just saying you know I'm trying to make a story out of that, but this is the opposite of the corner in in the the angle here. It's obviously it's a case of, you know it's an abusive situation. So I've been trying to make a story out of it. But in the end you go back to the actual situation to the context of the corner. And it's very difficult to make a story out of it. Ah hah. Because what's happening here is obviously a case of you know. He's not actually hiding his face, it's a case of, 'Just keep away, don't don't do that to me, don't don't don't show that to me. Don't...' (Long pause.) Maybe it's more of a case of, 'I don't want to see it. Don't show it to me. I don't want to know,' type of thing. It's more that. 'I don't want to know. I don't want to see. I don't don't...' It's obviously that. **[SF: What happened before?]** You know I find that really hard with this one. Cause I can't imagine anybody doing that to a kid, but um, I don't know. OK let's have a look. OK. What's happened here is.... (Long pause.) Let's take another one, so he's terrified of spiders. (Laugh.) Absolutely terrified of spiders. And um he's got this nasty little brother. And he's gone out of the house and he's collected all these spiders together. Right, OK. And he's going, 'Oh look at these.' And he's showing him all these spiders. And he's going 'No, no I don't want to see. I'm terrified. Don't don't don't don't don't get those near me.' And he's going like this. (Gestures hands up.) And his brother's there, literally, really the brother's enjoying himself, sort of tormenting him. I guess he's going, 'No, I hate this. Don't don't don't don't' like this. And ah eventually the brother just turns and says, 'You big softie. Can you not tell that they're just plastic? They're not real.' And he holds him up all these plastic spiders. And ah. He gets really angry then with his brother, and he busts out, and gets him down on the floor in a rugby tackle hold, and the boy

says 'I hate you! I hate you!' You know, the usual child torment scene. And um, then the brother just laughs. Because he just knows that that's his weakness, but ....there's no harm meant as such. The brother didn't....Just that he's got an exaggerated fear of spiders. (Long pause.) Hmmm. How come I couldn't do that one? I found it really difficult. My brain wasn't working.

At that point, I took the AAP card and suggested that Mary and I stop and talk:

M: How come I couldn't do that one?
SF: Yeah. I want to talk about that.
Mary: Yeah yeah. I found that one really difficult.
SF: Yeah, I saw.... What's your sense?
M: I don't know...I feel there's a tightness right in my back here, right in this... right in this area, right there, right in the neck. And I feel a bit nauseous as well. I can't really make a story of that because it just seems like such a real situation in a way, you can't really say anything about that. The boy's obviously being threatened in some way. I can't find a different story about that. I've tried the pantomime, I've tried the spiders, but it's a threatening situation. I can't get beyond that.
SF: Well it looks like it was hard to actually tell a story about that threatening scene.
Mary: Mmm... mmm... Yeah, to tell a story about that which... often happens in reality.
SF: It was almost like... I don't know what it felt like. It looked like your brain wouldn't go there.
Mary: No, it wouldn't. It wouldn't go there. It just wouldn't go there.
SF: So what are your thoughts about that?
Mary: Actually, the spider things, I don't love spiders, for example, so I invented something which is actually true...with the brother tormenting with the spiders.
SF: Yeah, a very creative story, really.
Mary: But I mean, it just didn't make sense to me when I was telling it even. I mean it was one alternative for this, "Oh, don't show me that, don't show me that." But it's... I can't get beyond the fact that the boy is... is... he's frightened and he's only young and... the fact that he's not looking. He's not looking like I didn't look. I think that's it...
SF: Go ahead.
Mary: Yeah, I think we're partly involved with that... that, I don't know why, I asked myself so many times after that rape, I said, "Why didn't I look? Why wasn't I able to identify this person?"
SF: I know.

Mary: Because that would have been the chance for me...because they actually interviewed people afterwards, so I would have been able to say "yes" or "no, it wasn't his friend" or "yes, it was." I didn't look.

At that point it was clear to me that Mary had connected her physiological response to the AAP drawing to her rape. I saw an opportunity to use scaffolding to help her understand how dissociation helped explain her inability to describe her rapist to the police. But rather than just tell her about Polyvagal Theory, I tried to use Mary's story to lead to a bottom-up learning.

SF: Yeah, and why isn't he looking?
Mary: Why isn't he looking? He doesn't want to see what's going to happen. He doesn't want to know. ...He's in a situation where he can't stop what's happening. He doesn't want it to be happening. He doesn't want it to happen to him whatever it is, and he just can't—there's nothing he can do.
SF: Exactly.
Mary: And he feels totally powerless.
SF: Exactly

Mary then went into a kind of flashback where she described seeing another man in the distance while she was being raped. She said she didn't shout out because she was afraid that "two men is potentially worse than one." I intervened to help bring her back into the room:

SF: Yes, it's a feeling of being totally powerless.
Mary: Powerless completely, and your mind's working and half of your mind closes down and the other half goes ahead.
SF: That's what it is. That's what I wanted you to understand.
Mary: Yeah, but I did. I recognized that half of my mind just closed down, and that was the half that didn't want to accept it or know what was happening. And the other half, which said how can I deal with this which was talking and saying, "It's not me," it was going ahead.

I saw how Mary's narrative still put responsibility on her for not having looked. This seemed the moment to introduce what I knew from Polyvagal Theory.

SF: But you are on automatic pilot at that point.
Mary: Yeah, you are on automatic pilot.
SF: Yeah, because you're...
Mary: You are fighting literally for your—not for your—maybe your life as well, but you're doing what you can.
SF: But you're in shock.

Mary: Yes, you're in shock. That's the word.
SF: Absolutely. It's an altered state.
Mary: Is it? Is that what it is? I was...yeah, you are in shock.
SF: Basically—And maybe another word might be that you're "dissociated."
Mary: Okay.
SF: And it's an automatic defense mechanism in our bodies that kicks in.
Mary: Is it?
SF: It's in your biology.
Mary: All right. Okay. So that not looking was not—because I thought that...
SF: It has nothing to do with your character.
Mary: All right. Because I thought that just must have been me.
SF: No. It's part of the freeze response. It's part of the shame in the moment... but none of that is conscious. It's an absolutely wired-in response when we feel like we're going to die.
Mary: Well, that was a real possibility.
SF: Yes!

At that point Mary flashed to the moment her latest boyfriend had cornered her in her kitchen, when she had cut him with the broken glass. She said she now realized that her she hated being forced into a corner physically because "that had happened to [her] before" with the rape. I chose to continue explaining Polyvagal Theory:

SF: I'll tell you a little more if you want.
Mary: Please tell me more because I'm just starting to make connections now.
SF: If we're watching animals, where an animal attacks—let's say, a wolf gets a rabbit or is about to get the rabbit. The rabbit will stop and freeze.
Mary: It stops and freezes.
SF: And it dissociates and there's a bunch of functions for it. It looks like it's playing dead, which sometimes will get the animal to leave it alone. And it goes into an altered state, so if it is about to be killed, it doesn't feel the pain as well as it would.
Mary: Really?
SF: Yes, really.

Right then, Mary's eyes widened, she took a huge breath, and let it out slowly. I saw her grasping what I had said and starting to have compassion for herself. She then switched to talking about her rage outbursts with her boyfriend when she felt cornered in her apartment. I listened, saw a chance to address Mary's Assessment Question about her uncontrolled anger outbursts, and again stepped in:

SF: Here is how we're wired in a life and death situation... to fight, flee, or freeze. When we can't fight, or fighting would put our life in danger, and there's no way out, we'll freeze and go into this kind of response (pointing to the AAP Corner drawing.)

Mary: That was that response there.

SF: That's the response there.

Mary: That was the freeze because...

SF: That was the freeze because you had no way out.

Mary: Yes, you know, with the hand around here, with the knee in there, I couldn't move and he was blocking everything. I knew that person was so much stronger than I was and there was no way of actually getting back.

SF: Exactly, and again this is what makes me so mad about the policeman asking you "Why didn't you look?" Because anybody who understands these trauma situations knows it is completely wired into you not to look.

Mary: Okay.

SF: You have no control over that. It's in your nerves.

Mary:That makes my reaction easier to accept.

SF: It is a completely normal reaction under the circumstances.

Mary: Okay.

SF: What's that like to hear?.

Mary: It helps, because that's been a part that was missing... It's been a question over the years, "Why didn't I look at this person? Why couldn't I identify the person?" And it partly explains that "why couldn't I..."—now partly I can explain that because I knew he was stronger than I was, but there were moments when, you know, I could have attempted to—but the doctor said " And you could also not be here telling your story."

SF: Exactly, so again, the evolutionarily built-in freeze response, just like for the rabbit, actually saved your life, perhaps.

Mary: Perhaps.

SF: But, but you had no control over it. That's an automatic kick-in response.

Mary and I continued to process what I had said, and I supported her as she began to cycle through a series of emotions: compassion for herself, relief that she now had an explanation for her behavior during the rape, anger at the police for not understanding what had happened, and anger at her friends and family for not supporting her emotionally. As Mary reached a calmer place, I wanted to see if I could pave the road to introduce an assessment finding I was afraid would be Level 3 information.

SF: And Mary, so the trouble you were having telling the story. What does that tell us?

Mary: It's the same trouble I had during the rape. With everything that has happened to me, it wasn't possible to tell a story.

SF: Exactly. So what it tells me is that the trauma is still very fresh.

Mary: Yeah, it seems to be, despite the years that have passed. I was very young.

SF: It's been years, yeah, but you haven't had a chance to heal from it.

Mary: Yes. I agree. How can I do that?

SF: Well, that's going to be my job at the end of the assessment—to give you next steps for healing this..

Mary: You've partly helped me there, by just describing that actual reaction which happens physiologically and it's a defense reaction, but I'm going to need to go beyond that as well.

She then talked more about her angry outbursts with her boyfriend and that she understood them better also.

SF: Well, there's the fight part of the fight—flight—freeze.

Mary: Yeah, that's the fight part. That was fairly strong in this last relationship with my partner.

SF: Mary, I know that was terribly painful for you, but I wonder if you've been trying to work through these traumas, and in the first event—in this one (pointing to the AAP card), *you have the freeze, and in this latest one you were trying out the fight. You're trying to heal from the trauma..*

Mary: Possibly.

SF: I wonder if one reason you couldn't leave your boyfriend is that you were trying to master the trauma this time.

Mary: Really?...Possibly...

Colleagues watching the video of this session have commented on how much "lighter" Mary looks at the end of this session, and I saw this too at the time.

After the AAP

This Extended Inquiry was a turning point in Mary's assessment and in her life. Mary repeatedly referred to our discussion throughout the rest of the TA and talked about how important it was for her. In a follow-up meeting we had five years later (as part of the termination process in her psychotherapy) she brought it up again. What I have come to understand is that the AAP and my explanation of Polyvagal Theory set in motion a process that finally allowed Mary to forgive herself, recognize the lack of support and protection she had received, and to grieve. After the TA Mary did not return to her boyfriend, although at one point he wanted to reconcile, and she continued working in therapy on her past traumas and getting more access to her feelings. She and her therapist agreed

Table 13.1 Coding Summary Sheet for Mary's AAP

Dyadic	*Personal Exp*	*Synch*	*Ds*	*E*	*Seg*	*Alone*	*Agency*	*Personal Exp*	*Connected*	*Ds*	*E*	*Seg*
Deprt (3)	0	1	Ds	E	R	Window (2)	"2"	1	2	Ds	E	U in PE
		Married couple					She		Desire to be in touch with others			
		Go to Paris					Back to think					
Bed (5)	0	1	Ds	E		Bench (4)	2	0	3	Ds	E	R
		Babysitter tells story					ISB					
							Woman works thing out					
							1					
							CTA					
							Goes home					
Ambul (6)	1	1	Ds	E	R	Cemtry (7)	2	0	-	Ds	E	
		Granny stops Martin					Man thinks to himself					
						Corner (8)	1	0	-	Ds	E	R
							Little boy					
							CTA					

that she would not date for several years, and Mary held to this. She also stopped drinking alcohol for a period of time. Not surprisingly, her work life also became more successful and when she finally began another romantic relationship it was with a man who was very kind to her.

What I wish to emphasize about this assessment event is that it was powerful and healing—I believe—not just because Mary got information about dissociation and the fight-flight-freeze response to traumatic events, but because this information was coupled with a vivid, emotionally meaningful experience—dissociation—that was evoked by the AAP in a controlled fashion. This occurred because the card elicited emotions and memories about an earlier trauma (the rape), and Mary and I were able to discuss the incident in a new way, which brought her relief and shifted her narrative about the event. Mary could tolerate this experience and not be traumatized by it because I was there to witness it and support her and because of the careful work I had done previously in establishing a safe and trusting relationship with her. And clearly it was not just my words that were important in this interaction, but also my affective resonance, support, and attitude of caring. I am grateful to Porges for his Polyvagal Theory with its clear conceptualization of the adaptive function of dissociation, and for George and West for the AAP, which did its job of eliciting a past trauma so Mary could reexperience it in a safe way.

Postscript: AAP Coding

Although I focused mainly on what happened during the AAP administration, for those readers who are interested, here is the coding for Mary's AAP protocol, done by Dr. Adriana Lis and colleagues. As Table 13.1 shows, Mary was Unresolved on the AAP, and even more importantly, there were seven trauma-based segregated systems in Mary's stories, as well as three E3 sexual trauma markers. Also, notice the pervasiveness of the trauma-based segregated systems—they occur starting with the first card and continue through the last, they occur on both the Alone and the Dyadic cards, and they occur both in the story content and in the personal experience content. If I hadn't known it before, Mary's AAP "screams" to me that many of her difficulties were related to unresolved traumas, including those of a sexual nature, and to the failure of her attachment figures to help her cope with those traumas

Note

1 Parts of Polyvagal Theory have been challenged in recent years based on new scientific evidence (Grossman, 2023) but those aspects I write about here are still generally considered valid (Porges, 2025).

References

Bucheim, A., Erk, S., George, C., Kächele, H., Ruchsow, M., Spitzer, M., Kircher, T., & Walter, H. (2005). Measuring attachment representation in an fMRI environment: A pilot study. *Psychopathology, 589*, 1–9.

Bruhn, A. R. (1990). *Earliest childhood memories: Vol. 1. Theory and application to clinical practice*. Praeger.

Ferenczi, S. (1932/1988). *The clinical diary of Sandor Ferenczi*. Harvard University Press.

George, C., & West, M. (2012). *The Adult Attachment Projective Picture System*. Guilford.

Grossman, Paul (2023). Fundamental challenges and likely refutations of the five basic premises of the polyvagal theory. *Biological Psychology, 180*. https://doi.org/10.1016/j.biopsycho.2023.108589

Janet, P. (1889). *L'automatisme psychologique: essai de psychologie expérimentale sur les formes inférieures de l'activité humaine*. Alcan.

Porges, S. W. (1995). Orienting in a defensive world: Mammalian modifications of our evolutionary heritage. A polyvagal theory. *Psychophysiology, 32*, 301–318.

Porges, S. W. (2025). Polyvagal theory: Current status, clinical applications, and future directions. *Clinical Neuropsychiatry, 22*(3), 169–184.

Chapter 14

Are the Sudden Transformations Seen at Times in Therapeutic Assessment Due to Memory Reconsolidation?

Several years ago, I found myself looking over records from past Therapeutic Assessments and pondering a question. "Why did some clients have sudden transformations after or during their TAs, while others did not?" Almost all the clients whose assessments I reviewed had clearly benefited from TA, but many did so slowly over time, while others had shown sudden positive changes—where longstanding problems-in-living appeared to get better almost overnight. What were the therapeutic mechanisms at work in this second group of clients? In the past I had explained such effects by dramatic alterations in clients' narrative identities (Finn, 2007), and this possibility still seemed important. But many TA clients had made substantial shifts in the ways they thought about themselves. Why did a subgroup of them become asymptomatic so rapidly?

Around this time, a colleague sent me an article that had interested her and invited me to read it (Lane et al., 2015). Lane and his colleagues proposed that a natural neurobiological process called *memory reconsolidation* was responsible for therapeutic change in many treatment modalities. I was intrigued, and as I read more about memory reconsolidation, it seemed very likely that it was the therapeutic element I had been trying to identify in those TAs in which clients suddenly got better. Since then, I have become even more intrigued about this possibility, and learning about memory reconsolidation has increased the impact of my work with clients both in TA and in psychotherapy.

What Is Memory Reconsolidation?

Memory reconsolidation is the name given to the recent discovery that the brain is capable of "rewriting" emotional learnings that are at the core of many clients' central problems-in-living, thereby resulting in rapid transformations in emotions and behaviors. This type of neuroplasticity is rather surprising because for years it was assumed that memories (especially traumatic ones) cannot be changed directly, but that we can help clients regulate the emotions connected to them (see Wampold & Imel, 2015). In contrast, many of the developers of modern psychotherapies I referred to in Chapter 1 now explicitly aspire to

DOI: 10.4324/9781003602231-14

permanently alter traumatic memories or report instances that are compatible with memory reconsolidation, including experts in Somatic Experiencing (SE; Levine & Frederick, 1997), Sensorimotor Psychotherapy (Ogden & Fisher, 2015), Accelerated Experiential Dynamic Psychotherapy (AEDP; Fosha, 2000); Emotion-Focused Therapy (EFT; Greenberg & Watson, 2006); Eye Movement Desensitization and Reprocessing (EMDR; Shapiro, 2001); Intensive Short-Term Dynamic Psychotherapy (ISTDP; Davanloo, 2001; Frederickson, 2013), Internal Family Systems Therapy (IFS; Schwarz, 1995); Gestalt Therapy (Polster & Polster, 1973), and Psychedelic Assisted Psychotherapy (González et al., 2022). The person most associated with the term memory reconsolidation in recent years is Bruce Ecker, who reviewed the scientific research in both animals and humans, identified the essential ingredients necessary for transformational change, and developed a psychotherapy model based on these elements, called Coherence Therapy (Ecker, Ticic, & Hulley, 2024). Before I discuss similarities between Coherence Therapy and Therapeutic Assessment, let me first summarize the research related to memory reconsolidation.

The Neurobiological Underpinnings of Memory Reconsolidation

Human memory is a complex process, and at this point we still don't know exactly how the different types of memory are organized, which neurologic systems are involved, and what molecular processes are at work (Nadel & Hardt, 2011). What has been understood for some time is that memories take time to consolidate, typically going through a series of steps traditionally labeled: (1) encoding, (2) working memory, (3) consolidation, and (4) long-term memory (Nadel & Hardt, 2011). Imagine that you are asked to remember a new phone number. Probably you will first understand it (encoding), rehearse it in your mind (working memory), then store it (consolidation), and eventually be able to recall it even hours later (long-term memory). It is known that the hippocampus plays a crucial role in the consolidation of memories; however, after consolidation, long-term memories are no longer dependent on the hippocampus and are stored in various places in the brain.

One important distinction is between what has been called *episodic* (or *autobiographical*) *memory* and *semantic memory* (Tulving, 1983). Episodic memory is our recall of specific events, such as "I remember my mother punishing me for asking for peanut and butter sandwiches from the neighbor" (see Chapter 7), while semantic memory involves lessons developed from multiple life events (e.g., "Asking for help from others is shameful and is likely to bring rejection from important others").[1] It is also understood that emotions have a significant influence on memory reconsolidation. Generally, there is better long-term encoding and consolidation of emotionally stimulating information (Cahill, 2000; Murty et al., 2010; Phelps, 2004; Vyas et al., 2002). However, events that are affectively overwhelming will produce powerful emotional learnings (semantic memories) accompanied by limited access to the details of those experiences (presumably because of dissociation). Importantly, memory is also dynamic and "reconstructive" (Bartlett, 1932); Rather than perfectly recalling past events, we revise memories as they get older and particularly each time that we retrieve them (Phelps, 2004). Overall, the adaptive function of memory is to help us: (1) recall things that are important for our survival, (2) build a coherent sense of self, and (3) provide a narrative that gives meaning to our experiences and protects us from overwhelming emotions (Nairne & Pandeirada, 2008).

The term *memory reconsolidation* comes from research first done in animals that showed that established and well-learned emotional learnings (i.e., semantic memories derived from highly affectively arousing events) could be profoundly altered by first retrieving those memories and then using chemical agents known to destroy unstable synapses (e.g., Sekiguchi, Yamada, & Suzuki, 1997). For example, Nader, Schafe, and LeDoux (2000) conditioned rats to expect a foot shock after a single tone and first observed freezing to the sound of the tone as a sign of consolidated learning. Next, they activated the fear memory by playing the tone and then immediately injected the rats' lateral and basal nuclei of the amygdala (LBA)—believed to be the site of memory storage in fear learning—with an antibiotic (anisomycin) known to inhibit protein synthesis. When the tone was played again, the rats showed amnesia for the original learning and this effect continued at subsequent retests.

Another important discovery was that the original memory had to be elicited first for memory reconsolidation to occur and that there was a "reconsolidation window" of five hours during which the reactivated memory was "labile" and could be altered (Pedreira, Pérez-Cuesta, & Maldonado, 2002). If the elicited memory was not interrupted during this time period, a new natural "locking" would occur that returned the memory to a stable state, and it was no longer susceptible to change until it was reactivated again. This five-hour reconsolidation window has since been confirmed in both animals and humans. Apparently when a previously consolidated memory is elicited, the hippocampus again becomes involved, allowing the memory to be altered.

The next breakthrough came when researchers discovered that it was possible to reconsolidate memories *without using chemical agents* by first reactivating the traumatic memory through contextual cues and then disconfirming it—within the five-hour reconsolidation window—via a contradictory experience that did not match what was expected (Pedreira, Pérez-Cuesta, & Maldonado, 2004). This "prediction error" would cause the original memory to reconsolidate and the traumatic emotional learning would no longer operate. Again, later research confirmed that this effect was true for humans as well (e.g., Hupbach et al., 2007; Schiller et al., 2010). Kindt, Seter, and Vervliet (2009) further demonstrated that cancellation of a fear reaction (the implicit emotional learning) doesn't compromise the *autobiographical* memory of the experience in which the person learned to be afraid of a particular stimulus. The memory of having been afraid stays intact, but the stimulus no longer elicits fear.

Coherence Therapy: Essential Therapeutic Elements in Memory Reconsolidation

As mentioned earlier, memory reconsolidation may be a common factor operating in many forms of psychotherapy, and some psychotherapy models now explicitly incorporate memory reconsolidation as one of their major goals, e.g., EMDR (Chamberlin, 2019). However, as mentioned earlier, one person has extensively mined the animal and human research on memory reconsolidation to create a clear and effective psychotherapy: Bruce Ecker, developer with Laura Hulley of *Coherence Therapy* (Ecker, 2013, 2015a, 2015b, 2015c, 2018; Ecker, Ticic, & Hulley, 2024). There is now a Coherence Psychology Institute (www.coherencetherapy.org) that sponsors training and supervision in Coherence Therapy and has assembled evidence that Coherence Therapy can be effective with a multiplicity of symptoms.

Coherence Therapy's name reflects its fundamental assumption that almost all our clients' problems-in-living are the result of implicit emotional schemas that were adaptive (coherent) at one point in time. As mentioned earlier, these schemas or mental models are stored in semantic memory and generally are not conscious without therapeutic intervention. The first major goals of Coherence Therapy are to help clients identify a symptom they want to change and then use experiential methods to discover the "necessity of the symptom," i.e., the unconscious emotional schema that generates the problematic emotional response or behavior. Ecker and colleagues use a variety of bottom-up techniques for discovering the "symptom-requiring schema," including, (1) asking the client to slowly recount in present tense a recent time when the symptom was present and imagining what they would feel if it weren't, (2) inviting the client to envision talking to significant family members about their symptom (e.g., "Mom, I'll never be happy because if I were, you…"), or (3) asking the client to spontaneously finish an incomplete sentence provided by the clinician (e.g., "Even though I get into trouble because of my anger, it's really important for me to have it because…"). Typically, once the underlying emotional schema becomes apparent, clients have much less shame and more self-compassion, since behaviors and emotional reactions that seemed irrational and "crazy" suddenly make sense.

After the implicit emotional learning is identified, clinicians trained in Coherence Therapy help clients recognize past or current experiences that directly contradict this schema and then hold the two pieces of information in mind at the same time. This is called a "juxtaposition experience," and there are various forms it can take, depending on the underlying emotional learning and the client's past experiences. If the client's implicit narrative is, "If I ever stand up for myself in relationships, I will surely be rejected and likely will be alone the rest of my life," the clinician might ask if there are times when the client was assertive and it helped them become closer to someone. If the client has had experiences like this, the clinician will then first activate the symptom-requiring schema and then ask the client to hold these contradictory experiences in mind at the same time. If the client has never had contradictory experiences, the clinician might invite the client to imagine expressing anger to a major attachment figure and then notice how they feel. If the client feels less anxious and more hopeful, their noticing this creates the juxtaposition experience. Other juxtaposition experiences can be staged by inviting a client to express previously punished emotions with the therapist, or with loved ones in family therapy, or with fellow therapy group members, and then helping the client notice what happens. If others' reactions run counter to those expected by the previous emotional learning, memory reconsolidation may take place. The conscious awareness of a prediction error—at the same time the symptom-requiring schema is activated—is seen as the key to memory reconsolidation and the disappearance of the presenting symptom. If the symptom is still present at that point, this is taken as a sign that there is one or more emotional learnings still driving it, and the clinician then guides the client in additional exercises to discover these "deeper" schemas (Ecker, Ticic, & Hulley, 2024). While this formula to achieve memory reconsolidation is relatively simple, Ecker and colleagues have provided many fascinating examples of how to implement it with different types of clients with varied problems-in-living. See www.coherencetherapy.org for more information and for a downloadable Coherence Therapy treatment manual (Ecker & Hulley, 2011).

Memory Reconsolidation in Therapeutic Assessment

As I read about Coherence Therapy and memory reconsolidation, there were clear parallels with TA that struck me, as well as a few differences:

1) Both theories propose that clients' problems-in-living often stem from schemas developed through past experiences that were once adaptive, that these schemas are outside of conscious awareness, and that clients can be helped if they can become aware of those schemas and update them.
2) Both TA and Coherence Therapy are client-centered and begin by asking clients to identify problematic patterns or symptoms they want to understand better and/or change. One apparent difference is that in TA we pay much more attention to developing therapeutic alliance and creating epistemic trust, especially at the beginning of our work with clients.

3) Both models emphasize the importance of bottom-up experiences in helping clients identify and change implicit narratives, coupled with later meta-processing of those in-vivo events. In TA, psychological tests are the main tools employed to create those emotionally arousing experiences, with meta-processing taking place via scaffolding during Extended Inquiries and Assessment Intervention Sessions.
4) Both methods aim to create emotionally powerful experiences that contradict clients' out-of-date implicit narratives. In fact, this is often one of the major goals of Assessment Intervention Sessions in Therapeutic Assessment.

As mentioned above, memory reconsolidation proved to be a very useful "lens" when I reviewed Therapeutic Assessments where clients showed sudden and dramatic improvements. Table 14.1 analyzes the successful TAs referred to in this volume and shows the emotional learnings discovered via the TA, how those came to light, through what means juxtaposition experiences might have been created, and the new schemas clients had after their TAs.

Jim's TA: The Power of Creating In Vivo Juxtaposition Experiences

I now wish to reshare an account of a TA that led to a sudden, powerful transformation in a client that I now believe was due to memory reconsolidation. I have written about this TA briefly before (see Chapter 8 of Finn, 2007) but now provide more details. In my mind, this TA demonstrates the power of first discovering clients' underlying emotional schemas and then creating juxtaposition experiences using psychological tests.

Background Information

"Jim" was 24 years old when he was referred by his psychotherapist, Dr. Hake, for a Therapeutic Assessment. Dr. Hake described Jim as "a lost boy" who was "unable to find a direction in life." Apparently, Jim had graduated from high school, despite a history of severe dyslexia, but had miserably failed his first semester of college and returned to his parents' home. Since then, Jim was unable to hold down a job and spent much of his time in his room. Dr. Hake also told me that Jim's parents were "high achieving" and "rather critical," and that Jim had "low self-esteem" that psychotherapy "had been unable to address." He also suspected that Jim suffered from an anxiety disorder or was clinically depressed. Months earlier, Dr. Hake had referred Jim to a psychiatrist who had prescribed antidepressant medication, but it had not led to any significant improvement in Jim's motivation and ability to find direction.

Table 14.1 Mapping concepts from Coherence Therapy on TA Cases in this book

TA client	*Chapter(s)*	*Major symptom*	*Underlying emotional schema*	*How discovered*	*New schema after juxtaposition experience*	*Outcome*
Thomas	4	Inability to maintain long-term romantic relationship	"My early surgeries have left me damaged and ugly, and no one will ever desire me. I must be content with brief sexual encounters."	Extended Inquiry of Rorschach	"My early surgeries were traumatizing, and it is OK for me to be angry about the way they were handled. I am not defective and there are men who will find me attractive."	Less body shame and success in establishing a long-term romantic relationship.
Ben	5, 9	Dangerous sexual acting out	"Whenever I get in touch with painful feelings, I have to act out sexually, or I will constantly hate myself and be depressed."	Assessment Intervention Session using dysphoric TAT cards	"I can experience painful emotions and tolerate them with support from another. Talking helps me feel better."	Desire for anonymous sexual encounters went away.
Sally	6	Tendency to become involved with highly narcissistic men	"I must be blind to the narcissism of male attachment figures, otherwise I will see my father in a new way, and I cannot tolerate that."	Extended Inquiry of Rorschach	"I can tolerate seeing my father's defects and be angry about the way he suicided. I can correctly assess whether men I am dating are narcissistic."	Able to select a romantic partner who truly cared for her. Able to see father's defects.

(*Continued*)

Table 14.1 (Continued)

TA client	*Chapter(s)*	*Major symptom*	*Underlying emotional schema*	*How discovered*	*New schema after juxtaposition experience*	*Outcome*
Tim	7	Inability to ask others for help	"Asking others for help is deeply wrong and humiliating, and I will lose my independence if I start relying on others."	Extended Inquiry of EMP	"My mother felt shame about asking others for help. I can ask others for help without losing my independence."	Able to ask others for help without shame or anxiety.
Al	8	Lack of success in promoting his art	"I am bad and lazy and do not deserve success."	Extended Inquiry of WAIS-IV	"My learning disability does not mean I am bad and lazy. Also, I can learn ways of handling my dyscalculia."	Able to promote self and to remediate his learning disability.
Hana	8	Compulsive checking behaviors for fear of hurting someone	"Even though compulsive checking is problematic, I must use this behavior to distract from painful feelings I cannot handle."	Extended Inquiry of AAP	"With support I can handle painful feelings from current and past losses."	Compulsive checking behaviors disappeared.
Jeff	9	Lack of empathy for wife's depression	"I must ignore my own needs and support Ann in her depression, even though I find it frustrating."	Extended Inquiry of Rorschach	"I too deserve acknowledgement for my depression and should not sacrifice all my needs for Ann's."	More able to share distress with wife and get support from her. More empathy and less frustration with wife.

(Continued)

Table 14.1 (Continued)

TA client	*Chapter(s)*	*Major symptom*	*Underlying emotional schema*	*How discovered*	*New schema after juxtaposition experience*	*Outcome*
Mike	11	Excessive independence and inability to commit in romantic relationships and in psychotherapy	"If I commit and allow myself to engage in close relationships, I will be overwhelmed by grief and depression and will be unable to function."	Written report focused on AAP results	"I can tolerate feelings of grief and depression and survive. I can get close to others without losing my ability to function."	Ability to commit to long-term therapy and to a romantic relationship.
Susan	12	Angry pursuing behaviors with husband that led to his avoiding closeness	"Even though I know that pursuing my husband pushes him away, I must continue to express my anger and disappointment at him, or I will be in touch with overwhelming feelings of grief about my childhood."	Extended Inquiry of AAP	"I can tolerate being alone without being overwhelmed and traumatized by feelings of grief. I can risk being close to my husband."	Able to be alone and to interact with husband in a much more inviting way.
Mary	13	Long term relationships with men who physically abused her	"I am a coward for not having looked at my rapist and I must keep subjecting myself to physical abuse in order to prove that I am brave."	Extended Inquiry of AAP	"My not looking at my rapist was not my fault; it was a natural neurobiological response. I no longer need to prove that I am not a coward."	Decreased longing to be with abusive men.

When I met Jim for the initial session I was struck by his inability to maintain eye contact and his difficulties putting his thoughts into words. He was soft-spoken and struggled to express himself, often resulting in long pauses in his discourse. I felt an urge to jump in and finish Jim's phrases but held back as I wanted to see what Jim could do on his own. He eventually was able to articulate three Assessment Questions:

Do I still have a learning disability?

I discovered that Jim had had difficulties with reading and math since elementary school but that he had not received special tutoring or accommodations, in part because he attended private schools without special education programs. Jim said he had heard most people "outgrow" their learning disabilities, but he still had problems with reading and writing. He wondered, did he still suffer from dyslexia, and would this be true his whole life?

Why can't I succeed at anything?

Jim recounted a long list of failures, including barely graduating from high school, failing a first semester at university, dropping courses multiple times at the local community college, and having been fired from a series of jobs. He told me he no longer "believed in himself" and that this made it difficult to try new things, as he was sure he would fail. I asked if there was any activity Jim did where he felt good about himself and learned that he spent hours in his room playing guitar. He told me, "I'm good at music, but that doesn't count." When I inquired further, Jim told me that his parents would never approve of him pursuing a career in music. His father and grandfather had been attorneys, and Jim had been expected to study law and eventually take over the family firm. His mother was a highly successful financial consultant and had also been disappointed by Jim not doing well in school.

Why am I so scared about talking to girls?

Jim had never had a girlfriend, and he told me that he grew incredibly anxious and tongue-tied when he tried to speak to women. He said this had happened even when a friend told him a certain woman thought Jim was "cute." Encouraged by this, Jim tried to converse with her at a party but felt so awkward and embarrassed that he fled after a few minutes and immediately went home feeling "like a jerk."

Early Testing Sessions

Early in the TA I asked Jim to do the WAIS-III (Wechsler, 1997) with me—because of his question about a possible learning disability—and it was a very enlightening experience. Jim struggled a great deal with the verbal subtests, achieving a Verbal IQ of only 92. His shame was palpable when we did those tests; he frequently shook his head and criticized himself when he didn't know an answer, particularly during the Information subtest, where he called himself an "idiot" several times. But he did much better on the nonverbal tests, earning a Performance IQ of 124. Jim's nonverbal abilities were especially evident on Block Design, for which his scaled score was 14! It was impressive and heartening to see Jim smiling and enjoying himself on the more difficult items of the subtest, effortlessly and quickly putting the blocks together in complex patterns that matched the test stimuli. This enjoyment was short-lived, however. When I asked Jim afterwards how he thought he had done on Block Design, he said he was, "pretty hopeless." When I said that in fact he had done very well, he looked uncomfortable and said he was sure this result was a "fluke." I was struck by how impenetrable Jim's negative view of himself was, and I began to have more compassion for Dr. Hake.

Next, I asked Jim to complete the MMPI-2 (Butcher et al., 1989), and the resulting profile (see Figure 14.1) helped me further get in his shoes. His scores were consistent with severe depression, anxiety, and incredible demoralization, lethargy, and hopelessness. (See Figure 14.1.) Jim also endorsed every item on the Low Self-Esteem (LSE) scale, reaching the highest possible score (T=97). I understood better why Jim was spending most of his time in his room! In my experience, this MMPI-2 profile is often associated with unresolved trauma, and this made me curious, as I was not aware that Jim had been physically or sexually abused. Thus, I chose the Early Memory Procedure (EMP; Bruhn, 1990) as our next task. Because of his difficulties with writing, I had Jim dictate his memories. This is his clearest, most negative memory, from when he was 12 years old:

> I'm at the dining room table after dinner. My father was "helping" me with my homework. I was supposed to be writing a book report about some book we read at school, and I couldn't do it. He was red in the face and screaming at me and yelled, "I can't believe a son of mine is such an idiot!" In the background I heard my mother crying in the bedroom.

When asked about the strongest feeling associated with the memory, Jim said, "I felt so bad that I couldn't write the report, that I was stupid, and that I was hurting my mother." When I asked how he would change the memory if he could, Jim immediately responded, "I would be able to write the report." It saddened me that Jim clearly blamed himself, rather than his parents, for this event. A second incident emerged when Jim told another memory—of winning a race at an athletic event in 7th grade—while his parents looked on. His mother had been very excited about his win and had praised him after, but his father had become

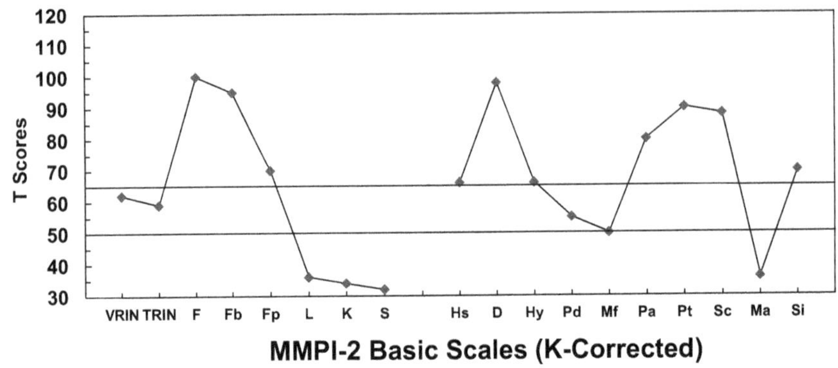

Figure 14.1 Jim's MMPI–2 profile.

Notes: VRIN = Variable Response Inconsistency scale; TRIN = True-Response Inconsistency scale; F = Infrequency; Fb = Back F; Fp = Infrequency Psychopathology; L = Lie; K = Defensiveness; S = Superlative Self-Presentation; Hs = Scale 1, Hypochondriasis; D = Scale 2, Depression; Hy = Scale 3, Hysteria; Pd = Scale 4, Psychopathic Deviate; Mf = Scale 5, Masculinity-Femininity; Pa = Scale 6, Paranoia; Pt = Scale 7, Psychasthenia; Sc = Scale 8, Schizophrenia; Ma = Scale 9, Hypomania; Si = Scale 0, Social Introversion. Minnesota Multiphasic Personality Inventory-2 (MMPI-2) Profile for Basic Scales.

angry and said, "My God, don't make such a big deal over this! It doesn't mean anything, and he [Jim] will get a big head." Jim reported that his mother had gotten very depressed afterward and spent the next few days in bed, which really scared him. This time, when I asked how he would change the memory, Jim said, "That I hadn't run the race." I remember thinking, "No wonder he can't let himself succeed at anything!"

Plan for Assessment Intervention Session (AIS)

At this point in the TA, my case conceptualization was that Jim was severely depressed and that years of academic failure and emotional abuse by his father had led him to develop an implicit narrative that he couldn't do anything well. The testing suggested that anger and healthy grandiosity were structurally dissociated, split-off affects for Jim, an accommodation that had helped him survive his childhood but that was keeping him from ever succeeding now. I also suspected his ongoing lack of direction served the family system by giving his parents a focus for their disappointment that helped them stay together and that kept his father from attacking his mother and her falling into depression. Jim's dilemma of change could be expressed in this way:

> To feel good about myself, I must recognize my strengths and find an area where I can achieve. But if I do this my dad would feel inferior and attack my mom, and my mom would fall into a deep depression. It's better for me to think I can never be good at anything.

To move forward, Jim would need an enormous amount of support, and his parents would need help dealing with their own conflictual relationship and grieving Jim's not being able to carry on the family law business.

My plan for the Assessment Intervention Session was to tell Jim that I wanted to explore his Assessment Question, "Why can't I do anything right?" I would then ask Jim to do a task I was almost certain he would be good at and afterwards ask him (as I had done after the WAIS-III Block Design subtest) how he had done. I predicted that even if Jim did well, he would evaluate his performance negatively and might even distort reality to conform with his shame and low self-esteem. I then planned to confront Jim with incontrovertible evidence that his self-assessment about the task was incorrect, support any emotions that emerged, while also emphasizing that Jim's negative self-views had been adaptive in the past. I also planned to help Jim connect this experience to how he handled other achievement situations in his life.

The task I chose for the AIS was the Bender Visual Motor Gestalt Test (Bender, 1938). This is a nonverbal test where the client is presented one at a time with nine index cards depicting geometrical figures. The client is asked to copy each design on a piece of paper. After the client has copied all nine figures, the assessor then asks them to draw on another sheet of paper as many designs as they can remember. The client's performance is scored according to how accurately they draw the figures and how many of the figures they recall afterwards. Given Jim's Performance IQ on the WAIS-III, I was almost certain he would do well on the test.

Assessment Intervention Session

Jim arrived the day of the AIS looking particularly down. I asked how he was doing, and he admitted that his father had been "hassling" that morning about not having a job and he felt "like shit." When I expressed compassion, Jim immediately said it was his "own fault" that his father was angry. I let this topic drop and said I wanted to do something that day to help us answer his question, "Why can't I succeed at anything?" He appeared to get a bit curious and agreed. As I explained the instructions to the Bender-Gestalt, Jim winced, hung his head, and said, "I'm no good at drawing." He then proceeded to draw the nine geometric figures almost perfectly, erasing several times and frequently sighing in a pained way. I took away his copied drawings and handed him a blank piece of paper, saying, "Now please draw as many of those as you can from memory." Jim winced again, looked a bit panicked, and said, "I already know I can't do this," to which I replied, "Just do the best you can." He then drew four of the nine drawings and pushed his paper toward me, saying that was all he could remember. I told him that was fine but asked him to take a few more minutes to see if he could recall any others. With my encouragement, he eventually recalled eight of the nine figures—an excellent performance (Bender, 1938). As planned, I then asked Jim how he thought he had done:

Jim: Terrible. I'm so stupid I couldn't remember any of them.
SF: Really? Is that what you think?
Jim: I already know I forgot a couple. I already know.
SF: How does it feel to know that?
Jim: Frustrating.
SF: Frustrating?
Jim: Yeah. I thought there weren't that many, but I can never remember all that. I always forget something.
SF: So how do you think you did on that one?
Jim: I think I forgot some, but, you know, I think I didn't even put some... more than one on there, maybe, maybe more, but... I think probably only about half or right or what they're supposed to be. Only about half of them are right.
SF: How many do you think there were?
Jim: I don't know... 14 or 15.
SF: And when you think that, how do you feel?
Jim: I'm just mad at myself, which, you know, happens a lot. And I don't know if I'm not smart enough to do that or if I just get nervous and can't remember or what. It's very frustrating.

Again, I was struck by how Jim's underlying narrative shaped his very perception of reality. I then turned over his initial drawings, put them next to the figures he had recalled, and laid out the Bender-Gestalt cards.

SF: Actually, let me show you how you did. Here are your initial drawings, the ones you remembered, and the cards I gave you to copy. There were only 9 cards and as you can see, your drawings were really accurate, and you got almost all of them when you had to remember them. Most people only remember 6 or 7 of them and you got 8. That's an excellent performance.... Really, I'm telling you the truth.

At that point Jim grew very still and fell silent. I wasn't sure what he was experiencing, so after a minute I inquired what it was like to see how he had done. Jim didn't reply, so I tried to name what he might be feeling:

SF: It looks like it's kind of a surprise.
Jim: Yeah.
SF: You didn't know that you had done that well.

Again, Jim didn't reply, and I realized he was dissociated.

SF: It looks like this is kind of a shock.
Jim: Well, kinda, yeah!
SF: So, you thought you'd done really badly?
Jim: Yeah. Well, you know, I thought it was really hard. I thought it was really hard.
SF: You didn't think you'd gotten this many right on the recall.
Jim: No.
SF: I saw that. Yeah.

I continued in a soft voice:

SF: I keep thinking about that question you had asked ... you know, why you do things so poorly and what's going on for you. And one of the things I'm wondering is if actually you feel so negatively about yourself that you can't tell what you're good at and what you're not... If I hadn't encouraged you, you would have given up after four designs, but I was pretty sure you could do this so I asked you to keep going. And even when you do something well, you'll see it negatively. So that just reinforces the idea that you can't do anything well.

Jim began to weep and covered his face with his hands, in the classic shame posture. I handed him some tissues and got him a glass of water, which he took and sipped from. As he composed himself Jim began to complain about how he could "never do anything right" for his mother, even putting a water pitcher back in the refrigerator. I said how frustrating that must be, and this time he agreed. He then spontaneously began to talk about his tears:

Jim: I was crying because nobody has ever told me that I did something good. I just couldn't believe it at first... but then I saw it is true. I started wondering about what else I can do that I don't know about.
SF: I'm thinking the exact same thing. It's like because of what you were told about yourself early on, you don't know what you're good at. You see everything through a distorted "lens."

Jim: Yes, a "loser lens!"

SF: I can see how you needed that lens early on, to fit with what the adults were telling you. It was really essential as a child, and it probably still serves you while you live at home with your parents. But that loser lens surely gets in your way now of figuring out what you want to do with yourself!

I then asked Jim if he could think of other times when he had misjudged himself, and he told of learning to play horseshoes at camp when he was 9 years old. Initially, he hadn't wanted to even try the activity, sure that he wouldn't do well. But a camp counselor encouraged him, and by the end of the week, Jim was beating everyone else—including the counselor! Jim and I continued to meta-process the AIS, and I even asked him to do a long-term recall of the Bender-Gestalt figures. He caught himself thinking he couldn't do it but kept going and eventually drew all nine figures correctly. This time, he smiled as I cheered, perhaps experiencing pride for the first time in many years without accompanying shame and anxiety. As Jim left the session, I too felt pride—that we had shed a light on his distorted self-narrative and how it affected him. I hoped this would free Jim from the prison of his shame and help him begin to find his way.

Outcome

In fact, Jim showed a surprising transformation after his TA that resembled the effects described by Ecker, Ticic, and Hulley (2024) when memory reconsolidation occurs. He was immediately less depressed and anxious and much more open and curious through the completion of the TA and in his psychotherapy afterwards. Dr. Hake told me he could barely believe how much Jim had changed. Several months after the TA, Jim was able to find a job he liked, and he moved out of his parents' house to live with friends. When I saw him for his three-month follow-up session, Jim had also formed a band with friends and was starting to get gigs in Austin. To my amazement, several years later the band had a record deal, and they are now internationally famous. What a testimony to the power of memory reconsolidation! I now see that without my knowing anything about Coherence Therapy, Jim and I had managed to identify a central symptom (his lack of success), discover the underlying emotional learning connected to the symptom (the importance of seeing himself negatively), activate the implicit schema (when I asked him to do the Bender-Gestalt—similar to when he did homework with his father), and pair that with a powerful juxtaposition experience (his competence on the Bender-Gestalt and my pleasure at his doing well). Also, the meta-processing that Jim did with me and with Dr. Hake after the TA helped Jim manage the many emotions that emerged as he changed his self-narrative and dealt with the implications of this shift on the family.

Jim continued to visit me occasionally for some years after his TA, and he often talked about how important the AIS had been to him. He said he had been shocked to realize that his perceptions of himself were so inaccurate, and that this led him to a place of being willing to ignore the negative voice inside his head and try almost anything. Around the same time, Jim had the fortune to meet several friends who wanted to start a band together, and as he said, "the rest was history." Sadly, I learned that several years after Jim left home, his parents had divorced. When I asked Jim how he felt about this he said, "Sad for them. But they made their own beds, I can't help them, and living with them was killing me." I agreed.[2]

Ways to Enhance TA to Maximize Memory Reconsolidation

As I explained above, Jim's TA and the others referenced in this book took place before I ever learned about Coherence Therapy. Yet I believe the major changes I witnessed in many of these clients are likely due to memory reconsolidation. In keeping with this belief, I have begun to make small changes in my TAs to intentionally incorporate aspects of Coherence Therapy:

1) I have become even more focused on working experientially with clients in hopes of activating implicit emotional schemas. For example, when discussing events clients have written about for the Early Memory Procedure, I now ask them at some point to recount the scene *in present tense*, as if it is occurring now, e.g., "I'm at the dining room table after dinner. My father is there sitting next to me 'helping' me. I am supposed to be writing a book report…" Afterwards I might ask the client, "What do you think you learned from that event?" Another subtle change I've made involves the Extended Inquiry of the Rorschach. Long ago I developed the custom of asking clients to put the phrase "I am a…" before their percepts and see if that metaphor was apt for their situation. For example, for Card I, "I am a... bat that is returning home after a war…." Now I tend to go one step further and ask the client to stand and put themselves in the physical position of the flying bat and then begin talking. By working less cognitively and more with the body and with emotions, I find that the client and I discover implicit emotional schemas more readily.
2) A fundamental principle of Coherence Therapy is that symptoms are "necessary," i.e., they serve(d) an adaptive function that part of the client's brain still thinks is important. I have long believed that even the most puzzling and obnoxious problems in living could be understood as having some purpose, and that it was the job of the client and assessor working together to

discover this function. Now I am even more focused on finding the "necessity" of my client's symptoms and helping them to see this too.

3) In Coherence Therapy, as implicit emotional learnings come to light, therapists typically write them down and ask clients to read them daily before the next session, to prevent clients from dissociating those insights. During the pandemic, I started asking clients at the end of each session to write brief answers to three questions: "How are you feeling right after the session?," "What sticks in your mind from the session?," and "Are there any important things you learned?". I have come to believe this practice serves the same purpose—of helping clients hold onto important things they learned—and I have made it a routine part of my TAs.
4) Now that I understand better the function of juxtaposition experiences in memory reconsolidation, I have become even more focused on using Assessment Intervention Sessions to contradict clients' underlying emotional schemas. This might involve helping clients express previously split-off affects, either by proxy—as in rewriting submissive responses to scenes in the Rosenzweig Picture Frustration Study (Rosenzweig, 1978) to be more assertive—or directly, by engaging in enactments of responses to the Adult Attachment Projective Picture System (George & West, 2012.) (See Finn, 2023 for an example.)
5) Another fundamental part of juxtaposition experiences in Coherence Therapy is that during meta-processing, clients are invited to simultaneously consider the implicit emotional learning that led to the target symptom along with the new experience/information that contradicts that learning. For example, with Jim, after the Bender-Gestalt I might have invited him: "Try now to hold these two things in mind at the same time: your absolute certainty that you can't do anything right, with the evidence that you did well on this test. What do you experience when you hold both things in mind?" Also, since many juxtaposition experiences in TA appear to involve the client feeling understood and accepted for the first time, I find it valuable to explicitly highlight this experience when it occurs: "What is it like to talk to me today about this topic you have felt so much shame about and see that I don't judge you negatively?" In my experience clients often experience some combination of positive emotions at that point, including awe, relief, happiness, or joy.

Notes

1 Bruhn's (1990) Early Memory Procedure (EMP) makes a distinction between clients' autobiographical memories (their accounts of specific one-time events) and the "précis" (semantic memories) derived from those experiences, i.e., general learnings of the form "When....then."

2 I wonder now if Jim's parents' marriage might have been saved if I had taken a more family systems approach to his TA. Nowadays in similar situations I use the model of TA with adolescents, in which parents are much more actively involved (Tharinger, Gentry, & Finn, 2013).

References

Bartlett, F. C. (1932). *Remembering: A study in experimental and social psychology.* Cambridge University Press.

Bender, L. (1938). *A visual motor gestalt test and its clinical use.* American Orthopsychiatric Association, Research Monographs (No. 3). American Orthopsychiatric Association.

Bruhn, A. R. (1990). *Earliest childhood memories, Vol. 1: Theory and application to clinical practice.* Praeger.

Butcher, J. N., Dahlstrom, W. G., Graham, J. R., Tellegen, A., & Kaemmer, B. (1989). *MMPI–2: Minnesota Multiphasic Personality Inventory–2: Manual for administration and scoring.* University of Minnesota Press.

Cahill, L. (2000). Neurobiological mechanisms of emotionally-influenced, long-term memory. *Progress in Brain Research, 126,* 29–37.

Chamberlin, D. E. (2019). The predictive processing model of EMDR. *Frontiers in Psychology: Hypothesis and Theory.* https://doi.org/10.3389/fpsyg.2019.02267

Davanloo, H. (2001). Intensive Short-term Dynamic Psychotherapy: Extended major direct access to the unconscious. *European Psychotherapy, 2*(1), 25–70.

Ecker, B. (2013). Nonspecific common factors theory meets memory reconsolidation: A game-changing encounter? *The Neuropsychotherapist, 2,* 134–137.

Ecker, B. (2015a). Memory reconsolidation understood and misunderstood. *International Journal of Neuropsychotherapy, 3,* 2–46.

Ecker, B. (2015b). Psychotherapy's mysterious efficacy ceiling: Is memory reconsolidation the breakthrough? *The Neuropsychotherapist, 16,* 6–24.

Ecker, B. (2015c). Using NLP for memory reconsolidation: A glimpse of intergrating the panoply of psychotherapies. *The Neuropsychotherapist, 10,* 50–56.

Ecker, B. (2018). Clinical translation of memory reconsolidation research: Therapeutic methodology for transformational change by erasing implicit emotional learnings driving symptom production. *International Journal of Psychotherapy, 6*(1), 1092.

Ecker, B., & Hulley, L. (2011). *Coherence Therapy practice manual and training guide.* Coherence Psychology Institute, LLC.

Ecker, B., Ticic, R., & Hulley, L. (2024). *Unlocking the emotional brain: Memory reconsolidation and the psychotherapy of transformational change* (2nd ed.). Routledge.

Finn, S. E. (2007). *In our clients' shoes: Theory and techniques of Therapeutic Assessment.* Erlbaum.

Finn, S. E. (2023). From unresolved to earned secure attachment: The AAP as a powerful clinical tool in psychotherapy. In C. George, J. Wargo Aikens, & M. Lehmann (Eds.), *Clinical application of the Adult Attachment Projective Picture System* (pp. 97–109). Routledge.

Fosha, D. (2000). *The transforming power of affect: A model for accelerated change.* Basic Books.

Frederickson, J. (2013). *Co-creating change: Effective dynamic therapy techniques.* Seven Leaves Press.
George, C., & West, M. (2012). *The Adult Attachment Projective Picture System: Attachment theory and assessment in adults.* Guilford.
González, D. Aixalà, M. B., Neimeyer, R. A., Cantillo, J., Nicolson, D., & Farré, M. (2022). Restorative retelling for processing psychedelic experiences: Rationale and case study of complicated grief. *Frontiers in Psychology, 13*, 832879. https://doi.org/10.3389/fpsyg.2022.832879
Greenberg, L., & Watson, J. (2006). *Emotion-Focused Therapy of depression.* American Psychological Association Books.
Hupbach, A., Gomez, R., Hardt, O., & Nadel, L. (2007). Reconsolidation of episodic memories: A subtle reminder triggers integration of new information. *Learning and Memory, 14*(1–2), 47–53.
Kindt, M., Soeter, M., & Verlviet, B. (2009). Beyond extinction: Erasing human fear responses and preventing the return of fear. *Nature Neuroscience, 12*, 256–258.
Lane, R. D., Ryan, L., Nadel, L, & Greenberg, L. (2015). Memory reconsolidation, emotional arousal, and the process of change in psychotherapy: New insights from brain science. *Behavioral and Brain Sciences.* https://doi.org/10.1017/S0140525X14000041
Levine, P. A., & Frederick, A. (1997). *Waking the tiger: Healing trauma.* North Atlantic Books.
Murty, V. P., Ritchey, M., Adcock, R. A., & Labar, K. S. (2010). fMRI studies of successful emotional memory encoding: A quantitative meta-analysis. *Neuropsychologia, 48*(12), 3459–3469.
Nadel, L., & Hardt, O. (2011). Update on memory systems and processes. *Neuropsychopharmacology, 36,* 251–273.
Nader, K., Schafe, G. E., & Le Doux, J. E. (2000) Fear memories require protein synthesis in the amygdala for reconsolidation after retrieval. *Nature, 406,* 722–726.
Nairne, J. S., & Pandeirada, J. (2008). Adaptive memory: Is survival processing special? *Journal of Memory and Language, 59*(3), 377–385.
Ogden, P., & Fisher, J. (2015). *Sensorimotor Psychotherapy: Interventions for trauma and attachment.* Norton.
Pedreira, M. E., Pérez-Cuesta, L. M., & Maldonado, H. (2002). Reactivation and reconsolidation of long-term memory in the crab Chasmagnathus: Protein synthesis requirement and mediation by NMDA-type glutamatergic receptors. *Journal of Neuroscience, 22*, 8305–8311.
Pedreira, M. E., Pérez-Cuesta, L. M., & Maldonado, H. (2004). Mismatch between what is expected and what occurs triggers memory reconsolidation or extinction. *Learning and Memory, 11*, 579–585.
Phelps, E. A. (2004). Human emotion and memory: Interactions of the amygdala and hippocampal complex. *Current Opinion in Neurobiology, 14*(2), 198–202.
Polster, E., & Polster. M. (1973). *Gestalt Therapy: Contours of theory and practice.* Brunner/Mazel.
Rosenzweig, S. (1978). *The Rosenzweig Picture Frustration Study basic manual.* Rana House.

Schiller D., Monfils M. H., Raio C. M., Johnson D. C., LeDoux, J. E., & Phelps, E. A. (2010). Preventing the return of fear in humans using reconsolidation update mechanisms. *Nature, 463,* 49–53.

Schwartz, R. (1995). *Internal Family Systems Therapy.* Guilford.

Shapiro, F. (2001). *Eye Movement Desensitization and Reprocessing: Basic principles, protocols, and procedures* (2nd ed.). Guilford.

Sekiguchi, T., Yamada, A., & Suzuki, H. (1997). Reactivation-dependent changes in memory states in the terrestrial slug Limas flavus. *Learning and Memory, 4,* 356–364.

Tharinger, D. J., Gentry, L., & Finn, S. E. (2013). Therapeutic Assessment with adolescents and their parents: A comprehensive model. In SaklofskeD. , C. R. Reynolds, & V. L. Schwean (Eds.), *Oxford Press handbook of psychological assessment of children and adolescents* (pp. 385–422). Oxford University Press.

Tulving, E. (1983). *Elements of episodic memory.* Oxford University Press.

Vyas, A., Mitra, R., Rao, B. S.Shankaranarayana , & Chattarji, S. (2002). Chronic stress induces contrasting patterns of dendritic remodeling in hippocampal and amygdaloid neurons. *The Journal of Neuroscience, 22,* 6810–6818.

Wampold, B. E., & Imel, Z. E. (2015). *The great psychotherapy debate: The evidence for what makes psychotherapy work.* Routledge.

Wechsler, D. (1997). *WAIS-III administration and scoring manual.* Psychological Corporation.

Chapter 15

Reflections on the Future of Psychological Assessment

At the time I am writing this chapter, I have been studying and practicing psychological assessment for over 47 years. During this period, I have witnessed enormous shifts in how psychological assessment is viewed and implemented, and current developments such as the increasing use of Artificial Intelligence make me certain that additional, significant changes are coming. Often, I find myself wondering, "What is the future of psychological assessment?" and "What will happen to Therapeutic Assessment?"

An Overview

When I entered graduate school in clinical psychology in 1979, psychological assessment—including personality assessment—was central to the identity of clinical, counseling, and educational psychologists, and graduate training programs devoted a great deal of coursework to teaching the administration and interpretation of major psychological tests (Evans & Finn, 2017).[1] The University of Minnesota, where I studied, was particularly well-known for psychological assessment, and my fellow graduate students and I were required to take two years of assessment courses, covering diagnostic interviewing, basic cognitive and neuropsychological tests, self-report tests, and several performance-based tests (the Rorschach and TAT). These courses were accompanied by practica in the Twin Cities community, where we got experience assessing many different types of clients. The supervisors at these practicum placements were graduates of the University of Minnesota, and most were expert assessors who made their living by doing assessment and some psychotherapy. In the hospitals and clinics where I trained, it was usual for every client to be given psychological tests, with many receiving a complete battery involving self-report, cognitive, and performance-based personality tests. Competition for psychology internships was intense, and it was understood that applicants with more assessment experience would be most likely to be accepted (Watkins, 1991). I, like many of my graduate school cohort, chose a dissertation topic related to psychological assessment (Finn, 1984), and I got my first job after my Ph.D. at the University

DOI: 10.4324/9781003602231-15

of Texas at Austin, with the understanding that I would teach psychological assessment. Even in graduate school I developed misgivings about the way psychological assessment was practiced. I began to call for an individualized approach to psychodiagnosis (Finn, 1982). I have written elsewhere about the development of Therapeutic Assessment (Finn, 2022), and how my thinking was fostered by contacts with top clinical psychologists in the field through the Society for Personality Assessment, which had over 2000 members. It was a thrilling time to be researching and practicing psychological assessment, and I found it easy to find colleagues who shared my passion.

As many others have noted, the place of psychological assessment in clinical and counseling psychology has changed enormously over the past 60 years (Merenda, 2007; Weiner, 2007; Handler & Smith, 2012; Evans & Finn, 2023). In the U.S., although some areas of assessment—particularly neuropsychological assessment and forensic assessment—appear to remain strong, the number of clients undergoing psychological assessment in general clinical settings has greatly declined, and perhaps as a result, many psychology training programs devote much less time to teaching assessment than they did in the past. This decrease in training and use is particularly acute for performance-based personality tests (Piotrowski, 2015). Given all these factors, it is not surprising that organizations such as the Society for Personality Assessment are contending with declining membership (SPA, 2025).

Many others have analyzed reasons for the decline in psychological assessment (Evans & Finn, 2023; Merenda, 2007; Weiner, 2007), which include lack of reimbursement for psychological assessment by insurance providers, skepticism (among both the lay public and psychologists) about the validity of psychological tests, the rise of cognitive behaviorism and biological psychiatry, and the relative ease and attractiveness for practicing psychologists of only doing psychotherapy. I have spent my career championing psychological testing, for example by chairing the Psychological Assessment Work Group (PAWG) in the mid-1990s for the American Psychological Association to investigate the declining use of psychological assessment. PAWG published two reports (Eisman et al., 2000; Kubiszyn et al., 2000), as well as a frequently cited article showing that the validity and reliability of major psychological tests is equal to that of most medical tests, and decision-making in mental health settings is greatly improved by incorporating information from psychological tests (Meyer et al., 2001). I had high hopes that the data and recommendations in these articles would lead to a resurgence of interest and use of psychological assessment, but it did not. And while, as mentioned in Chapter 1, the efforts my colleagues and I have put into developing, researching, and teaching Therapeutic Assessment have certainly had an impact, we are nevertheless contending with the reality that fewer graduating psychologists are interested in or well trained in psychological assessment, especially personality assessment. I do not mean to imply that psychological assessment is dead or dying. It is not. But I fear that its true potential as a powerful life-changing intervention is far from being recognized. Why has this been so difficult?

Therapeutic Assessment's Dilemma of Change

To use a rubric that has proven valuable in working with clients, I decided to examine Therapeutic Assessment's "dilemma of change." This is a framework from family therapy (Papp, 1983) and other systems therapies (Agazarian, 2018) that helps conceptualize systems that appear "stuck" in their development, i.e., unable to fulfill their promise. The process involves specifying a goal and listing the "driving forces" and "restraining forces" currently relevant to the goal, and then examining these for possible "tipping points," where viable interventions might shift the balance of these forces to allow the system to move toward its goal.

To comment briefly on this table, one could further the spread of TA by strengthening some of the driving forces, for example, by publishing more books and articles about the method or sponsoring more training workshops. But another potential way of "tipping" the system would be to reduce one or more of the restraining forces. Some of these constraints are probably fixed and not amenable to intervention, e.g., psychological tests are costly, and therefore assessment entails a high overhead. But I wonder if other impediments might be moderated more easily? For example, my colleagues and I are developing briefer forms of TA that are less costly (e.g., Sun et al., 2024). AI might be used as a support for novice assessors (although not as a substitute for relational understandings). Among these restraining forces, however, the prevailing epistemological view of assessment as an information-gathering activity stands out because it shapes how all the other constraints are understood and justified. My sense is that this view is held by many psychologists as well as by auxiliary professionals such as psychiatrists and social workers. Other professions clearly follow psychology's lead on this topic, so the main question is, "What are the main reasons why psychologists are so wedded to this view?" It could be that they have not been exposed to TA, but this cannot be the only cause, as I have witnessed many assessment colleagues who read or see presentations about TA and then continue to see tests mainly as tools for labeling clients.

Mainstream Psychology's Fixation with Being a Natural Science

Of course, I am speculating here, but I am struck that mainstream psychology continues to aspire to natural science goals (prediction, quantification, standardization, and group-comparison experimental designs), and I believe this greatly influences the field of psychological assessment. For example, in 2005 the American Psychological Association approved a policy about "evidence-based

Table 15.1 Driving and restraining forces for recognizing psychological assessment as a life-changing intervention

Goal: Psychological assessment is widely recognized as a life-changing intervention.	
Driving forces	**Restraining forces**
Clients long to be seen accurately, treated respectfully, and get help with problems-in-living (see Chapter 1)	Clients may distrust psychological assessment because of experiencing or witnessing bad assessment in the past
Many mental health professionals want help with their clients	Professionals may be skeptical of assessment because they have not found it helpful previously
There is a great need for brief effective mental health interventions	It takes years to learn and become expert in psychological tests
Psychological assessment should attract psychologists as a unique domain of competence	Therapeutic Assessment requires training in tests *and* in psychotherapy; fewer graduate programs provide training in tests
Psychological tests are as valid as many medical tests and provide information not easily available in other ways (Meyer et al., 2001)	The prevailing view of psychological tests is that they are useful for information gathering, not tools for direct intervention
When used collaboratively, tests often provide powerful bottom-up-learning experiences (see Chapters 6, 10, 13, 14)	Therapeutic Assessment is emotionally challenging and requires a great deal of flexibility on the part of assessors
There is evidence that TA is effective (see Finn, 2023) even with clients who are difficult to treat (De Saeger et al., 2016)	It is difficult to secure funding for Therapeutic Assessment research
Students enjoy learning Therapeutic Assessment (see Smith & Egan, 2015; Pade et al., 2021)	Very few graduate instructors feel competent to teach or supervise TA
Therapeutic Assessment is applicable to clients from many different cultures and is recognized as being culturally sensitive (e.g., Finn & Holman, in press; Mercer, Macdonald, & Purves, 2022; Pade & Holman, in press)	TA is costly compared to other brief interventions; clients in disadvantaged groups may have little access to TA
There are now many articles and books on Therapeutic Assessment	Many psychologists trained in psychological assessment are not aware of the latest developments in interpersonal neurobiology and their implications for intervention
The TAI sponsors TA training around the world and there are now 43 professionals certified in TA in 9 different countries	Many local areas have no psychologists knowledgeable about Therapeutic Assessment

practice" (APA, 2006) in which psychological assessment is mentioned multiple times as an information-gathering activity but nowhere as a possible intervention. Furthermore, evidence-based practice was defined as integrating "the best available research" with clinical practice, with the gold standard for research being randomized controlled trials (RCT) and meta-analyses. Similarly, a recent major article on "best practice" in "evidence based clinical psychological assessment" does mention Therapeutic Assessment but focuses mainly on recommendations for improving the "empirical basis" of psychological assessment as an information-gathering tool (Wright et al., 2022).

Perez-Alvarez (2018) and others have suggested that psychology's adoption of the scientific method of logical positivism and of an epistemology that emphasizes control and prediction contributed to its prestige, and I believe that this is true of psychological assessment also. Psychologists were rightfully proud of the contributions they made to screening military applicants in WWII, and many experts believe this work launched clinical psychology as a field (Weiner, 2007). Psychological assessment as a professional activity differentiated psychologists as "scientists," and this view has permeated training models for years. Why, then, are more graduate students not drawn to assessment now? One possibility is that assessment, as currently conceptualized, no longer speaks to psychologists' desire to engage meaningfully with human suffering.

I believe we have reached the point at which psychological assessment has reached its limit as a predictive science and where a deeper, more complex understanding of assessment and of human nature is needed. Even in physics it is now recognized that attempting to measure something may change its properties. Why then do we reject this idea when attempting to assess human beings? We humans are known as "meaning makers," constantly construing the world around us to create narratives that affect us and others. For psychological assessment to remain current and exciting, I think we need to acknowledge that our traditional approach has yielded important insights into human nature, but that we need a model where no test score has a fixed meaning (Cf. Finn, 2007), assessment results can *only* be understood through dialogue with a client (Fischer, 1985/1994), awareness of the client's familial, cultural, and personal context is essential for interpreting test results (Wright, 2021; Wright, 2024), and assessment is recognized as impacting both clients *and* assessors (Finn, 2007). We must go beyond "the myth of the isolated mind" (Stolorow & Atwood, 1992) and develop another model of psychological assessment.

As described in Chapter 8, Constance Fischer articulated an approach to psychological assessment that meets these criteria, and which was embedded in a larger view of psychology as a "human science." As she described, this model is "not an opposite of object science, but rather a more adequate and comprehensive view of humans" (Fischer, 2017, p. 50). Fischer's view was not driven by a desire to be humanistic, but rather by her attempt to more accurately describe what occurs in psychological assessment, and it was grounded in the writings of a minority strand in psychology broadly described as "qualitative inquiry" (Giorgi, 1970; Wertz, 2014). When one views the world through the lens of Fischer's phenomenological psychology, the individualized, collaborative assessment practices she developed not only make sense, but are essential for the ethical use of psychological tests. For example, one would never attempt to interpret a test finding (i.e., "The patient saw no whole humans on the Rorschach…") without first discussing this event with the client and trying to understand its significance in their daily life. And it becomes a matter of common sense to collect clients' comments on psychological reports before they are sent to referring professionals. Although Fischer did not at first recognize her individualized, collaborative assessment approach as a potential therapeutic intervention, she was aware that many clients benefited from participating in psychological assessment when it was conducted according to these phenomenological principles. Again, I want to emphasize that a human-science paradigm is not blind to nomothetic meanings of psychological test scores, it just strives to integrate these into an understanding of clients' lived experiences. As Finn and Tonsager (1997) asserted, traditional and Therapeutic Assessment are "complementary paradigms" rather than being at odds with each other. Aschieri (2012) expressed this view even more elegantly with the metaphor of a "piano duet for 4 hands," where the assessor engages in "epistemological triangulation" between three types of stories: "the stories written with numbers (the test data), the stories written with personal meanings…., and the stories 'written by four hands" (the interactions between client and clinician)" (p. 356).

Intersubjectivity, Therapeutic Assessment, and Interpersonal Neurobiology

For me, it is only through this human-science intersubjective perspective that I can begin to appreciate the experiences I have had with clients through Therapeutic Assessment. When I think of the journey Thomas and I had to uncovering his medical trauma via the Rorschach (Chapter 4), Ben's sudden understanding via the TAT of the function of his sexual acting out (Chapter 5), Mary's finally realizing through the AAP of why she "didn't look" at her rapist (Chapter 13), and the impact all these events and others mentioned in this book have had on me, I experience awe and a kind of spiritual connection. By this I mean that I am left with a greater awareness of the interconnectedness of all human beings, the fragility of life, my own strengths and limitations, the people who helped me over the years, and the amazing human capacity to survive and heal. I find this perspective enlivening, but I am also aware of the difficulties of being conscious of the "unbearable embeddedness of being" (Stolorow & Atwood, 1992). If we truly think relationally about psychological assessment, we enter a world of being much less sure of the meaning of our MMPI scores; realizing that it is near impossible to understand how our personal stimulus value influences our clients' Rorschachs; humbly appreciating that our clients have a lot to teach us; and recognizing that uncertainty is not a weakness of assessment, but an honest reflection of its relational nature. I personally think psychology is at a place where we can tolerate this more accurate view of psychological assessment, but I have witnessed psychologists having near disintegration experiences when their traditional view of tests is challenged (e.g., Del Corno, 2009). I do not scorn their struggles, because it is truly difficult to maintain a worldview in which reality is co-constructed. It is easy to fall back on a view of psychological assessment as accurately measuring inherent traits and predicting behavior and adopting a kind of "deliberate ignorance" (Hertwig & Engel, 2016) that ignores many evident facts and serves a host of functions. A traditional view of assessment helps us fit into a world that largely thinks mechanistically, thereby protecting our self-esteem, regulating our emotions, avoiding regret, and eschewing responsibility for the effects of our assessment approach on clients.

I hope that more awareness of the latest research and theories of interpersonal neurobiology will help. While interpersonal neurobiology does not "prove" Fischer's human science approach to psychological assessment, it does corroborate her point of view. For example, reading Alan Schore's (2012) elegant volume, *The Science of the Art of Psychotherapy*, one comes away convinced of the primacy of emotion and unconscious "enactments" in clinician-client interactions and of the inevitable "right-brain to right-brain" communications that take place not only in daily life but also in psychotherapy and psychological assessment. The traditional view of psychological tests as measuring traits and qualities that "reside" in individuals strikes me as a more "left-brain" perspective. Whereas McGilchrist (2019) masterfully assembled evidence that the right hemisphere is dominant and that empathy and intersubjectivity are the "ground of consciousness," which dovetails well with a human-science perspective on psychological assessment. I had the same experience of awe I described above when first reading Daniel Siegel's (1999) book, *The Developing Mind.* As Siegel described evidence for the amazing connectedness of minds (intersubjectivity) and how this is related to mirror neurons and right-hemisphere brain structures, I immediately began to think about psychological assessment and Fischer's phenomenological stance. I was further encouraged when fMRI studies emerged of clients taking psychological tests (e.g., Asari et al., 2008, Bucheim et al., 2005, Giromini et al., 2017). It seems to me that this research both grounds psychological assessment in a natural science approach while allowing for a deeper understanding of how intersubjectivity is a major factor in assessment.

In my mind, interpersonal neurobiology does not merely show that relationships influence neural functioning; it demonstrates that affect regulation, meaning-making, and learning emerge within relational systems. If psychological assessment aims to understand meaning, adaptation, and change—and not merely to quantify between-person variance—then assessment findings cannot be understood as properties of isolated individuals. Test results emerge within intersubjective fields that include the client, the assessor, the testing situation, and the cultural meanings embedded in the instruments themselves. From this perspective, an intersubjective epistemology is not an optional philosophical overlay, but a necessary implication of what interpersonal neurobiology reveals. Once assessment is viewed in this way, its true power as a life-changing intervention becomes evident.

A Vision of a Modern Training Program in Assessment

If we want to cultivate this modern, complex, and exciting view of psychological assessment as a psychological intervention, as well as an information-gathering tool, what would be the best way to train early career psychologists in assessment? First, I think we would have to abandon the idea that psychology graduate schools have the time and resources to turn out fully formed psychological assessors. Graduate programs certainly can teach basic principles of psychometrics, begin introducing tests, and expose students to phenomenological psychology as a counterpoint to the logical positivist perspective they almost certainly learned in their undergraduate psychology courses. Students could also witness and take part in Therapeutic Assessments in a way I have written about previously (Finn, 1998). But assessment would become recognized as a post-graduate specialty (see Evans & Finn, 2023) where interested psychologists would engage in four or five years of intense study at an assessment "institute" after they have their psychology license. This model would complement, rather than replace, existing graduate and postdoctoral pathways to professional competence in assessment.

In these institutes, psychological tests would be taught in depth, along with collaborative assessment practices such as gathering Assessment Questions, conducting Extended Inquiries, planning and conducting Assessment Intervention Sessions and Summary/Discussion Sessions, and providing written feedback. Assessors in training would alternate between observing assessments conducted by the expert faculty, co-conducting assessments with faculty on a variety of clients, and doing their own Therapeutic Assessments under close supervision. Students would also learn different psychotherapy modalities that are useful in assessment and study important topics such as epistemic trust, attachment, and shame. Importantly, supervision would be offered in a way that conforms to the core values of Therapeutic Assessment (see Finn, 2019) with faculty helping students identify their own unresolved traumas and shame so that they can work on these in psychotherapy. Last, a great emphasis would be placed on building a resilient and safe community so that trainees could form the supportive collegial connections they need to practice Therapeutic Assessment on their own after graduating.

I realize this vision of modern assessment training may seem like a grandiose pipe dream, and I, being toward the end of my career, am not the person to attempt to implement it fully. But I believe it is important to let ourselves dream or the world would never move forward, and I humbly offer these ideas for you to reflect on—as I have reflected on what psychological assessment has been, and what it might yet become.

Note

1. I am aware that already at this time various writers (e.g., Lewandowski & Saccuzzo, 1976) decried the declining status of psychological assessment.

References

Agazarian, Y. M. (2018). *Systems-Centered Therapy for groups*. Routledge.Aschieri, F. (2012). Epistemological and ethical challenges in standardized testing and collaborative assessment. *Journal of Humanistic Psychology, 52*(3), 350–368.

American Psychological Association. (2006). Evidence-based practice in psychology. *American Psychologist, 61*(4), 271–285.

Asari, T., Konishi, S., Jimura, K., Chkazoe, J., Nakamura, N., & Miyashita, Y. (2008). Amygdalar enlargement associated with unique perception. *Cortex, 30*, 1–6.

Bucheim, A., Erk, S., George, C., Kächele, H., Ruchsow, M., Spitzer, M., Kircher, T., & Walter, H. (2005). Measuring attachment representation in an fMRI environment: A pilot study. *Psychopathology, 589*, 1–9.

De Saeger, H., Bartak, A., Eder, E. E., & Kamphuis, J. H., (2016). Memorable experiences in Therapeutic Assessment: Inviting the patient's perspective following a pretreatment randomized controlled trial. *Journal of Personality Assessment, 98*(5), 472–479.

Del Corno, F. (2009, January). *Vincoli metodologici nell'uso del test di Rorschach [Methodological constraints for using the Rorschach*]. In S. Di Nuovo (Chair), "Il Test di Rorschach e il Therapeutic Assessment" [The Rorschach Test and Therapeutic Assessment]. Symposium conducted at the meeting of Istituto Italiano Rorschach e Psicodiagnostica Integrata, Milan, Italy.

Eisman, E., Dies, R. R., Finn, S. E., Eyde, L. D., Kay, G. G., Kubiszyn, T. W., Meyer, G. J., & Moreland, K. L. (2000). Problems and limitations in using psychological assessment in the contemporary healthcare delivery system. *Professional Psychology: Research and Practice, 31*, 131–140.

Evans, F. B., & Finn, S. E. (2017). Training and consultation in psychological assessment with professionalpsychologists: Suggestions for enhancing the profession and individual practices. *Journal of Personality Assessment*, 99(2), 175–185.

Evans, F. B., & Finn, S. E. (2023). Training and consultation in psychological assessment with professional psychologists: Suggestions for enhancing the professional and individual practice. *Journal of Personality Assessment, 99*(2), 175–185.

Finn, S. E. (1982). Base rates, utilities, and DSM-III: On the shortcomings of fixed-rule systems of psychodiagnosis. *Journal of Abnormal Psychology, 91*, 294–302.

Finn, S. E. (1984). *A partial cross-sequential analysis of personality ratings on 400 men*. Unpublished doctoral dissertation, University of Minnesota.
Finn, S. E. (1998). Teaching Therapeutic Assessment in a required graduate course. In L. Handler & M. Hilsenroth (Eds.), *Teaching and learning personality assessment* (pp. 359–373). Erlbaum.
Finn, S. E. (2007). *In our clients' shoes: Theory and techniques of Therapeutic Assessment*. Erlbaum.
Finn, S. E. (2019). Supervision of Therapeutic Assessment. In A. J. Wright (Ed.), *Essentials of psychological assessment supervision* (pp. 221–242). Wiley.
Finn, S. E. (2022). The development of Therapeutic Assessment: From shame and isolation to connection and love. In C. Hopwood (Ed.), *The evolution of personality assessment in the 21st century: Understanding the people who understand people* (pp. 12–39). Routledge.
Finn, S. E., & Holman, A. R. (in press). Culturally sensitive collaborative/therapeutic assessment. In L. A. Suzuki & KrishnamurthyR. (Eds.), *Handbook of multicultural assessment* (4th ed.). Wiley.
Finn, S. E., & Tonsager, M. E. (1997). Information-gathering and therapeutic models of assessment: Complementary paradigms. *Psychological Assessment, 9*, 374–385.
Fischer, C. T. (1985/1994). *Individualizing psychological assessment*. Routledge.
Fischer, C. T. (2017). *On the way to collaborative psychological assessment: Selected papers of Constance T. Fischer*. Routledge.
Giromini, L., Viglione, D. J., Zannaro, A., & Cuada, F. (2017). Neural activation during production of Rorschach responses: An fMRI study. *Psychiatry Research: Neuroimaging, 262*, 25–31.
Giorgi, A. (1970). *Psychology as a human science: A phenomenological approach*. Harper and Row.
Handler, L., & Smith, J. D. (2012). Education and training in psychological assessment. In J. R. Graham & J. A. Naglieri (Eds.), *Handbook of assessment psychology* (Vol. 10, 2nd ed., pp. 211–238). Wiley.
Hertwig, R., & Engel, C. (2016). Homo ignorans: Deliberately choosing not to know. *Perspectives on Psychological Science, 11*(3), 359–372.
Kubiszyn, T. W., Meyer, G. J., Finn, S. E., Eyde, L. D., Kay, G. G., Moreland, K. L., Dies, R. R., & Eisman, E. J. (2000). Empirical support for psychological assessment in clinical health care settings. *Professional Psychology: Research and Practice, 31*, 119–130.
Lewandowski, D. G., & Saccuzzo, D. P. (1976). The decline of psychological testing. *Professional Psychology, 7*(2), 177–184.
McGilchrist, I. (2019). *The master and his emissary: The divided brain and the making of the western world*. Yale University Press.
Mercer, B. L., Macdonald, H., & Purves, C. (Eds.). (2022). *Psychological interventions from six continents: Culture, collaboration, and community*. Routledge.
Merenda, P. F. (2007). Update on the decline in the education and training in psychological measurement and assessment. *Psychological Reports, 101*(1), 153–155.
Meyer, G. J., Finn, S. E., Eyde, L. D., Kay, G. G., Moreland, K. L., Dies, R. R., Eisman, E. J., Kubiszyn, T. W., & Reed, G. M. (2001). Psychological testing and psychological assessment: A review of evidence and issues. *American Psychologist, 56*, 128–65.

Pade, H., & Holman, A. (in press). Collaborative assessment. In L. Hoffman (Ed.), *APA handbook of humanistic and existential psychology*. APA Press.

Pade, H., Martin, H., Lewis, J., Bigalke, L., & Tavari, A. (2021). Exposure to collaborative therapeutic assessment in early graduate training through therapeutic letters. *The TA Connection, 9*(2), 19–24.

Papp, P. (1983). *The process of change*. Guilford.

Pérez-Álvarez, M. (2018). Psychology as a science of subject and comportment, beyond the mind and behavior. *Integrative Psychological and Behavioral Science, 52*, 25–51.

Piotrowski, C. (2015). Projective techniques usage worldwide: A review of applied settings 1995–2015. *Journal of the Indian Academy of Applied Psychology, 41*(3), 9–19.

Schore, A. N. (2012). *The science of the art of psychotherapy*. Norton.

Siegel, D. J. (1999). *The developing mind: Toward a neurobiology of interpersonal experience*. Guilford.

Smith, J. D. & Egan, K. N. (2015). Trainee and client experiences of Therapeutic Assessment in a required graduate course: A qualitative analysis. *Journal of Personality Assessment*, 99(2),126–135.

Society for Personality Assessment. (2025). SPA strategic framework 2022–2027. Downloaded from www.personality.org

Stolorow, R. D., & Atwood, G. E. (1992). *Contexts of being: The intersubjective foundations of psychological life*. Erlbaum.

Sun, Q., Wang, Z., Wang, M., & Finn, S. E. (2024). Ultra-brief Therapeutic Assessment with three Chinese adult clients: A case-based time series pilot study. *Journal of Personality Assessment, 107*(3), 406–417.

Watkins, C. E., Jr. (1991). What have surveys taught us about the teaching and practice of psychological assessment? *Journal of Personality Assessment, 56*, 426–435.

Weiner, I. B. (2007). President's message: Education and training in personality assessment. *The SPA Exchange, 19*(1), 11.

Wertz, F. J. (2014). Qualitative inquiry in the history of psychology. *Qualitative Psychology, 1*(1), 4–16.

Wright, A. J. (2021). Deliberate context-driven conceptualization in psychological assessment. *Journal of Personality Assessment, 104*(5), 700–709.

Wright, A. J. (2024). Queering psychological assessment. *Professional Psychology: Research and Practice, 55*(6), 529–536.

Wright, A. J., Pade, H., Gottfried, E. D., Arbisi, P. A., McCord, D. M., & Wygant, D. B. (2022). Evidence-based clinical psychological assessment (EBCPA): Review of current state of the literature and best practices. *Professional Psychology: Research and Practice, 53*(4), 372–386.

Index

Note: Page numbers in **bold** and in italics indicates tables and figures respectively.

For Product Safety Concerns and Information please contact our EU representative GPSR@taylorandfrancis.com
Taylor & Francis Verlag GmbH, Kaufingerstraße 24, 80331 München, Germany

www.ingramcontent.com/pod-product-compliance
Ingram Content Group UK Ltd.
Pitfield, Milton Keynes, MK11 3LW, UK
UKHW022351190926
475702UK00015B/2236
9781032990910